ID # BENJAMIN FRANKLIN
American and World Educator

By LOUIS K. WECHSLER

TWAYNE PUBLISHERS
A DIVISION OF G. K. HALL & CO., BOSTON

Copyright © 1976 by G. K. Hall & Co.

All Rights Reserved

First Printing

Library of Congress Cataloging in Publication Data

Wechsler, Louis K
    Benjamin Franklin : American and world educator.

    (Twayne's world leaders series ; TWLS 56)
    Bibliography: p. 198–201.
    Includes index.
    1.   Franklin, Benjamin, 1706–1790.
E302.6.F8W3   973.3'092'4 [B]   76-2679
ISBN 0-8057-7667-2

MANUFACTURED IN THE UNITED STATES OF AMERICA

TWAYNE'S WORLD LEADERS SERIES

EDITORS OF THIS VOLUME
Samuel Smith, Ph.D.
Gladys Walterhouse, Ph.D.

Benjamin Franklin

TWLS 56

*The Metropolitan Museum of Art,
Gift of John Bard, 1872.*

Benjamin Franklin
Sculpture by Jean Antoine Houdon, 1778.

Contents

About the Author

Preface

Acknowledgments

Chronology

1. Exploration and Discovery: Early Years, 1706–1727 — 13
2. Independence and Expansion: Manhood, 1727–1746 — 44
3. Emancipation: Middle Years, 1746–1764 — 79
4. World Influence: Later Years, 1764–1790 — 116
5. Inspiration to the Common Man — 157
6. Guide on Education and Other Problems Today: An Extrapolation — 172

Notes and References — 186
Selected Bibliography — 198
Index — 202

About the Author

It has been the good fortune of Louis K. Wechsler to enjoy the advantages of the two cities that have probably had the greatest influence on American life and culture: he was born in New York City and raised in Boston (Boston Latin School and Harvard). He returned to New York to continue his education (B. A., College of the City of New York; M. A. in Latin, Columbia; and graduate study in English at Harvard and in education at Fordham, New York University, and Columbia), and remained to teach Latin and English in the public high schools of the city for twenty-five years and to serve as a junior and a senior high school principal for eighteen years before his retirement from the High School of Music and the Arts.

He has had a lifelong admiration and affection for Benjamin Franklin ever since he was a student at the Boston Latin School, which Franklin attended for one year. He has written reviews, a study of the Colonial almanacs of America (Harvard doctoral dissertation), and textbooks on college entrance examinations and counseling. He is a fellow of the Royal Society of Arts (London) and a member of the New York Academy of Sciences.

Preface

Benjamin Franklin, though not a professional educator, spent his life in educating both himself and others. A born teacher, he loved to learn and to teach. At first his pupils were his neighborhood friends, and then the people of Philadelphia and Pennsylvania, and in time America and the world.

He was a child of the Puritan Revolution and the Enlightenment, deeply imbued with the desire to serve God by serving his fellowmen. He was saved by circumstance from the formal education of his time, which might have cast him as a Congregational minister in New England. Instead he came to regard mankind as his congregation and prepared to make himself worthy of his purpose in life by acquiring the education and developing the character necessary for service to God and man. What he had achieved by and for himself, he sought to accomplish for others who faced the disadvantages he had known.

Living in a frontier society where the means of education were accessible to very few, he satisfied his compulsion to teach and help others and to promote education by improvising many unconventional educational aids—the letter to the press, the mutual-improvement club, the satirical or serious topical pamphlet, the newspaper, the subscription library, the almanac, the voluntary association for mutual benefit, the learned society, and his own extensive correspondence. He was also the planner and the prime mover in the founding of a new kind of school, the English School, for the youth of Pennsylvania who did not or could not contemplate a professional career.

All his activities were molded and permeated by the use of his many talents—educational, literary, psychological, scientific, and political—for the benefit of his fellowmen, and he strove constantly and consistently in every way possible to teach them the way to their own best self-interest.

One cannot fully appreciate Franklin as an educator or understand his vast influence in education and other fields during his lifetime and since, unless his life, his character, his goals, and his multiple talents are viewed in their organic interaction with one another, each irradiating and sustaining and motivating the rest. In harmonious coordination, they gave his personality the unique power it exerted and still exerts on all kinds of people in all parts of the world.

Acknowledgments

I am glad to express my deep appreciation to the Columbia University Library for extending to me the convenience of unrestricted access to its rich Franklin collection, which made my research task much easier.

It is also a pleasure to acknowledge my special debt to the editors of *The Papers of Benjamin Franklin,* whose monumental work will provide a model of historical and literary scholarship for future generations, particularly William B. Willcox and Claude-Anne Lopez for their many courtesies, and to the Yale University Press for permission to quote from the *Papers* published to date.

No author could be more fortunate than I in the editorial assistance I received from Dr. Samuel Smith, editor-in-chief, and Dr. Gladys Walterhouse, assistant editor, of the Twayne series of great educators, and Alice D. Phalen, managing editor of Twayne Publishers. Their critical suggestions and unfailing encouragement were of inestimable value. I am also greatly indebted to Dr. Walterhouse for preparing the index.

It would be ungrateful of me not to add that I am profoundly obliged to the many authors, of whom I can mention only a few here (men like Carl Van Doren, John Hardin Best, F. L. Lucas, and Carl Becker), who helped me to gain a deeper insight into Franklin, and to the sage himself, whose writings made it possible for me to enjoy four happy years in his company.

And to my wife Tatyana Podryska, who graciously endured the role of book widow, and who gave unstintingly of her sound criticism and literary taste in reviewing the manuscript as it slowly grew, I owe, in this instance as often before, my heartfelt gratitude.

L. K. W.

Chronology

1706	Born in Boston January 17.
1714	Attended Boston Latin Grammar School for a year.
1718	Bound as printer's apprentice to brother James.
1722	Writing as "Silence Dogood," had several pieces published in brother's newspaper, *New-England Courant*.
1723	Left Boston secretly and after short stay in New York continued to Philadelphia.
1724	Worked for printer S. Keimer.
	Sent to England by Governor of Pennsylvania.
1725	Published *A Dissertation on Liberty and Necessity*, then suppressed it.
1726	Returned to America to work as clerk for Philadelphia merchant.
1727	Founded Junto Club.
1728	Started his own printing business with partner.
1729	Purchased *Pennsylvania Gazette* from Keimer.
	Published *The Nature and Necessity of a Paper Currency*.
1730	Married Deborah Read.
	Became sole proprietor of printing business.
1731	Son William born.
	Established Library Company of Philadelphia, first subscription library in North America.
1732	Son Francis born.
	First *Poor Richard: An Almanack* (for 1733) published.
1736	Chosen clerk of the General Assembly of the colony.
	Organized Union Fire Company.
	Death of son Francis.
1737	Appointed deputy postmaster of Philadelphia.
1739	Invented "Franklin stove."
1740	
1741	Started *The General Magazine*; discontinued it after six issues.
1743	Daughter Sarah born.
	One of founders of American Philosophical Society.
1747	Organized "The Association" for defense of Pennsylvania.
1748	Retired as active partner in printing business.
	Elected to Philadelphia Common Council.

1749 Founded Academy of Philadelphia (now University of Pennsylvania), opened in 1751.
1751 *Experiments and Observations on Electricity* published in London (begun 1746–1747).
Member of Pennsylvania Assembly.
1752 Performed "kite experiment."
Invented lightning rod.
1753 Awarded Copley Medal by Royal Society.
Received honorary master of arts degrees from Harvard and Yale.
Appointed deputy postmaster general for North America jointly with William Hunter.
1754 Delegate to Albany Congress.
1756 Elected fellow of Royal Society.
Received honorary master of arts degree from College of William and Mary.
1757 Sailed for England to serve as agent of Pennsylvania Assembly in dispute with Penn family, Proprietors of the colony.
Wrote "Father Abraham" preface to *Poor Richard* for 1758, frequently reprinted under title of *The Way to Wealth*.
1759 Received honorary doctoral degree from University of St. Andrews.
Traveled in northern England and Scotland.
1760 Traveled in western England and Wales.
1761 Visited Flanders and Holland.
1762 Son William appointed royal governor of New Jersey.
Returned to Philadelphia from successful mission in England.
1764 Elected Speaker of Pennsylvania Assembly.
Appointed again as agent of Pennsylvania Assembly in England; stayed there until 1775.
1766 Traveled in Germany.
His "Examination" before the House of Commons very helpful in the repeal of the Stamp Act.
1767 Visited Paris.
Daughter Sarah married to Richard Bache.
1768 Appointed agent of province of Georgia.
1769 Traveled in France.
Appointed agent of New Jersey House of Representatives in England.
1770 Appointed agent of Massachusetts House of Representatives in England.

1771	Part One of *Autobiography* written at Twyford, England. Traveled in Ireland and Scotland.
1772	Elected member of French Academy of Sciences.
1773	Translation of his works into French by Dubourg.
1774	Death of wife Deborah in Philadelphia. Humiliated before Privy Council because of connection with publication of "Hutchinson Letters." Dismissed as deputy postmaster general for North America.
1775	Returned from England to Philadelphia. Delegate to second Continental Congress. Elected postmaster general for American Colonies by Continental Congress.
1776	Served on committee of Continental Congress chosen to prepare Declaration of Independence. Appointed one of three commissioners to France; remained until 1785.
1777	His great influence decisive in preparing ground for alliance with France.
1779	Appointed sole minister to France.
1781	Appointed one of commissioners to conduct peace negotiations with England.
1782–1783	Played leading role in peace negotiations with England.
1784	Part Two of *Autobiography* written at Passy, France.
1785	Returned to Philadelphia from France. Chosen president of Supreme Executive Council (chief executive) of Pennsylvania; served three years.
1787	Delegate to Constitutional Convention from Pennsylvania. Elected president of Pennsylvania Society for Promoting the Abolition of Slavery. Elected first president of newly founded Society for Political Enquiries.
1788	Part Three of *Autobiography* written in Philadelphia.
1789	Part Four of *Autobiography* written in Philadelphia.
1790	Signed petition to Congress for abolition of slavery and slave trade. Wrote satire, *On the Slave Trade*, less than a month before his death. Died in Philadelphia April 17.

CHAPTER 1

Exploration and Discovery: Early Years, 1706–1727

Proem

IN the present season of our disenchantment with formal schooling and professional educators, Benjamin Franklin, the generalist, the self-educated printer, who exposed the inadequacies of the formal education of his time and who introduced seminal concepts and new ways and means into education, has again come to life for us, as he has for many previous generations since his death.

Partly because he had to educate himself, partly because he delighted in people and nature, education for him was life, and life was education, and he could never separate the two. His pleasure in teaching himself and others began early in his life and continued without diminution as long as he lived. The rhythms of his education were not determined by graduations and commencements, but by the seasonal changes of his life cycle, and as the margin of his involvements widened, living and learning and teaching expanded and fused into an inexhaustible stream of activity and influence.

To cap his many natural gifts with a special gift, chance placed him at birth in an obscure but sturdy family in Boston, Massachusetts, the "New Jerusalem," a family belonging to the class of tradesmen and traders that were destined to transform society and rise to power during the century in which he lived. While the upward movement of Franklin and the middle class was mutually helpful, it was his genius as a writer and educator that made him the foremost spokesman and noblest exemplar of his class.

And after his death, for generation after generation, through his *Autobiography* and the inspiration of his legendary life, he continued to teach the way to personal independence and self-respect wherever youth was deprived of educational and individual opportunity because of poverty, prejudice, geography, or other conditions of servitude.

I *Boyhood (1706–1718)*

The saga began on January 17, 1706, when the Sunday peace in the Franklin household on Milk Street was disrupted by the birth of another boy, the fifteenth child of Josiah Franklin and the eighth of his second wife, Abiah Folger Franklin. Mother and son having come through the ordeal in good condition, the infant was carried on that wintry day to the Old South Church across the street and promptly baptized. He was named Benjamin after his father's favorite brother, then living in England.

It was a vastly different world from ours that he was born into. The colony of Massachusetts, his "country," was all empty wilderness and seacoast, except for Boston and a few scattered settlements in the eastern part. Plymouth was farther away in time than Los Angeles, and London more distant than the moon, today. Poverty was widespread; disease and death were devastatingly frequent, especially for women and children, jobs scarce, working hours long, and schools and books accessible to only a few.

The disadvantages that he faced are obvious, but the advantages could not be fully appreciated until recently: a secure and literate large family; the natural world of water, woods, and animals close by; a community of neighbors supporting themselves by their own labor and tools and governing themselves by generally accepted principles; respect for authority worthy of respect; a young country with limits, responsibilities, mutual obligations, and increasing opportunities and hopes; and a familiar universe ruled by a good and wise God. In this world a child grew up amid the natural hazards of life, unscarred by the man-made evils of our age—broken homes, friendless cities, fear of strangers, the absence of clear guidelines (except for traffic rules), unclean surroundings, mischievous idleness or meaningless work, the satieties of affluence and pleasure, alienation from nature, and an inconceivably immense universe in the scale of which mankind, the earth, our solar system, and the Milky Way seem to have an almost equal insignificance.

On the surface there was little to distinguish the Franklins from the other tradesmen's families in the town. Josiah was a maker and seller of candles and soap, and Abiah was the daugher of an indentured servant who had married her master, Peter Folger of Martha's Vineyard and Nantucket. They were devout and hard-working people. But if we look behind the exterior aspect of the family, we find considerable evidence of ability and individuality, and the first traces of many exceptional qualities that later distinguished Benjamin. His father, who was nearly fifty when Benjamin was born, was a man of independence and judgment, with a talent for making friends and a natural turn for counseling and teaching. "At his table," Franklin remembered,

he lik'd to have as often as he could, some sensible friend or neighbour, to converse with, and always took care to start some ingenious [i.e., learned] or useful topic for discourse, which might tend to improve the minds of his children.[1]

His mother was a woman of "sound judgment and steady calm." His Folger grandfather had been a schoolmaster, a pacifist, a Puritan advocate of "liberty of conscience," and a writer of "homespun verse" (in his grandson's charitable phrase). His Uncle Thomas, a prosperous tobacco merchant in England, who had been a self-educated schoolmaster, was remembered long after his death as "a chief mover of all publick-spirited undertakings" in his town and county.[2] And his eccentric, peace-loving Uncle Benjamin was an assiduous student of religion and politics, the inventor of a personal shorthand system, and an inveterate versifier.

Outwardly the youngest Franklin boy was not noticeably different from the neighbors' boys of his age. He went swimming and boating and fishing with them, kept pets, made and flew kites, occasionally got into trouble with grown-ups, and dreamed sometimes of a free life on the never-resting sea that he loved. As it became evident that he excelled in those traits that boys have always admired—physical strength, daring, athletic ability, and ingenuity, he became a leader among the boys and at times "led them into scrapes."

The boys knew he was "smarter" than they were, but it did not make any difference to them since he did not *act* any differently and did not seem to *feel* different. The only difference he was aware of at first was an extraordinary affinity between himself and books. He had discovered this when he learned to read at a very early age and began to explore the Bible and any other books in his father's small library. He was delighted to find reading—and writing—as easy as speaking was difficult for him, and before long he was composing verse like Uncle Benjamin and Grandfather Folger. "My father's little library," he recalled,

consisted chiefly of books in polemic divinity, most of which I read, and have since often regretted, that at a time when I had such a thirst for knowledge, more proper books had not fallen in my way. . . . Plutarch's Lives there was, in which I read abundantly, and I still think that time spent to great advantage. There was also a book of Defoe's, called an Essay on Projects, and another of Dr. Mather's, called Essays to do Good [Cotton Mather, *Bonifacius. An Essay Upon the Good* . . .] . . . .[3]

The books that he read in these impressionable years account to some extent for his lifelong aversion to religious disputation and his dedication to devising projects for improving society and doing good to his fellowmen.

His love of reading, being the main outlet for his mental energy, became a passion, a habit, that grew stronger with the years. In alliance with his phenomenal memory, it was a formidable factor in his self-education. When the books in his father's library were exhausted, he saved his pennies to buy more books. His first purchase, prompted by his enjoyment of *Pilgrim's Progress,* was a secondhand set of John Bunyan's works, which he frugally sold to buy Burton's *Historical Collections,* consisting of forty-five inexpensive chapbooks that contained popular compendia of English history. The limitations of time and money, combined with his own intelligence, compelled Franklin, young as he was, to select books for reading that would give him both instruction and pleasure, the pleasure coming from his interest in the content and the writer's felicity of expression.

Impressed by Ben's remarkable ability and interest in reading and writing and encouraged by friends of the family, his Puritan father was persuaded, though he could hardly afford the gesture, to give his precocious tenth son "as the tithe of his sons to the service of the Church." He was therefore enrolled at the age of eight in the Boston Grammar School. The first year in school was a self-testing experience for this son of an immigrant who unexpectedly had to measure himself against the young scions of the intellectual aristocracy of Boston in the best and toughest college preparatory school in the Colonies. When the year was nearly over, he stood, perhaps to his own surprise, at the head of his class and marked for double promotion to the third year!

Exploration and Discovery: Early Years, 1706–1727 17

At this moment his father suddenly withdrew him from the scene of his triumph and registered him in a business school, giving as his reasons that he could not afford the expense of a college education and that graduates of Harvard often made a poor living. Ben dutifully accepted the decision without overt protest, but the extent of his disappointment may be indicated by the fact that the number one scholar in the grammar school failed in arithmetic in the business school.

The only place to go—except to sea, which his father vehemently opposed—was into the family business. Since he revered his father, he stuck it out for two years, though he detested the work. He cut wick for the candles, filled the molds, waited on customers, went on errands, and read and fretted and thought of running away to sea, like his half-brother Josiah, who had not been heard from since his last visit home. His wise father could read the danger signals and prudently began to take him along whenever he had occasion to call on various tradesmen in town in the hope that his restive youngest son would show an interest in one of the trades and forget the sea. It was a sound method, but the adventurous heart of Ben was set on casting loose and sailing away from home and Boston. Looking back on those exploratory excursions with his father, he admitted that he had learned a good deal from them:

It has ever since been a pleasure to me to see good workmen handle their tools; and it has been useful to me, having learnt so much by it, as to be able to do little jobs my self in my house, when a workman could not readily be got; and to construct little machines for my experiments while the intention of making the experiment was fresh and warm in my mind.[4]

But he also found time for diverting excursions with the boys, on one of which he performed a memorable experiment. As he was flying a kite near a pond about a mile wide, he conceived the idea of using the kite to transport him across the pond while he lay on his back in the water and held the stick at the end of the string that was attached to the kite. In that way, he recalled, he was ferried across "without the least fatigue, and with the greatest pleasure imaginable."[5]

The return from England of his brother James, a master printer, finally settled his father's problem of finding a suitable trade that would keep Ben safely close to home. James had brought back a press and equipment to set up his own printing business in Boston and agreed to take his brother as an apprentice. Ben, still possessed by "a hankering for the sea," held out for a while, though attracted by a trade in which his facility in reading and writing would be an advantage. His father, observing this interest, pressed hard, and Ben yielded at last, signing up reluctantly for a term of nine long years.

James, who was twenty-one and had been away from home for a long time, had had little opportunity to become acquainted with his twelve-year-old brother, whose uncommon intellect and intelligence were eclipsed for those who did not know him well by his difficulty in speaking. His father was right in thinking that these abilities would be valued more highly in Boston than at sea, and that the printing trade, although not one of the most lucrative, was well suited to Ben's abilities.

II *Youth (1718–1727)*

The printing venture of James Franklin quickly proved to be an unexpectedly stimulating workshop for the young apprentice who craved nourishment and exercise for his active mind. James had brought back from London not only a printing press but also a headful of advanced ideas, attitudes, and plans, which before long attracted a circle of dissidents chafing under Puritan repressions and platitudes. Ben, fresh from his father's tallow shop and Puritan orthodoxy, listened to the stirring talk of the freethinking circle and responded with all the enthusiasm of his youth and nature.

He enjoyed the work, and had access to more and better books. Before the first year of service was over, he composed and printed, with his brother's encouragement, who thought they might be profitable, two ballads about recent sensational happenings, which he peddled on the streets. They sold well, and he was so puffed up by his successful debut as a "poet" that his sensible father felt compelled to take him down a few pegs by ridiculing his doggerel verse. "I escap'd being a poet," he remarked in grateful retrospect, "most probably a very bad one."[6]

When he was not working, he was reading and studying—at night after work, in the morning before work, and on Sundays, alone and undisturbed in the shop, which he attended on his day of rest more regularly than church. The boy who had flunked arithmetic to vent a grievance, finding now that he needed it, mastered a standard arithmetic textbook by himself "with great ease," and for good measure a book on navigation. The necessities of the printing trade likewise made him apply himself assiduously to the study of English grammar, rhetoric, and logic, and by extension the Socratic dialogue, a type of reasoning that he found fascinating in itself and personally useful outside his trade.

As a student of the noted deists Shaftesbury and Anthony Collins and an outspoken convert to their ideas, he had been attracting unfavorable notice among the orthodox Puritans of Boston, including his father, who thought he was too much given to contradiction and argument. He was quick to perceive in these circumstances that the Socratic method of arriving at a conclusion by asking questions and adopting a posture of inquiry rather than assertion would be both helpful and congenial to him, for it would enable him to argue without appearing argumentative and to exercise his mental agility unhampered by his verbal awkwardness. By constant practice he made himself embarrassingly proficient in the method, winning many victories and few friends in discussions. It took time and experience to teach him that the search for truth and not the pursuit of victory was the proper function of the Socratic method and that victory for its own sake was a form of defeat.

At about this time, he happened to buy "an odd volume of the Spectator," which he had never seen before. It was a case of love at first sight. He read the papers over and over again, savoring their lucidity, reasonableness, urbanity, amiable satire, and happy blend of instruction and entertainment with an intensity of pleasure that revealed a deep affinity between the English *Spectator* and his distant American admirer. Here was the kind of writer he would like to be, the providential model that fitted his needs and capabilities and that he "wish'd if possible to imitate." "With that view," he wrote,

I took some of the papers, and making short hints of the sentiment in each sentence, laid them by a few days, and then without looking at the book, try'd to compleat the papers again. . . .

Then I compar'd my Spectator with the original, discover'd some of my faults and corrected them. But I found I wanted a stock of words or a readiness in recollecting and using them. . . . Therefore I took some of the tales and turn'd them into verse: and after a time, when I had pretty well forgotten the prose, turn'd them back again. I also sometimes jumbled my collection of hints into confusion, and after some weeks, endeavour'd to reduce them into the best order, before I began to form the full sentences, and compleat the paper. This was to teach me method [i.e., organization] in the arrangement of thoughts. By comparing my work afterwards with the original, I discover'd many faults and amended them. . . ."

And, smiling at his boyish vanity, he added: "But I sometimes had the pleasure of fancying that in certain particulars of small import, I had been lucky enough to improve the method or the language. . . ."[7]

This brief reference in the *Autobiography* introduces us for the first time to some of the methods of study that Franklin developed in educating himself. In carrying out the study project on the *Spectator*, he first set his aims as determined by his needs: improving his style and organization and enlarging his vocabulary. Then he analyzed the learning processes involved: imitation of a model, using new words, and arranging ideas and topics in reasonable order. Next he devised a variety of exercises or activities to stimulate and advance the learning processes: outlining, recall, comparing and contrasting, two-way conversion to a different medium, and rearranging scrambled parts.

This self-directed program reveals more than the achievement of a bright boy of fifteen with only one year of academic schooling. It would do credit to a gifted teacher with many years of experience. Implicit in the project are principles and methods of education which Franklin would later practice or advocate, and some of which have not been fully recognized and adopted to this day:

1. Education is a function of the individual; a teacher may inspire and guide, but the individual still must educate himself.

2. Education should be related to the needs and desires of the individual.

3. Education involves individual activity; one learns by doing and masters what is learned by practice and use, which require hard work and perseverance on the part of the learner.

4. Education is most effective when it seeks to uncover and develop the talents of the individual; talent is developed by study and imitation of those who have developed the same talent to a high degree of excellence; imitation of excellence does not inhibit originality, which is a gift, not a goal.

5. Improvement of English can be achieved by the study of English literary models as well as Latin or Greek models.

In England James Franklin, an admirer of the sprightly London *Daily Courant*, had conceived the ambitious plan of starting a weekly like it in Boston, which had nothing better to offer than the *News-Letter* and the *Gazette*, both of them thoroughly arid recorders of officially acceptable news. In the summer of 1721, three years after opening his printing shop, James decided to go ahead with his plan and began publication of the *New-England Courant*, which was intended, with the help of his circle of freethinking friends, to be as independent and entertaining as the London model, and which was fated to have a decisive influence on the future of his apprentice.

An epidemic of smallpox and a heated controversy over inoculation were raging in Boston that summer. The printer of the *Courant,* with his usual impulsiveness, came out at once on the side of the anti-inoculationists—which happened to be the wrong side scientifically and politically. It was apparently enough for him and his coterie that the redoubtable Cotton Mather, symbol of repressive Puritanism, was sponsoring the cause of inoculation, but they overlooked the fact that Mather was also a scientist and fellow of the Royal Society of London and a powerful spokesman of the governing class of the Colony. Before long he dubbed them the "Hell-Fire Club" and urged all good Puritans to avoid contamination by the Satanic *Courant.*

As the epidemic receded, interest in inoculation waned, and the *Courant* began to supplement the scanty news of the week with spirited Addisonian essays in the form of pseudonymous letters to the editor signed "Abigail Afterwit" (James Franklin), "Tabitha Talkative," "Harry Meanwell," and the like. The subjects, borrowed from the *Spectator* and adapted to local conditions, were the frailties and follies of men and women, as seen in their manners, scandals, vanities, and pretensions. They proved as popular in Boston as they had been in London, and the Mather interdiction on the *Courant* was ignored by a great many newspaper readers, adding fuel to the feud between the Mathers and the Franklin clique.

Ben was impressed by the popularity of the "letters" and in the spring of 1722 was ready to enter upon the final step in his method of study, further practice and use. He was fairly confident that he could do as well as his brother's friends, but there was a serious obstacle. He knew that his brother would never publish an essay written by his sixteen-year-old apprentice. To conceal his identity he would not only have to drop the paper at the shop when no one was around, but also, as he realized, disguise his handwriting beyond recognition by his brother or anyone else who was familiar with it. It would be fun to play a role and, for extra measure, to fool his brother, who was often heavy-handed in dealing with his proud apprentice. He would not merely adopt a pseudonym, but, following the example of Addison and Defoe, give his fictitious letter-writer a history and a personality to match her happily chosen New England name: "Silence Dogood," middle-aged widow, with three children, a sharp tongue, a humorous eye, and a generous heart. She would naturally reflect traits of people he knew, himself most of all. Like him, for example, she would take "more than ordinary delight in reading ingenious books," and be self-educated, and like his Folger grandmother she would be apprenticed as a servant who later married her master.[8]

When he had finished writing the first essay, in which Silence introduced herself, and had copied it in disguised form, he slipped the first half of the "letter" furtively under the door of the shop late at night and awaited the verdict with apprehensive confidence. "It was found in the morning," he recalled,

and communicated to his [brother's] writing friends when they call'd in as usual. They read it, commented on it in my hearing, and I had the exquisite pleasure, of finding it met with their approbation, and that in their different guesses at the author none were named but men of some character among us for learning and ingenuity.* [9]

*Used in Franklin's time to mean "distinguished intellectual capacity; genius, talent, quickness of wit," as well as in 'present'-day sense of "capacity for invention or construction." (O.E.D.)

Encouraged by the flattering reception of his unidentified production, he resumed Silence Dogood's story in the second paper, concluding it with a striking description of her that bore a remarkable resemblance to the author:

... *Know then*, That I am an enemy to vice, and a friend to vertue. I am one of an extensive charity, and a great forgiver of *private* injuries: a hearty lover of the clergy and all good men, and a mortal enemy to arbitrary government and unlimited power. I am naturally very jealous for the rights and liberties of my country; and the least appearance of an incroachment on those invaluable priviledges, is apt to make my blood boil exceedingly. I have likewise a natural inclination to observe and reprove the faults of others, at which I have an excellent faculty. I speak this by way of warning to all such whose offences shall come under my cognizance, for I never intend to wrap my talent in a napkin. To be brief: I am courteous and affable, good-humour'd (unless I am first provoked,) and handsome, and sometimes witty.[10]

No one recognized the young apprentice in this portrait because no one could imagine that the tongue-tied boy in the printing shop could write with such power and so mischievous an air of maturity and self-awareness. The self-portrait of Silence Dogood, but actually of her creator, was completed in the short third letter, in which she promised that she would aim at entertainment as well as instruction in her writing and would "do for the future all that *lies in my way* for the service of my countrymen"[11]—two promises that Franklin was to keep with rare consistency in his later life and work.

An attack on the *Courant* by Cotton Mather's son Samuel, signing himself "John Harvard," had been published in the rival *Gazette* several months before the appearance of "Silence Dogood." Ben now saw a chance in the fourth essay to get even with the Mathers and John Harvard with less risk and greater subtlety than in open combat, in which they had the advantage of bigger guns and higher ground. He would retaliate with satire camouflaged by allegory, and he would direct a surprise attack against the very citadel of their power, which he judged to be more vulnerable than people thought. The opening volley was a quotation from Cicero, which freely translated asked a historic question: "Am I to be taught even now to speak in my native language or in a foreign tongue?" ("An sum etiam nunc vel Graece loqui vel Latine docendus?"). It struck at the least guarded gate of the college and at the same time concealed the identity of the attacker, who had studied Latin for only one year, from the Mathers and the Courant Club.

Let us now join "Silence Dogood."[12] Unable to make up her mind whether to send her son to college, she had sought the advice of the minister of the town, who was a boarder at her house. He thought the boy should go to Harvard since he was studious and would "not idle away his time as too many there now-a-days do." When she inquired more closely into conditions at "that famous seminary of learning . . . the information which he gave . . . was neither pleasant," nor what she had expected. After their talk she went for a stroll in her orchard and, coming to her favorite retreat, "the great apple-tree," lay down "on a verdant bank" to review her troubled thoughts, fell asleep, and had a dream:

I fancy'd I was travelling over pleasant and delightful fields and meadows, and thro' many small country towns and villages; and as I pass'd along, all places resounded with the fame of the Temple of Learning: Every peasant, who had wherewithal, was preparing to send one of his children at least to this famous place; and in this case most of them consulted their own purses instead of their childrens capacities: So that I observed, a great many, yea, the most part of those who were travelling thither, were little better than dunces and blockheads.

As she approached the gate of the Temple, where young men from all parts of the country were gathered seeking admission, she noticed that it was guarded by "two sturdy porters named *Riches* and *Poverty* . . . and the latter obstinately refused to give entrance to any one who had not first gain'd the favour of the former: so that . . . many who came even to the very gate, were obliged to travel back again as ignorant as they came, for want of this necessary qualification."

Allowed to enter as a visitor, she came to a great hall containing "a stately and magnificent throne," on which Learning sat dressed entirely in black and surrounded by "innumerable volumes in all languages." On her right sat English, "with a pleasant smiling countenance," and on her left Latin, Greek, and Hebrew, "with their faces vail'd." They "seldom or never unvail'd their faces here, and then to few or none. . . ." When she asked why they remained veiled, she was told to look at the foot of the throne, where she noticed "*Idleness*, attended with *Ignorance* . . . who first vail'd them, and still kept them so."

Most of those admitted to the Temple, soon finding the work too onerous and difficult, were content to take it easy in the company of "Madam *Idleness* and her maid *Ignorance*," but as the time neared for ascending the first step, they sought the assistance of those who by "diligence and a docible temper" had nearly climbed the step "and who, for the reward perhaps of a *pint of milk*, or a *piece of plumb cake*, lent the lubbers a helping hand, and sat them in the eye of the world, upon a level with themselves." The procedure was repeated for the next step, after which the usual terminal ceremonies were held and "every beetle-scull seem'd well satisfy'd with his own portion of learning, tho' perhaps he was *e'en just* as ignorant as ever."

Silence then followed the company that was leaving to see where they were going.

Some . . . took to merchandizing, others to travelling . . . and some to nothing; and many of them from henceforth, for want of patrimony, liv'd as poor as church mice, being unable to dig, and asham'd to beg, and to live by their wits it was impossible. But the most part of the crowd went along a large beaten path, which led to a temple at the further end of the plain, call'd, *The Temple of Theology*. The business of those who were employ'd in this temple being laborious and painful, I wonder'd exceedingly to see so many go towards it; but while I was pondering this matter in my mind, I spy'd Pecunia [goddess of money] behind a curtain, beckoning to them with her hand, which sight immediately satisfy'd me for whose sake it was, that a great part of them (I will not say all) travel'd that road.

As she turned homeward in her dream, she reflected sadly that so many attending the Temple, since they lacked the requisite ability and inclination, "learn little more than how to carry themselves handsomely, and enter a room genteely, (which might as well be acquir'd at a dancing-school,) and from whence they return, after abundance of trouble and charge, as great blockheads as ever, only more proud and self-conceited."

At this moment she was accidentally awakened by her boarder, to whom she related the events and scenes of her dream. He assured her that "it was a lively representation of Harvard College. . . ."

Though the allegory is rather transparent (Bunyan had not received the intensive study given to the *Spectator*), the result, considering the refractory nature of the material, is an ingenious and effective tour de force, if not a specimen of alchemy. The satirical charge Franklin had launched had hit home, as "John Harvard" acknowledged in the *Gazette*, but he could do no better than to answer it with a feeble shot of stylistic criticism that evaded the basic issue—the value of an education at Harvard College. Stripped of its allegorical embroidery and satirical interest, the fourth Dogood paper presented an indictment of Harvard on four counts:

1. The college admits young men of insufficient academic ability whose parents can afford the expense while it keeps out gifted children of poor parents.

2. English studies, which would be more interesting and useful, are subordinated to Latin, Greek, and Hebrew studies in spite of the fact that the latter are beyond the capacity of most of the students.

3. The narrow course of study prepares students only for the ministry, which too many enter because of financial necessity, though unqualified for its demands and rigors.

4. Those who do not have an independent income and cannot bring themselves to follow an ecclesiastical career have to go into business without adequate preparation.

In brief, Harvard does not meet the needs of most of the students or of the Colony. Though Franklin is not ready at the age of sixteen to make specific proposals for the improvement of education, his educational philosophy has already taken shape: *A proper education is related to the capacities, interests, and needs of people and to the goals of the society in which they live, and should not be denied to anyone because of insufficient means.* Here is the seed of a far-reaching revolutionary idea which we are still struggling to realize 250 years later.

The issue of the *Courant* in which the sixth letter of "Silence Dogood" was printed also contained a harmless bit of fictitious news twitting the authorities for dragging their feet in the search for pirates. Had the Mathers not been waiting for a chance to clip the wings of the high-flying *Courant*, the government would probably have shrugged off the trifle. Instead, the Council chose to regard it as a case of contempt and arrested James. When he refused to disclose the author of the item, he was put in jail, and Ben had to run the paper and the printing shop alone, an opportunity which he welcomed. Whether he was discreet or too busy or both, his eighth *Dogood* contribution is an "abstract from the London Journal" on freedom of thought and speech, the point of which no one could miss. However incendiary it may have been, it was less subversive in the view of the hierarchy than the ninth on "hypocritical pretenders to religion," which mounted a scarcely veiled attack on the Mathers prudently screened by another excerpt from the *London Journal* on the same theme. As might be expected, Benjamin-Dogood, while professing to be "a hearty lover of the clergy," was enraged by the Mathers' abuse of their political power. Everyone knew whom he meant when he declared: "A man compounded of law and Gospel, is able to cheat a whole country with his religion, and then destroy them under *colour of law*."[13] His brother, who expressed approval of the two hard-hitting papers, did not fully appreciate, as did their author, the importance of this first skirmish in America on the issue of freedom of the press. James apologized to the authorities for printing the offensive piece and gained his release after a month.

Although none of the other Dogood articles approaches the significance of the fourth, they reveal additional facets of Franklin's early thinking and writing. The fifth, ostensibly dealing with the female faults of idleness and pride, a theme that he owed to the *Spectator*, was turned into a plea for equal education for women; he quoted liberally from Defoe's *Essay on Projects*, one of the books in his father's library that left a permanent imprint on his thinking. The seventh paper, a satire on current New England poetry, is the most original literary achievement of the Dogood series and created a considerable stir among the local wits lasting several months. He proposed in the tenth

Dogood essay a plan of insurance to mitigate the "lamentable condition of widows" (again borrowed from the *Essay on Projects*).

The reader of these essays will easily note their immaturities and imperfections, but he will soon overlook these as he admires the undeniable originality and vigor of their thought and expression. Though the young author may have borrowed from Bunyan, Defoe, Addison, Locke, Socrates, and Shaftesbury, he adapted and transmuted what he took to his own interests and ends. The resulting person is not an amalgam of these men, overpowering as they could have been, but uniquely Ben Franklin of Boston, printer's apprentice extraordinary—already wise beyond his years in the ways of men and women and inclined to see them in the clear light of day rather than the enchanting light of the moon or the beatified light of heaven, viewing the world with humor and good will, jealous of his own and his neighbors' freedom, eager to raise himself and others out of poverty and ignorance, and superbly equipped to realize his powers and purposes by means of the written word.

After four years of able service, including the management of the business and the paper during James's imprisonment, Ben considered himself qualified and entitled to do the work of a journeyman; yet he was constantly asked to perform the most menial tasks, and was further humiliated by being beaten at times. When, therefore, his apprenticeship contract was legally terminated by James (though not morally), he was in a position "to assert his freedom," and, having taken one beating too many, felt compelled to leave his rigorous master. Looking back long after, he reflected: "I fancy his harsh and tyrannical treatment of me might be a means of impressing me with that aversion to arbitrary power that has stuck to me thro' my whole life."[14] He later regretted having taken advantage of his brother, but he was not sorry that he had been unable to find work as a journeyman printer in Boston, where his prospects were rather dim because of his reputation as a rebel and an atheist.

The lure of the sea had faded for him with the acquisition of a trade that he loved. Knowing that there was a printer in New York, he decided to try his luck there. Since his father could and would legally stop him, it would be necessary for him to get away secretly. That was arranged by his persuasive friend, John Collins, who explained to the sympathetic captain of a boat bound for New York that his friend could not take passage openly because he "had got a naughty girl with child, whose friends would compel . . . [him] to marry her."[15] Ben sold some of his books to pay for his passage and take care of anticipated expenses and left Boston, friends, and family without saying goodbye to them.

At the end of September, 1723, an advertisement appeared in the *Courant:* "James Franklin, printer in Queen's Street, wants a likely lad for an apprentice." But neither he nor any other printer would ever again find an apprentice to compare with Ben Franklin.

The voyage to New York lasted three days—time enough for a boy of seventeen to feel both the poignancy of separation and the exhilaration of freedom. He was alone and "without the least recommendation to or knowledge of any person in the place" where he was going and "with very little money." But he was on his own at last, no father to lean on, no brother to order him around, no neighbors to constrain him, and a world of strangers to learn to feel at home with.

Come to think of it, he was lucky to have had four years of association with his gritty brother, even though James may have been bossy and ill-tempered at times. Thanks in part to him, Ben was now a competent printer capable of supporting himself, familiar with many of the best minds of the time, and with some experience in journalism, business, and politics. He had been given an opportunity to meet men of substantial learning and devotion to the public welfare, to test himself as a writer, to manage briefly a spirited and independent newspaper, and, not least, to observe the contradictions of human nature. He had been both student and teacher of himself, and now this was his commencement. He judged he was as well prepared as one can be before taking the inevitable plunge into the unknown.

It was also his first taste of travel, with its beckoning prospect of new places, new "lovers of reading," new forms of "ingenuity," new opportunities for learning. His nature seemed to crave change and movement; perhaps that was why he had long loved the sea. Permanence made him uneasy.

William Bradford, the veteran printer in New York, received the young stranger warmly but could not offer him a job and advised that he might find work in Philadelphia, where Bradford's son, a printer and newspaper publisher, had recently lost the best man in his shop. Franklin decided to go on to the Quaker town by way of New Jersey, walking the fifty miles from Amboy to Burlington to save money. Though he suffered many hardships along the way, he arrived safely at his destination, but dirty, hungry, and exhausted, on a cold Sunday morning in October. He never forgot that first morning in Philadelphia:

> I was in my working dress, my best cloaths being to come around by sea. I was dirty from my journey; my pockets were stuff'd out with shirts and stockings; . . . I was fatigu'd with travelling, rowing and want of rest. I was very hungry, and my whole stock of cash consisted of a Dutch dollar and about a shilling in copper. The latter I gave the people of the boat for my passage, who at first refus'd it on account of my rowing; but I insisted on their taking it, a man being sometimes more generous when he has but a little money than when he has plenty, perhaps thro' fear of being thought to have little.[16]

Meeting a boy with bread, he was directed to a baker's shop, where he asked for "three penny worth" of bread and was given "three great puffy rolls." Having no room in his pockets, he walked away "with a roll under each arm, and eating the other." On his way he passed the house of the Reads, in front of which their daughter was standing, who thought he made "a most awkward ridiculous appearance," and finally entered the meetinghouse of the Quakers, where the reverent silence and his state of exhaustion put him soundly to sleep.

He did not find employment with Andrew Bradford, as he had hoped, but with another printer, Samuel Keimer, a religious eccentric, who had recently gone into business with an old printing press that did not work. The clever young journeyman made it operable and had a job. Lonely and a little homesick, and therefore less inclined to read, he sought out and soon made the acquaintance of several congenial young lovers of reading in town, with whom he spent his evenings "very pleasantly" during this first winter away from home.

Philadelphia had much to commend it at that time. Though smaller and less stimulating intellectually than Boston, it was much younger—only twenty-four years older than Ben was—and, owing to the principles of its great Quaker founder, William Penn, the most democratic, cosmopolitan, and tolerant settlement in the Colonies. None of its residents were as yet very rich or very poor, those who had more money than their neighbors had worked hard themselves to make it, each man was of necessity valued for what he was, and everybody was an ancestor rather than a descendant. This condition was generally true of all the settlements in America, but truer of Philadelphia than of Boston, and much truer of both than of London or other old European cities—a most favorable condition for a poor underprivileged boy with Franklin's gifts and ambitions. He had also coolly observed that the two printers in Philadelphia, who were twice his age, would offer no serious competition to any able printer who might wish to challenge them in the future.

The future suddenly became the present when Sir William Keith, the well-intentioned governor of Pennsylvania, who had by chance read a letter written by Franklin setting forth his reasons for leaving Boston, sought *his* acquaintance. He described their first meeting at Keimer's shop with obvious relish: . . . "[The Governor] would have me away with him to the tavern . . . to taste as he said some excellent Madeira. I was not a little surpriz'd, and Keimer star'd like a pig poison'd."[17]

Warmed by the Madeira, the governor, long dissatisfied with the poor quality of printing in the Colony, proposed nothing less than that his charming and talented young drinking companion open his own printing shop, with his father's financial backing, of course, and with the assurance that the governor would help in getting printing orders from the government. It was agreed that he should return to Boston as soon as passage could be arranged. In the meantime the project would be kept secret between them, and he would continue to work for Keimer as usual. He sailed late in April and after a stormy voyage reached Boston about two weeks later.

When he suddenly appeared after seven long months of complete silence flaunting a brand-new suit and watch, his family was happily surprised. But not "grum and sullen" brother James, whom he went to see at the printing shop: "He receiv'd me not very frankly, look'd me all over, and turn'd to his work again."[18] Ben, who was usually not one to bear a grudge, responded in kind. With an air of condescension he treated the men to a drink "and took his leave." It was more obvious than ever that the two brothers were still irreconcilable. His father penned a courteous letter to the governor, thanking him for his interest in Ben, but respectfully declining to finance his son of only eighteen "as yet." Franklin undoubtedly felt let down, but not entirely convinced that his father was wrong.

During a stopover in Newport on the way to New York, he visited his married brother John, and was entrusted by a friend of his brother, Samuel Vernon, with the task of collecting a considerable sum of money in Pennsylvania. He evidently inspired trust in men of substance in spite of his youth. His childhood friend Collins, a brilliant mathematician, who had decided also to seek his fortune in Philadelphia, was waiting for him in New York. His friend had been drunk every day since arriving there and had gambled all his money away.

Before leaving New York, Franklin paid off Collins's debts and on the way home picked up the money owed to Vernon. In Philadelphia, while Collins was vainly looking for work, he borrowed money for board and lodging and brandy from Franklin and the Vernon fund, which was soon so depleted that its custodian, not knowing when he would have to return it, began to be very much worried. There were frequent quarrels and recriminations, especially when Collins was drunk and irascible. He finally left for Barbados, where he had been offered a position as a tutor, promising faithfully to pay back all he owed. Franklin never heard from him again. At that point he was ready to agree with his father that he was still too young to manage a business requiring judgment and discretion.

But Governor Keith did not agree, contending that Ben's father was "too prudent." He advised his protégé to shop for printing equipment and other supplies in England and offered to give him the necessary letters of recommendation and credit. Franklin's happiness would have been perfect were it not for the fear that nibbled away at it every day—what if Vernon should ask for his money before he sailed? (As it happened, he did not.)

Still, the days passed quickly and pleasantly. The burden of the unhappy Collins had been lifted from his shoulders, he was courting Deborah Read, and he often took walks on Sundays with his good friends, Charles Osborne, Joseph Watson, and James Ralph, in "the woods near Skuylkill," where they read to each other and discussed what they had read. He remembered Osborne for another reason:

Osborne went to the West Indies, where he became an eminent lawyer and made money, but died young. He and I had made a serious agreement that the one who happen'd first to die, should if possible make a friendly visit to the other and acquaint him how he found things in that Separate State. But he never fullfill'd his promise.[19]

The governor, being fond of Franklin's company, often invited him to his house and always mentioned the letters he had promised, but invariably in the indefinite future. Just before the ship was to sail Franklin again called for the letters and was told that the governor was busy but would deliver them at the next stop. At the next stop he was informed that the governor was in but was "engag'd in business of the utmost importance," and would send them on board. Franklin returned to the ship "a little puzzled, but still not doubting." When the mail was brought on board, he asked the captain for his letters and was told they were in one bag together with the other mail and would not be available until the mail was sorted out before their landing in England.

Without misgiving, he put the letters out of mind. Among the passengers were Thomas Denham, a benevolent Philadelphia merchant, and, unexpectedly, his friend James Ralph, traveling without his wife and child. Crossing the Atlantic then was a tedious and hazardous journey lasting two to three months, but to Franklin, crossing it for the first time at the age of eighteen, it was the unbelievable realization of many dreams,—going to sea, visiting London and the mother country, and achieving independence in his own business. Toward the end of the voyage, the mailbag was opened, but there were no letters from the governor.

Though deeply hurt and indignant, he tried to understand why Keith had behaved so cruelly. "What shall we think," he cried,

of a Governor's playing such pitiful tricks, and imposing so grossly on a poor ignorant boy! It was a habit he had acquired. He wish'd to please every body; and having little to give, he gave expectations. He was otherwise an ingenious sensible man, a pretty good writer, and a good governor for the people. . . . Several of our best laws were of his planning, and pass'd during his administration.[20]

Like his creation, "Silence Dogood," Franklin was a person "of an extensive charity, and a great forgiver of *private* injuries."

He arrived in London on Christmas Eve, invincibly imbued with good will toward men but somewhat less trustful of them than when he had set sail for the Old World. His first year of independence had been largely one of adjustment and discovery rather than growth. He had learned he could support himself as a printer and had a remarkable talent for making and keeping friends. He was beginning to be aware of the hazards as well as the rewards of friendship but had not yet found a way to protect himself against the hazards and luckily, perhaps, would never quite succeed. Most important of all, he had discovered that he felt at home with all classes of people. Though he was slow in conversation, his quick wit and high spirits, combined with a range of knowledge and understanding unusual for his age and background, attracted men and women to him of all ages and stations in life.

In retrospect, Governor Keith had been a benefactor. His good intentions, though as insubstantial as the clouds, had lifted Franklin out of provincial Philadelphia before he was twenty and transported him to the most advanced city and country in Europe. This feat could hardly have been accomplished if the governor had been a man of integrity.

During the long sea voyage Franklin and Denham had become good friends, and Denham now wisely advised him to seek employment only among the reputable printing firms of London, contending that, since he planned to set up his own printing shop when he returned home, it would be a mistake for him to look for any other kind of work when he had this opportunity to improve his competence in the printing trade. Within a short time he was taken on by Samuel Palmer, a well-known printer in the city. Franklin rented cheap quarters for himself and his friend Ralph, who had confided to him that he had no intention of returning to Philadelphia and wife and child. He planned to achieve success as a poet some day. Having spent all his money to pay for the passage to London, he had to borrow from Franklin's slender reserve, while looking for work suitable for a future poet, in the pattern made familiar by Collins.

Freed from religious scruples, family restraint, and prying neighbors, the two small-town chums set out to sample the novel pleasures offered by the city, visiting the notable sights and "going to plays and other places of amusement." When Franklin's reserve was exhausted, they could still manage on his earnings at Palmer's. Among the many pleasures they encountered was a charming young woman, "Mrs. T.," living in the house where they lodged, who had a millinery shop and a child. Ralph, being a man of leisure and a fascinating talker, had the advantage over his boon companion. "[Ralph] . . . read plays to her in the evenings, they grew intimate, she took another lodging, and he follow'd her."[21] Prompted by Ralph's example, as similar occasions presented themselves, Franklin reconsidered the understanding he had with Miss Read and wrote to her—it was the only letter he sent her while he was in London—that he was not likely to return for some time.

During his first year in London, Franklin wrote a philosophical paper on free will, entitled *A Dissertation on Liberty and Necessity*. He ran off 100 copies, a few of which he hesitantly handed out to friends. Drawing upon his earlier studies in Locke, Shaftesbury, Anthony Collins, and syllogistic logic, he started out with the prime axiom of the deists, that God was "all-wise, all-good, all-powerful," and, by what seemed to him ironclad logic at the time, reached the conclusion that evil could not exist in the universe and that men did not truly possess free will. As often happens when logic is applied to metaphysics, Franklin found himself at the end exactly where he wanted to be—free to pursue his pleasures in a God-dominated world without free will and evil. The paper brought him introductions to Bernard Mandeville, the cynical Dutch philosopher, and to Henry Pemberton, a fellow of the Royal Society and a friend of Newton.

Things were not going well with his friend Ralph. He was still out of work, and the milliner's shop was "not sufficient to maintain them with her child." In desperation he turned to teaching, the last resort of the needy writer. "This," Franklin remarked with modest irony, "he deem'd a business below him, and confident of future better fortune when he should be unwilling to have it known that he once was so meanly employ'd, he changed his name, and did me the honor to assume mine."[22] But without asking leave to use it!

Meanwhile, in Ralph's absence, the milliner turned often to Franklin for aid and comfort. He gave her as much money as he could spare and, misconstruing her acceptance of it, attempted to take his friend's place. Indignantly, she rejected his advances and promptly informed her lover, who, with a nice sense of compensation, let Franklin know that his perfidy had canceled the substantial loans received from him. It was a lesson in human relations, which, Franklin concluded, have a special logic not taught in books.

With a feeling of relief that matched his loss, he set about putting his affairs in better order. In the expectation of better work and training, he transferred from Palmer to the printer John Watts, who ran one of the largest and most important printing firms in London. He moved to lodgings nearer Watts; he visited his friend Denham more often. Now that he was on his own, without the drag of Ralph and his entanglements, he could be himself again.

Though a newcomer, he could not resist suggesting several improvements in the shop rules at Watts and "carried them against all opposition." Reformers and teachers are often insufferable to work or live with, but "Dogood" Franklin escaped this fate because he was free of self-righteousness, convivial, warm-hearted, and as ready to poke fun at himself as at others. Above all, he was genuinely fond of people, including those who had taken advantage of him. In spite of the fact that Ralph had sponged on him outrageously, he confessed that he loved him, "for he had many amiable qualities." He particularly enjoyed the company of people who loved reading or had a marked talent or skill of any kind, and he came upon them in the most unexpected places, as in the case of the lame elderly widow who kept the house he had moved to after the break with Ralph. She had lived "much among people of distinction, and knew a 1000 anecdotes of them as far back as the time of Charles the Second" 50 years before. He was glad to keep her company at supper, he remembered, " . . . whenever she desired it. Our supper was only half an anchovy each, on a very little strip of bread and butter, and half a pint of ale between us. But the entertainment was in her conversation."[23]

A fellow printer and friend at Watts, whom he had taught to swim, proposed that they travel together through Europe, supporting themselves (the Collins-Ralph syndrome arising again) by giving instruction and conducting exhibitions in swimming. The idea appealed to Franklin, ready for a change regardless of where it might lead, until he mentioned it to his friend Denham, who earnestly advised him to give it up and return home. Fortunately, Denham was in a position to offer more than advice. He was opening a store in Philadelphia and invited Franklin to return with him as his assistant, with the promise of teaching him the mercantile business and helping him in time to go into business for himself. The offer was accepted with alacrity: "The thing pleas'd me, for I was grown tired of London, remember'd with pleasure the happy months I had spent in Pennsylvania, and wish'd again to see it."[24] He welcomed this chance to be associated in business with the friend who had been an anchor of integrity for him during these precarious months of freedom in London. He resigned at once from Watts and, as he then thought, from the printing trade, in order to help Denham make final purchases and deliveries to the ship. They sailed from London on July 21, 1726, in the *Berkshire*, of which Denham was half-owner. As the wind filled the sails and the pier crowded with people quickly receded, the malaise he had felt in recent months abated somewhat. It was good to be afloat again, to have the illusion that he was motionless while the little houses and people went sailing by. That night they anchored off Gravesend.

Looking back at the year and a half he had lived in London, he sensed that it had been a rich, though unsettling, experience. The complete freedom he had enjoyed in the ancient storied city had widened his horizon and introduced him to forbidden pleasures of mind and body. Like old wine, it had raised his spirits at first, as he savored new places, amusements, plays, acquaintances, and books. Staid Philadelphia and innocent Deborah Read had seemed a planet away. In the first flush of youthful release from sobriety and convention, he celebrated a universe suffused with the power, goodness, and wisdom of its Creator, a universe in which evil and inequality existed only in the eye of the beholder. In due course came the awakening and the hangover of the morning after—like the rebuff by Mrs. T. and the wrecking of his friendship with Ralph. The "truths" of logic and reason were less attractive in the uncosmetic light of day, and his paper on free will "appear'd now not so clever a performance as . . . [he] once thought it." Assailed by self-doubt and self-reproach, he burned all the remaining copies of the *Dissertation* save one. On the credit side, he reflected with some comfort, there had been work and people and books:

Most part of the time, I work'd hard at my business, and spent but little upon myself except in seeing plays and in books. . . . Tho' I had by no means improv'd my fortune . . . I had pick'd up some very ingenious acquaintance whose conversation was of great advantage to me, and I had read considerably.[25]

On the day after his departure, he started a journal, which he kept faithfully throughout his return voyage. It is the authentic voice of Franklin at the age of twenty, freshly recording without self-consciousness the events and impressions of each day, and incidentally affording him some daily relief from the troubled state of mind in which he had left London. Many of these entries are so vivid that time is erased, and we feel he is alive and talking to us.

When they turned into the Channel, he wrote:

And now whilst I write this, sitting upon the quarter-deck, I have methinks one of the pleasantest scenes in the world before me. 'Tis a fine clear day, and we are going away before the wind with an easy pleasant gale. We have near fifteen sail of ships in sight, and I may say in company. On the left hand appears the coast of France at a distance, and on the right is the town and castle of Dover, with the green hills and chalky cliffs of England, to which we must now bid farewell.[26]

For more than a week they were held up by contrary winds at the Isle of Wight. Visiting ancient Carisbrooke Castle, seat of the island's governors, he heard a story about one of them that apparently touched

Exploration and Discovery: Early Years, 1706–1727 37

a critical point in the turmoil that was churning in his mind, for it stirred him to an almost poetic intensity of expression:

At his death it appeared he was a great villain, and a great politician. . . . What surprised me was, that the silly old fellow, the keeper of the castle, who remembered him governor, should have so true a notion of his character as I perceived he had. In short I believe it is impossible for a man, though he has all the cunning of a devil, to live and die a villain, and yet conceal it so well as to carry the name of an honest fellow to the grave with him. Truth and sincerity have a certain distinguishing native-lustre about them which cannot be perfectly counterfeited, they are like fire and flame that cannot be painted.[27]

The wind turning suddenly favorable, they finally set sail on August 5. The days passed without incident until the eighteenth, when one of the passengers was accused of playing with marked cards. An informal "court of justice" was set up, and the culprit brought to trial. After weighing the evidence, the jury returned a verdict of guilty. He was sentenced to an appropriate punishment, including a fine of two bottles of brandy. Refusing to pay the fine, he was ostracized by the other passengers, who refrained from eating, drinking, conversing, or playing with him. He held out stubbornly for six days and then, unable to endure his isolation any longer, paid the fine. "Man is a social being," Franklin observed after this episode,

and it is for aught I know one of the worst of punishments to be excluded from society. . . . One of the philosophers, I think it was Plato, used to say, that he had rather be the veriest stupid block in nature, than the possessor of all knowledge without some intelligent being to communicate it to.[28]

Whether or not this is true for all, it was certainly true for Franklin, whose passion for knowledge was equaled only by his need to share it with others.

The days and the ship sailed on against the unchanging background of wind and sun, cloud and sea. On September 23, with the passengers irritable and uncommunicative after being cooped up together at sea for two months, they sighted another ship also sailing west. They "shortened sail" and, when it came close, learned that it was from Dublin bound for New York, with more than fifty indentured servants, men and women, aboard. The travelers on both ships were delighted to see each other. As Franklin observed:

When we have been for a considerable time tossing on the vast waters, far from the sight of any land or ships, or any mortal creature but ourselves (except a few fish and sea birds) the whole world, for aught we know, may be under a second deluge, and we (like Noah and his company in the Ark) the only surviving remnant of the human race.[29]

The two vessels continued in sight of each other for a week, running on "very lovingly together."

He noted a partial eclipse of the sun; a partial eclipse of the moon; and an interesting experiment he made with "gulf weed," on which embryos of tiny crabs were attached by stalks to the branches, like "a fruit of the animal kind." His descriptions of the dolphins and the flying fish that were caught also give us an early hint of his intense pleasure in observing and recording the phenomena of nature down to the minutest significant detail.

With the distractions of everyday living removed and the misty rampart of sky and sea inviting contemplation, Franklin continued to examine the dissatisfactions that had been nagging at him. He finally came to the conclusion that he had been sailing through life without compass and destination, carried wherever the winds of chance might blow him. During the long days and nights, as the procession of disparate places and persons trooped through his memory, constituting a confusion of factors seeking a solution, a plan gradually took shape in his mind and was entered in his journal. "Perhaps the most important part of that journal," he declared, "is the *plan* to be found in it which I formed at sea, for regulating my future conduct in life."[30] The "preamble" to the plan stated the problem as he saw it: "I have never fixed a regular design in life; by which means it has been a confused variety of different scenes."[31]

The solution he had worked out followed:

I am now entering upon a new . . . [life]: let me therefore make some resolutions, and form some scheme of action, that, henceforth, I may live in all respects like a rational creature.

1. It is necessary for me to be extremely frugal for some time, till I have paid what I owe.

2. To endeavour to speak truth in every instance; to give nobody expectations that are not likely to be answered, but aim at sincerity in every word and action—the most amiable excellence in a rational being.

3. To apply myself industriously to whatever business I take in hand, and not divert my mind from my business by any foolish project of growing suddenly rich; for industry and patience are the surest means of plenty.

4. I resolve to speak ill of no man whatever, not even in a matter of truth; but rather by some means excuse the faults I hear charged upon others, and upon proper occasions speak all the good I know of every body.[32]

He had not abandoned the ideal of reason; he had simply come to recognize from his own experience that by itself it was inadequate to deal with the problems that life presented. He saw now that he had converted or "perverted" some of his friends to deism, especially Collins and Ralph, with disastrous consequences:

Each of them [Collins and Ralph] . . . afterwards wronged me greatly without the least compunction and recollecting Keith's conduct towards me, (who was another Freethinker) and my own towards Vernon and Miss Read which at times gave me great trouble, I began to suspect that this doctrine tho' it might be true, was not very useful. . . . I grew convinc'd that *truth, sincerity* and *integrity* in dealings between man and man, were of the utmost importance to the felicity of life. . . .[33]

In human affairs, Franklin was implying, truth and reason must be justified in action by their effect on the welfare of the individual and society, or be put aside as irrelevant. His Plan of Conduct would have to meet the same test, or be discarded later for a better plan.

When land was sighted at last on October 9, he was overcome by emotion: "I could not discern it so soon as the rest; my eyes were dimmed with the suffusion of . . . [tears] of joy."[34] He wept with joy partly because he had come home after a long absence, having twice escaped the perils of the sea, but even more because he had survived the greater perils of the land and was at peace with himself at last. He had left Philadelphia a boy; he came back a man.

And then the story almost ended here.

Mr. Denham opened his store, and his assistant quickly learned the business and "grew in a little time expert at selling." "We lodg'd and boarded together," he added,

he counsell'd me as a father, having a sincere regard for me: I respected and lov'd him: and we might have gone on together very happily. . . .[35]

But soon after Franklin's twenty-first birthday, both were taken very seriously ill. His revered friend and counselor died, and he came close to following him. "I suffered a good deal," he recalled, gave up the point [i.e., conceded defeat, as in a game] in my own mind, and was rather disappointed when I found my self recovering; regretting in some degree that I must now some time or other have all that disagreeable work to do over again.[36]

III *Reprise*

Though the world of Benjamin Franklin's boyhood and adolescence seems light years distant from ours, the needs of the young and the conditions favorable for their education remain basically pretty much the same for any time or place. These factors are briefly reviewed under the following heads: Family, Nature, School and Studies, Work, Friends, Transplantation, and Religion and Philosophy, and considered with particular reference to their influence in Franklin's education.

Family

Franklin was fortunate in his family background. To begin with, his inheritance was good on both sides, Franklin and Folger, in strength of body and mind, intelligence, ability, and character. As a bonus, he was spared the extremes of poverty or wealth, which tend to foster distorted attitudes and emotional inertia in children. In his early years he enjoyed the essentials of good care, love, understanding, and the give-and-take of a large family. His mother and father respected and may even have loved each other. They could read and write, and they provided a home where books, music, and learning were valued. His father was a man of superior intelligence, independent judgment, and marked mechanical aptitude, his mother a woman of remarkable good sense and equanimity. They held the same religious and moral beliefs and exercised them in common with their neighbors. Consequently, as a child Benjamin did not suffer the traumatic confusion and isolation of children whose parents differ in fundamental outlook from each other or from the community in which they live. In addition, he grew up in an "open" home, where relatives and friends were welcomed and glad to come.

Nature

Franklin was lucky to have grown up in close proximity to the sea and the primeval forest and to the animals who share the land and sea with man. The child who has been separated from these natural influences is greatly handicapped in his development and education. Living wholly in a man-made and man-dominated world, he acquires unbalanced attitudes and values, sees things in a limited perspective, and lacks the wonder and reverence, as well as the total awareness of reality, that direct experience of nature instills.

School and Studies

Although he had only one year of academic schooling, he made up for this handicap by directing his own education. His secret weapon was reading, which he learned at a very early age, probably with some assistance from his father. Unretarded by the absence of "children's books," he pursued this natural interest with avidity and discrimination in the fields of biography, history, literature, and philosophy, being guided by the conviction that books should be useful and pleasurable. To improve his own writing, he also studied grammar, composition, logic, and the Socratic method of argumentation. Given the narrow curriculum of the schools of his youth, he probably fared better by self-education than he might have done by following the conventional course through the Boston Grammar School and Harvard College. Although compelled by necessity to take his education in his own hands, he had the advantage of consulting his own interests, needs, and capacities rather than having to adapt or subordinate them to the requirements of the school, and there was less danger in that time and place that he would ignore his obligation to society in following his individual interests.

Of course, the great risk in self-education is that not all young people are Benjamin Franklins, endowed with his passion for knowledge, his talents, discrimination, and perseverance. Still, if they possess these qualities in some measure, they stand a good chance of overcoming their initial handicaps.

Work

Franklin's work experience, starting at the age of ten, was an invaluable part of his education, as it is in the education of any young person who gets the chance through necessity or desire or parental wisdom to work while carrying on his studies. In the family chandlery, in the sampling of various trades arranged by his wise father, in the printing shops of Boston, Philadelphia, and London, and in Mr. Denham's store, he acquired a mastery of his trade and a knowledge of manufacture, journalism, business, politics, and people that cannot be gained in any school, together with the invaluable feeling of self-confidence and independence that competence in a trade or profession gives the beginner in life.

Friends

Like his father, Franklin had a talent for friendship, in spite of his speech handicap. His numerous brothers, sisters, and cousins were his first friends, and his "ingenious" Uncle Benjamin should be included in this company. As he grew older, he made friends among the neighbors' boys of his own age, learning in competition with them to swim and fish and manage a boat and acquiring self-confidence and influence in this way as he surpassed them. They probably started him on his hobbies of flying kites and training pigeons. Older men and women also were attracted to him and contributed to his education. The bridge and bond between him and his friends was most often a mutual love of reading, which recognizes no barriers of age or class. Through these friends of all ages and conditions, avenues leading to other interests and ways of life were opened to him: John Collins (the new mathematics and science); the Courant Club (radical new ideas from London); James Ralph (poetry and drama); Governor William Keith (government and the English aristocracy); Deborah Read and Mrs. T. (the ways of women); his lame widowed landlady in London (the world of fashion); Thomas Denham (integrity in business and friendship)—to mention a few of the many who enriched his education and life.

Transplantation

Another invigorating factor in his education was his exposure to different cultures, at first through his wide-ranging exploration of books that introduced him to unfamiliar viewpoints, customs, personalities, times, and places. While making these excursions in his imagination, he was establishing his roots and center of gravity in Puritan Boston. Steeped in the formidable native culture of Puritan orthodoxy, he would be better prepared to stand up to the impact of conflicting cultures in other households, cities, and countries. The fortunate timing of the accidents (abetted by his temperament) that transplanted him from Boston to Philadelphia and London was a special but substantial dividend in his education.

Religion and Philosophy

In his childhood Franklin found security in the religious faith of his home and community, and so was freed from the fear of the mysterious forces of nature and the universe. The peace of mind that he enjoyed in his years of immaturity is an essential element in the natural development of children. When he reached the age at which intelligent children commonly question the tenets of their traditional belief, he had the support of a strong foundation on which to build either a personal adaptation to his family's faith or a new personal faith or philosophy that met his own spiritual and intellectual needs. In either event he would have a moral stabilizer as he embarked on the responsibilities of manhood.

On closer examination it appears that Franklin's education, which on the surface might seem to have been seriously disadvantaged, was in reality uncommonly rich in those favorable influences that family, nature, study, work, friendship, travel, and religion and philosophy contribute to a well-rounded education at all times everywhere. It is therefore not entirely surprising that even at the age of sixteen Franklin, favored as he was by extraordinary circumstances and talents, produced his entertaining and far-sighted critique of education at Harvard College.

CHAPTER 2

Independence and Expansion: Manhood, 1727–1746

I *Educator of the Common People*

FRANKLIN'S plan to achieve economic independence and live "like a rational creature" on terms of truth, sincerity, and good will with his fellowmen was abruptly shattered by the death of Denham, his revered patron and friend, and he was left "once more to the wide world"—a depressing prospect at that time to a young man trying to make his way on his own. Unable to find employment in the mercantile field, as he would then have preferred, he went back reluctantly to the precarious printing trade, accepting an offer from Sam Keimer, who needed him to manage his shop and break in a motley staff of untrained men. This job would end, Franklin suspected, as soon as Keimer thought he could get along without him.

In the meantime his mind was not idle. His recent close brush with death had given him quite a jolt, forcing a new perspective on him and leading him to reexamine his beliefs and himself. The Plan of Conduct drawn up before his illness was still valid, but it was little more than a program geared for the immediate future. In his chastened frame of mind, he felt he also had to find answers to the fundamental questions that he had asked himself when he expected to die, questions concerning the place and meaning of man in the universal scheme of things. Unless he could answer these to his own satisfaction, he would not have a long-range rational basis for moral conduct.

Franklin's encounter with the ultimate had intensified his dissatisfaction with the deistic concept of God. In facing death, as well as life, he found the God of the deists too remote, too impersonal, for man's needs. Their concept "might be true, [but] was not very useful." He was also troubled by the internal tug-of-war between his ingrained Puritan ideal of virtue and his pleasure-loving temperament. When, as was his way, he discussed these problems with his friends, he found, of course, that he was not the only one who was asking these questions. Rather than engage in futile casual discussions, he proposed, and they agreed, that it would be more profitable to form a "club for mutual improvement" which would meet regularly to consider these and other questions of common interest in an orderly manner. He was chosen, or more probably volunteered, to draft the "rules" or constitution for the club, which was named the Junto. Most of the group were, like Franklin, young tradesmen, poor, talented, self-educated, and eager to improve their education and status.

In framing the constitution of the Junto, Franklin borrowed the best features of the clubs familiar to him—the organization and social orientation (minus the intolerance) of the neighborhood clubs described by Cotton Mather in his "Essays to do Good," which Franklin had read as a boy; the free thinking and mutual assistance (plus secret membership) of the Masonic lodges; and the conviviality of the London clubs he had visited—to which he added his own indispensable ingredients, mutual education, the inspiration of his questing mind, and his extraordinary awareness of, and ability to provide for, the human strains and weaknesses inherent in any social institution.

The rules of the Junto, designed to minimize these human factors, required each member to attend the weekly meeting held on Friday evening; to submit one or more questions on any topic relating to morality, politics, or science; and once every three months to present an original essay on any subject he pleased. Advance reading was recommended wherever possible to raise the level of discussion. This method of study with discussion and writing related to reading, which had been so valuable to Franklin in educating himself, was now extended by him to improve the education of the Junto members.

The rules for conducting debates bear the stamp of his recent personal Plan of Conduct—truth, sincerity, and good will—now expanded into a plan of social conduct:

Our debates were to be under the direction of a president, and to be conducted in the sincere spirit of inquiry after truth, without fondness for dispute, or desire of victory; and to prevent warmth all expressions of positiveness in opinion, or of direct contradiction, were . . . made contraband and prohibited. . . .[1]

They also reflect Franklin's unremitting struggle to bring his competitive spirit under control, replacing it with good will.

He had borrowed from Cotton Mather the scheme for the main business of each meeting—a set of twenty-four "standing queries" to be read at each meeting, with a pause between each for any reply. Examples of these questions follow:

1. Have you met with any thing in the author you last read, remarkable, or suitable to be communicated to the Junto? particularly in history, morality, poetry, physic [i.,e., natural science], travels, mechanic arts, or other parts of knowledge.

7. What unhappy effects of intemperance have you lately observed or heard? of imprudence? of passion? or of any other vice or folly.

11. Do you think of any thing at present, in which the Junto may be serviceable to mankind? to their country [i.,e., Pennsylvania], to their friends, or to themselves?

12. Do you know of any deserving young beginner lately set up, whom it lies in the power of the Junto any way to encourage?

15. Have you lately observed any encroachment in the just liberties of the people?

20. In what manner can the Junto, or any of them, assist you in any of your honourable designs?[2]

For relaxation in the intervals between questions, "one might fill and drink a glass of wine," and further to increase sociability, members met "once a month in spring, summer and fall . . . of a Sunday in the afternoon in some proper place cross the river for bodily exercise . . . "[3] and once a year celebrated the anniversary of the club with a dinner enlivened by wine and song.

All Franklin's persistent motivations up to that time appear in these rules of the Junto, presumably shared or at least accepted by the other members: his love of reading, his interest in every kind of "useful" knowledge (not excluding poetry), his concern for morality, his belief in doing good to others, and his natural disposition to instruct and entertain. All of these could now be expanded through the Junto "for mutual improvement" and the improvement of the community, and he hoped that the foundation of idealistic fellowship and the cement of "honourable" self-interest that was incorporated in the club would keep it strong.

In its educational aspect, the Junto was the first concrete elaboration of the principles of education that Franklin had originally intimated in his Harvard satire:

1. The inescapable interdependence of the individual and society.
2. The primacy of moral character.

Independence and Expansion: Manhood, 1727–1746

    3. The ideal of service to mankind, community, and friends.
    4. Provision in the program of study for the needs and interests of those seeking an education, with the corollary emphasis on English rather than Latin and Greek.
    5. The availability of appropriate education for all, without regard to economic condition.
    6. The value of organized reading, discussion, and writing in any plan of education.

The Junto brought to a head the religious and moral conflicts that Franklin's Plan of Conduct and nearly fatal illness had quickened. Though he had traveled a long way from the Puritan theology of his father, he had carried away with him much of the correlative Puritan idealism, its sense of mission, of having been "chosen" by God to build a New Jerusalem in the unspoiled wilderness of America. But Benjamin Franklin's noble city of the future, though no less virtuous, would be far more tolerant and humane than Cotton Mather's, far more considerate of the variety and complexity of man and nature.

What still troubled Franklin was that he was discontented with himself and with God. He had not yet succeeded in reconciling his love of virtue with his love of pleasure; and he had lost interest in the God of the deists because, as Creator of the immeasurable universe, He was too remote to be concerned, as Franklin was, with making better men and women of His human creatures. Unless he found a God he could love and a virtuous way of life he could embrace, he would be unworthy to participate in building the New Jerusalem by deed or word and unable to instruct and help others, for they would surely detect the hollowness of his teachings and actions.

Under the stimulus of the Junto, he therefore undertook to formulate, in accordance with his own emotional and rational needs, a Divine Being appointed by the Creator of the universe, who was too busy to run our solar system, and especially this planet earth, with goodness and wisdom. This surrogate Deity, having decreed that "without virtue man can have no happiness in this world," was concerned that Franklin, as well as other men, should be virtuous and happy and would therefore not be offended "when he sees his children solace themselves in any manner of pleasant exercises and innocent delights," that is, delights not harmful to others.[4]

Franklin then recorded, for his private use only, the principles of his personal religion, a unique blend of astronomy, polytheism,[5] deism, Puritanism, and Franklinism, entitled by him "Articles of Belief and

Acts of Religion."[6] To express his reverence and gratitude to this Deity, who had made our "glorious sun, attended with a beautiful and admirable system of planets," he included "a little liturgy" of prayer and thanksgiving, a part of which he repeated privately at the beginning of each day in full sincerity. He did not presume to think that his personal creed would fit or suit anyone else. It was enough for him that it did not offend his reason too much or repel his heart, and, above all, that it served "to inspire, promote or confirm morality" and to discourage the dogmatic differences that "divide us and make us unfriendly to one another."

Having arrived by need, the will to believe, and rationalization at a conception of God that allowed virtue to be pleasurable and pleasure to be virtuous, with reason assisting, he turned next to the task of devising for his own use a practical method of achieving virtue—and happiness. He had learned from observing himself and others that

> . . . the mere speculative conviction that it was our interest to be completely virtuous, was not sufficient to prevent our slipping, and that the contrary habits must be broken and good ones acquired and established, before we can have any dependence on a steady uniform rectitude of conduct.[7]

Franklin was not the kind of man who sets up his religious and moral faith in a private chapel of his mind where it is reverently kept for Sabbath comfort and never profaned by daily practice. From his limited experience as a teacher of men, he knew that what a man is, is the most convincing part of his teaching. If he has learning, they will admire *it;* if he has character, they will imitate *him.*

As he thought about teaching himself the habit of rectitude, he realized that "virtue" was a term that needed analysis. Drawing upon his reading and self-examination, he concluded that it actually stood for a cluster of thirteen individual "virtues," such as sincerity, frugality, justice, moderation, and humility (the last-named being added by him at the suggestion of a Quaker friend, who thought Franklin needed it). For each of these he composed a short "precept" clarifying its meaning. For example, Frugality—"Make no expence but to do good to others or yourself: i. e. Waste nothing"; Moderation—"Avoid extreams. Forbear resenting injuries so much as you think they deserve"; Humility—"Imitate Jesus and Socrates." With the optimism of youth he called his program a "project of arriving at moral perfection," meaning the highest degree of virtue that imperfect man is capable of, and not saintliness. Since he hoped that his method might be helpful to "people in all religions," he would avoid all sectarian modes of virtue.

With the educational insight and practical ingenuity that marked his study of the *Spectator*, Franklin worked out a course of training that could be completed in thirteen weeks, or a quarter of a year, with one week assigned to each virtue. He kept a daily record of transgressions—a well-known Puritan habit—in tabular form, concentrating his attention each week on a different virtue. If necessary, the course could be repeated four times a year until the habit of virtue as exemplified in its thirteen elements was firmly established. At the beginning he was amazed to discover that he had more faults than he had expected, but in time he had to repeat the course only once a year, and later only once in several years. Of all thirteen virtues, he found humility the most difficult to acquire in reality, though he was fairly successful in achieving the appearance of it, especially in private conversation and public speaking.

On the subject of this recalcitrant virtue he remarked candidly:

. . . there is perhaps no one of our natural passions so hard to subdue as *pride*. Disguise it, struggle with it, beat it down, stifle it, mortify it as much as one pleases, it is still alive, and will every now and then peep out and show itself. . . . For even if I could conceive that I had compleatly overcome it, I should probably be proud of my humility.[8]

In time he applied the virtue of moderation and the antidote of humor to his goal of "moral perfection" and thereby avoided the peril of becoming a prig. As he said in extenuation, "a benovolent man should allow a few faults in himself, to keep his friends in countenance."

As Franklin had anticipated, he and Keimer parted company within a year, and for the first time since he had run away from Boston, there was literally no employment in sight for him. He was so disheartened that he even considered going back to Boston. At this juncture, "the favour of God," as he chose to call his luck, rescued him from that impulse in the person of Hugh Meredith, a workman in Keimer's shop who had become quite attached to Franklin. Meredith suggested that they go into the printing business in partnership and said that his father, who had a high regard for Franklin's ability and character, was willing to stake them. Within a few months the firm of Franklin and Meredith opened its doors.

Though he was only twenty-two years old, Franklin had come a long way. He had been on his own for five eventful years in Philadelphia and London, during which he had become a master in the printing business, in the knowledge of himself, books, and men, in the art of writing, in self-education and the education of others, and in self-discipline. He had finally found his spiritual center of gravity and stability in a private religion that satisfied his emotional and rational requirements, and now, after successive disappointments and a nearly mortal illness, at last had an opportunity to find his economic center of gravity and stability in work that satisfied his interests and abilities. He was ready for the future, hopeful of living like a rational creature in useful harmony with himself, nature, and man.

When the first customer walked into his shop, the anxious young beginner signalized the memorable event as an example of the value of the twelfth of the "standing queries" of the Junto and its relation to his lifelong concern for "young beginners":

We had scarce opened our letters and put our press in order, before George House, an acquaintance of mine, brought a country-man to us; whom he had met in the street enquiring for a printer. All our cash was now expended . . . and this countryman's five shillings being our first fruits, and coming so seasonably, gave me more pleasure than any crown I have since earn'd; and from the gratitude I felt towards House, has made me often more ready than perhaps I should otherwise have been to assist young beginners.[9]

One of the early questions debated in the Junto was connected with a heated controversy over paper money then going on in the colony. Franklin was in favor of an increase in paper money, as he had observed that, since the first small issue a few years before, there had been a marked increase in population and employment in Philadelphia. Spurred by the discussions he plunged with zest into reading books on economics, a field new to him, and mastered it with the same ease as he had history, literature, morality, religion, and philosophy. When a bill was introduced in the Pennsylvania Assembly in 1729 authorizing a substantial increase in paper money, he quickly wrote a pamphlet setting forth his position, now confirmed by his readings in economics. It was printed anonymously by Franklin and Meredith, but everyone knew who the author was.

In this pamphlet, *The Nature and Necessity of a Paper-Currency*, in

Independence and Expansion: Manhood, 1727–1746

which Franklin made his political debut, the young printer sided with "the common people in general" against the chief centers of power in Pennsylvania—the local men of money, the lawyers, the officials of the British government, and the proprietary Penn family in England—not a very practical start, it would seem, for a beginner in the printing business without money and connections, except for the hardly influential members of the Junto. He had, however, several undercover allies—a mind enlarged by systematic study, a character stabilized by the integration of his religious and ethical principles and practices, a spirit dedicated to the common welfare, and a talent for writing trained to serve it.

Marshaling with consummate skill the complex technical material he had recently absorbed and digested in his reading, he transformed it to fit the local situation, employing simple language made vivid by familiar examples and comparisons that any intelligent farmer or tradesman could understand.

"There is no science," he began, "the study of which is more useful . . . than the knowledge of the true interest of one's country,"[10] and he went on to show by logical steps the advantages in farming, trade, and manufacturing that would accrue not only to the people of the colony, but even in time to the Proprietor and to England if an adequate supply of paper currency were in circulation.

It was a masterly popular lecture in economics geared to the time, place, and people. At the end he blandly invited the opposition to show where he was wrong in his judgment of "what is the true interest in Pennsylvania," knowing perhaps that there was no writer on the other side who could stand up to him, or possibly using the occasion to practice the difficult virtue of humility. After a few minor compromises, the money bill was passed by the assembly and signed by the governor. Franklin, under adverse conditions, had given the first public demonstration of his power as an educator of the common people, a man to be reckoned with by the popular and proprietary parties of the colony.

With Franklin's confidence in his ability to instruct and influence people strengthened by the favorable reception accorded to his pamphlet, and with the happy recollection of his work on the *Courant* fortifying his confidence, he inevitably began to consider the possibility of publishing his own newspaper and exercising that ability on a regular periodical basis. He was well aware:

... that the then only newspaper . . . [in Philadelphia], printed by Bradford was a paltry thing, wretchedly manag'd, and no way entertaining; and yet was profitable to him.[11]

But he made the mistake of confiding his hopes and plans to a friend—and a member of the Junto, who, though pledged to secrecy, promptly conveyed the information to Keimer—for a consideration. Keimer immediately announced and soon after started printing a weekly newspaper pretentiously entitled *The Universal Instructor in all Arts and Sciences: and Pennsylvania Gazette*. Stung by the treachery of his "friend" and the setback to his project, which he thought was very important to his future, Franklin struck back with unwonted animosity. To divert attention from the newcomer, he wrote several amusing essays for Bradford's *Mercury*, using the pseudonym "The Busy-Body." The hapless *Instructor*, lacking Franklin's ability to entertain, as well as his competence in business, folded in less than a year and was sold to him "for a trifle." Franklin continued publication without any interruption, but under the sensibly abbreviated title of *The Pennsylvania Gazette*. The change of ownership and management was immediately apparent not only in the title, but more significantly in the dramatic improvement of type, printing, and content and some weeks later in the shift from weekly to semiweekly publication.

Franklin was only sixteen when he first briefly tasted the pleasure of publishing a newspaper; and now seven years later he found himself the part owner and sole publisher of his own newspaper, in possession of an instrument with which he could freely exercise his best abilities—reading, writing, teaching, entertaining, reforming, and making friends. From the outset he looked upon his newspaper as a "means of communicating instruction"[12] as well as news to the farmers and tradesmen of the town and region who could afford to buy it or could borrow it from a neighbor.

The standard of instruction that he aimed at was implied in his concept of the qualifications that a newspaper editor should possess:

The author of a gazette . . . ought to be qualified with an extensive acquaintance with languages, a great easiness and command of writing and relating things cleanly and intelligently, and in a few words; he should be able to speak of war both by land and sea; be well acquainted with geography, with the history of the time, with the several interests of princes and states, the secrets of courts, and the manners and customs of all nations. Men thus accomplish'd are very rare in this remote part of the world; and it would be well if the writer of these papers could make up among his friends what is wanting in himself.[13]

Independence and Expansion: Manhood, 1727–1746

Nor did he overlook the other elements that he considered essential in the ideal editor, assuring his readers that:

. . . no care and pains shall be omitted, that may make the *Pennsylvania Gazette* as agreeable and useful an entertainment as the nature of the thing will allow.[14]

He made it plain to his readers that he believed deeply in freedom of press, speech, and thought, but he also let them know that freedom is not absolute and that, unless reasonable restraints on freedom are self-imposed by writers—and people, excessive government curbs are bound to be applied before long. "I myself have constantly refused," he told the readers of the *Gazette*,

to print any thing that might countenance vice, or promote immorality; tho' by complying in such cases with the corrupt taste of the majority, I might have got much money. I have also always refus'd to print such things as might do real injury to any person, how much soever I have been solicited, and tempted with offers of great pay; and how much soever I have by refusing got the ill-will of those who would have employ'd me.[15]

And when correspondents piously cited the principle of freedom of the press, as often happened, arguing that "a newspaper was like a stage coach in which any one who would pay had a right to a place,"[16] Franklin replied that he would gladly print the piece separately and give the complainant as many copies as he wanted, provided he would distribute them himself.

As an educator of the common people, he also did what educators (or newspaper editors) hardly ever do—he warned them to look out for bias or special interest in controversial matters, whether presented by him or others, and with faith in their intelligence endeavored to teach them to think for themselves. To give them practice in carrying on this rare activity, he reprinted in one of the early issues of the *Gazette* four reports on the controversial peace with Spain taken from four London newspapers (two "Government papers," one Whig paper, and one Tory paper), remarking: "When the reader has allowed for these distinctions, he will be better able to form his judgment on the affair."[17]

When his readers interpreted freedom of the press to mean freedom to print only what they agreed with, he published in the *Gazette* a good-humored "Apology for Printers,"[18] in which he reminded them that:

Printers are educated in the belief, that when men differ in opinion, both sides ought equally to have the advantage of being heard by the publick; and that when truth and error have fair play, the former is always an overmatch for the latter: Hence they chearfully serve all contending writers that pay them well, without regarding on which side they are of the question in dispute.[19]

That being the case, he "sometimes thought it might be necessary to make a standing apology for . . . [himself], and publish it once a year,"[20] adding amicably, but leaving no doubt about where he stood,

That if all the people of different opinions in this province would engage to give me as much for not printing things they don't like, as I can get by printing them, I should probably live a very easy life; and if all printers were every where so dealt by, there would be very little printed. . . . I consider the variety of humours among men, and despair of pleasing every body; yet I shall not therefore leave off printing. I shall continue my business. I shall not burn my press and melt my letters.[21]

Adherence to principle was less of a handicap to Franklin partly because the *Gazette* was incomparably more spirited and readable than his competitor's *Mercury*. Since the local news was often known to many of the readers before they received the paper, Franklin would season the familiar facts with fresh detail, homespun language, broad humor, and spiked irony, sometimes directed against himself.

He loved to play a role, as it enabled him to make a lesson or a hoax more interesting and convincing and gave him the freedom of anonymity. When extra space was available, Franklin filled it, as in the *Courant*, with letters to the editor, employing this means to introduce a serious or humorous topic to his readers. For example, he posed as "The Casuist" to discuss a legal question,[22] or used the initials "J. T." in expounding facetiously on printer's errors.[23]

One of the most successful hoaxes perpetrated by Franklin, "A Witch Trial at Mount Holly," which appeared as a news item in the *Gazette*, achieved the distinction soon after of being reprinted as the account of an actual trial by *The Gentleman's Magazine* in England. Written with mock seriousness buttressed by lifelike details, the article described the tests by Bible and by water to which several men and women, who were accused of causing their neighbors' sheep to dance and their hogs "to speak, and sing psalms," had agreed to submit themselves. Guilt would be proved in the first test if the Bible outweighed the accused person on the scales, and in the second test, if the accused, after being stripped and bound hand and foot, sank in the millpond—presumably with the weight of his sin. In the water test, the women were stripped down only to "their shifts." All the accused proved to be innocent of witchcraft, but the spectators, disappointed by the verdict, protested that the women had not been fully tested, as Franklin solemnly reported: ". . . it being the general belief of the populace, that the womens shifts, and the garters with which they were bound help'd to support them; it is said they are to be tried again the next warm weather, naked."[24] Perhaps, if the editor of the British magazine had deferred publication a little longer after reading the piece, he might have realized that his leg was being pulled. The readers of the *Gazette* did not have to wait to appreciate the unique flavor of this American tall tale. But in Franklin's hands it was more than a frontier hoax, for, while they were slapping their thighs in delight, a noxious superstition was being dissolved in laughter at the same time.

When Franklin sought to give the farmers and tradesmen who read the *Gazette* a sense of their common interest, or raise the level of their knowledge and taste, or enlarge the area of their concern for those who were less fortunate, or improve the conditions of living for all, his ever-present sense of humor was muted, and his constant dedication to the common welfare expressed itself with simple unaffected eloquence. Shortly after he took over the *Gazette*, he published his views on a critical constitutional dispute between the governor and the assembly of Massachusetts over its fiscal rights, rights which it insisted were confirmed by the charter of the colony, the Magna Carta, and—introducing a new principle of constitutional law—"the dictates of reason." Without explicitly disagreeing with Governor Burnet, Franklin, as might be expected, clearly indicated his wholehearted approval of the assembly's continuing "to abide by what *they think* their right, and that of the people they represent," and commended their "ardent spirit of liberty and . . . undaunted courage in the defence of it. . . ."[25] His stand in opposition to the royalist party brought him a great many new subscribers, to whom it was refreshing to have a newspaper at last that spoke without equivocation and subservience.

For Franklin, the art of writing was the key that might unlock the massive gate through which he hoped to escape from being a dependent to being his own master. He had taught himself how to write, and he now had the means and therefore the obligation to teach those who had grown up like himself, without the advantage of schooling, how to acquire this key to independence. He summed up what he had learned in an essay "On Literary Style," written originally for the benefit of the members of the Junto and later printed in the *Gazette* as a letter to the editor. "I have thought in general," he observed,

that whoever would write so as not to displease good judges, should have particular regard to these three things, viz. That his performance be *smooth, clear,* and *short:* For the contrary qualities are apt to offend, either the ear, the understanding, or the patience.[26]

The advice that followed, since it was designed to be practical, avoided generalities. To write smoothly one should not use a great number of monosyllabic words or parentheses. To write clearly one should choose "not only the most expressive, but the plainest words." To write concisely

. . . all should be retrenched, that does not directly conduce to the end design'd. . . . *Amplification,* or the art of saying little in much, should only be allowed to speakers. . . . If they plead in the courts, it is of use to speak abundance, tho' they reason little; for the ignorant in a jury, can scarcely believe it possible that a man can talk so much and so long without being in the right . . . yet a writer should take especial care on the other hand, that his brevity doth not hurt his perspicuity.[27]

Franklin did not consider his own class of English tradesmen and farmers the only children of God whom he should serve. His head and heart embraced all people who happened to fall under his notice. To the recent Irish immigrants whom the less recent immigrants looked down upon as inferior intruders, he extended his sympathy and understanding through the *Gazette,* "notwithstanding the general disrespect and aversion to their nation that they every where meet with among the inhabitants of the Plantations." In an article that he wrote for his paper on the affairs of Ireland,[28] he did his best to counteract this prejudice by describing "the unhappy circumstances of the common people of Ireland," which were driving them by the thousands to the English Colonies in spite of "long and miserable passages . . . [during which] many starve for want and many die of sickness." Two years later he exposed in the *Gazette* the incredible story of a shipload of 150 Germans who had been robbed by the captain and crew of the food, wine, and other belongings they had brought with them, and of whom fewer than 50 survived the ordeal.[29] In these instances Franklin's example may have done more than preaching and reproof could to recall his readers to the belief they professed in the fatherhood of God and the brotherhood of man.

Franklin had been taught by experience that the combination of ignorance and inertia rather than tradition was the chief obstacle to social change. If people only knew why a change was necessary and what the advantages to themselves *and* others would be if the change were made, they would be less inclined to oppose it. It was his conviction that enlightened self-interest was a powerful solvent for indurated selfishness, and that the *Gazette* was a very convenient instrument for applying it in the cause of serving God by doing good to man, starting with one's own neighbors and community. The matter needing improvement might be a common nuisance, like "slippery sidewalks" in winter[30] or people who talk too much. In these cases he blended instruction and laughter to effect a change, as in the scene in which two compulsive talkers meet:

. . . the vexation they both feel is visible in their looks and gestures; you shall see them gape and stare, and interrupt one another at every turn, and watch with the utmost impatience for a cough or a pause, when they may croud a word in edgeways; neither hears nor cares what the other says; but both talk on at any rate, and never fail to part highly disgusted with each other.[31]

In a more serious vein, often reflecting questions that had been discussed in the Junto, he would explain a plan for fighting fires or cite statistics to encourage smallpox inoculation or urge better care of the sick. Occasionally he insinuated his own rationalistic views on religion under the cover of reprints from other publications, as when he published three essays from the *London Journal* on the origins of Christianity,[32] but he gave up this youthful practice as he grew older and more tolerant.

Franklin was one of the first to recognize and enlist the power of the newspaper in influencing the minds of men, but he regarded this power as a trust to be exercised primarily for the common welfare, in education, government, morality, manners, and community betterment, and only secondarily for his own advancement. There was never any doubt or confusion in his mind about which came first. As the conflict sharpened between the interest of the people of Pennsylvania represented by their assembly and that of the absentee Proprietor represented by the descendants of William Penn, who lacked his magnanimity and wisdom, Franklin generally sided with the people of the colony and used the *Gazette* to educate them as to their "true interest" in the issues that arose.

1730 was a busy year of harvest for Franklin. Early in the year his firm was designated official printer for the assembly in recognition of the demonstrably superior quality of his printed work and his services to the majority party of the assembly. The event greatly improved his credit rating in the business community and by the same measure reduced his financial worries, especially the long overdue debt to Vernon, which he paid off soon after "with interest and many thanks." About a half-year later the uneasy partnership with Meredith was amicably dissolved to the satisfaction of both parties. Meredith, who had been quite unhappy in the printing business, migrated to North Carolina, where he went back to farming, which better suited his abilities and temperament. He sent Franklin two long letters the following year, "containing the best account that had been given of that country, the climate, soil, husbandry, &c.," which were published in the *Gazette* with "grate satisfaction to the publick."[33] And on the first of September, Deborah Read, who had been married and soon after deserted while Franklin was in London, agreed to become his common-law wife.

Because of her uncertain marital status, the legal difficulties that could have arisen from a conventional marriage were so great under Pennsylvania law that this informal arrangement was accepted by Deborah's family and all friends and neighbors of the couple as an adequate marriage.[34] At about the same time, his illegitimate son William was born, and with Deborah's reluctant consent, was acknowledged and raised as a member of the family. Whether or not the marriage of Deborah and Benjamin was made in heaven, it was rooted on earth in mutual affection, respect, and advantage, which are often more enduring than romantic love.

One of the most serious obstacles to the improvement of conditions in Pennsylvania was the fact, as Franklin wrote to an English correspondent, that there was ". . . no manner of provision made by the Government for publick education, either in this or the neighboring provinces, nor so much as a good booksellers shop nearer than Boston."[35] He had done as much as he could to make the *Gazette* an agency of public education, but it could not compare, as he knew, with books as a means of education, and these were accessible to very few, even in Boston. When he came to London, he found that the problem existed there too. There were plenty of books, new and secondhand,

Independence and Expansion: Manhood, 1727–1746

but few could afford to buy them. Franklin had hit on an ingenious way to get books cheap in London. He used the vast collection of secondhand books at Wilcox's as a lending library, from which for a small fee he borrowed any books that interested him. In Philadelphia the members of the Junto frequently exchanged books from each other's small collections, and later, when they acquired a permanent meetingplace, agreed at his suggestion to keep as many of their books as they could spare in a common library at one end of the room. However, the arrangement proved unsatisfactory.

Franklin's informal idea had been a good one, in spite of its apparent failure. What it lacked, he concluded, was the kind of practical organization that had made the Junto work—a carefully planned constitution that took human fallibility into account. Within a short time, he had drafted the plan, rules, and contract for a subscription library, his first public project, and the first of its kind in North America, to be named the Library Company of Philadelphia and run by a board of directors with the assistance of a secretary, a treasurer, and a paid part-time librarian, as soon as fifty subscribers could be signed up for a term of fifty years! Each subscriber had to bind himself to pay an enrollment fee "for the first purchase of books" and "an annual contribution for encreasing them."[36]

The Junto, as might be expected, became the nucleus of the company and helped to enroll others, but Franklin was the prime mover without whom this bold, unprecedented project could not have been successfully launched. He might still have failed had he not been a pragmatic idealist quick to observe and adapt himself to a facet of human nature that was new to him:

The objections and reluctances I met with in soliciting the subscriptions, made me soon feel the impropriety of presenting one's self as the proposer of any useful project that might be suppos'd to raise one's reputation in the smallest degree above that of one's neighbours, when one has need of their assistance to accomplish that project. I therefore put my self as much as I could out of sight, and stated it as a scheme of a *number of friends,* who had requested me to go about and propose it to such as they thought lovers of reading. In this way my affair went on more smoothly, and I ever after practis'd it on such occasions.[37]

The usefulness of the library, which opened late in the fall of 1731, was not intended to be limited to the subscribers only. Nonsubscribers could read the books in the library and under proper security could take out some of the books on a scheduled fee basis. With the assistance of James Logan, the distinguished Quaker scholar, a list of basic books in law, medicine, astronomy, government, mathematics, physical and biological science, and classics in modern and ancient literature was prepared, and the books were ordered through a London agent, Peter Collinson, a Quaker merchant and botanist.[38] Franklin added Montaigne's *Essays* as a gift, matching Collinson's donation of *A View of Sir Isaac Newton's Philosophy* by Henry Pemberton,[39] whom Franklin had met in London. "The institution," he wrote many years later,

soon manifested its utility, was imitated by other towns and in other provinces, the librarys were augmented by donations, reading became fashionable, and our people having no publick amusements to divert their attention from study became better acquainted with books, and in a few years were observ'd by strangers to be better instructed and more intelligent than people of the same rank generally are in other countries."[40]

The "public library" invented by Franklin became a school of the common people of Colonial America, providing the means of self-education and self-improvement for all those like him who had been unable to get a formal education. It was, of course, a boon to him, too. "This library," he said,

afforded me the means of improvement by constant study, for which I set apart an hour or two each day; and thus repair'd in some degree the loss of the learned education my father once intended for me. Reading was the only amusement I allow'd my self.[41]

Hitherto, Franklin's educational ventures had been directed to English-speaking people. His involvement through the *Gazette* in the plight of the German immigrants awakened his interest in the growing German community in Pennsylvania, which was isolated from the English majority. The need to establish a two-way bridge between the unregarded strangers and the English population and to convey news and instruction to them seemed to him quite urgent. Fortunately, one of his journeymen, Louis Timothée, who could write German, was available for this purpose. Though Franklin was occupied with the promotion of his library, he announced the publication of a German newspaper, *Philadelphische Zeitung*. The response was indifferent, perhaps because the Germans were too poor to subscribe in sufficient numbers. Publication was suspended after the second issue. The need was there, but the remedy was premature.

There was only one "book" in Franklin's time, other than the Bible, that could be found in practically every home—the annual calendar-almanac. With settlements and farms far from each other and from the coastal towns, with no calendars and often no clocks, and with most of the settlers poor and superstitious and generally believing in the influence of the moon and the planets on their work and welfare, the cheap little almanac containing the calendar and astrological guide for the year was a necessity. The itinerant peddlers carried it with the rest of their varied merchandise to the most remote and isolated districts of the frontier. It was our first periodical with mass circulation, the "secular Bible" of the Colonists,[42] and the bread-and-butter of Colonial printers. Bradford and Keimer printed almanacs, and Franklin & Meredith, as soon as they were able, broke into the profitable field with almanacs for 1730, 1731, and 1732 prepared by Thomas Godfrey, an original member of the Junto, and almanacs for 1731 and 1732 prepared by John Jerman. But in the fall of 1732 both almanac-makers switched to Bradford. Faced with this emergency, Franklin surprised his competitors by assuming a new role as "Richard Saunders, Philomath" and compiling his own almanac for 1733. If they had known Silence Dogood, they would have been better prepared for Richard Saunders ten years later.

For the first time he would be able to reach out to all the people, most of whom were too poor to buy a newspaper or books and unable to avail themselves of the new subscription library in Philadelphia. His almanac, he said, would therefore be "a proper vehicle for conveying instruction among the common people" in as entertaining a manner as possible and with top priority given to helping them escape like him from the prison of poverty to a life of independence, dignity, and "virtue."[43] In accordance with these aims he created an almanac-maker who was as poor as any of its readers. The image he sought to project was symbolized by the title chosen for his almanac, *Poor Richard*, and was sketched with ingratiating detail in the preface to the first almanac.

(1733) Courteous reader, I might in this place attempt to gain thy favour, by declaring that I write almanacks with no other view than that of the publick good; but in this I should not be sincere. . . . The plain truth of the matter is, I am excessive poor, and my wife, good woman, is, I tell her, excessive proud; . . . and has threatned more than once to burn all my books and rattling-traps (as she calls my instruments) if I do not make some profitable use of them for the good of my family.[44]

To gain attention and amuse his readers, he resorted to a type of hoax he had learned from Swift—predicting the death of a rival. He had Saunders explain in the first preface why, in view of his straitened circumstances, he had never before prepared any almanacs. The reason, he said, was his profound regard for his "good friend and fellow-student, Mr. Titan Leeds" (incidentally Franklin's chief rival as almanac-maker), but, since his friend was destined to die on October 17, 1733, at 3:49 P.M., he finally felt "free to take up the task," adding mischievously that Leeds himself calculated that he would live until October 26. "This small difference between us," he remarked with tongue in cheek, "we have disputed whenever we have met these 9 years past; but at length he is inclinable to agree with my judgment."[45] Indignant denial only made matters worse, as it gave Franklin free advertising in his competitor's almanac.

Franklin wisely refrained from tampering with the conventional facade of the almanac, retaining the familiar title-page; "Man of the Signs" and other astrological data; calendar-pages for each month with verses at the top and compact weather predictions or sayings interspersed down the page; and near the end of the twenty-four pages, dates of eclipses, court sessions, and other important events. But once the reader was inside, the indelible stamp of Franklin's personality and purpose was quickly apparent in the three traditional features that would lend themselves to alterations: the preface, the verses, and the sayings.

The preface became in his hands a potent means of entertainment, advertising, competition, or instruction through the *dramatis persona* of Poor Richard. The verses, instead of describing the seasonal changes of nature, were chosen to present instructive aspects of human nature, often with genial irony or satire. And the proverbs and other kernels of folk wisdom, drawn from "many ages and nations," had as their basic aim the inculcation of ". . . industry and frugality, as the means of procuring wealth and thereby securing virtue, it being more difficult for a man in want to act always honestly, as . . . *it is hard for an empty sack to stand upright.*"[46]

Only those who have been as poor as most of Franklin's contemporaries can fully understand the helplessness and humiliation of owning nothing, neither property nor money nor talent, and of having to depend on the bitter bounty of others, whether individuals or governments. For them Franklin's prescription of "industry and frugality" was not a penny-pinching end, but a liberating means of achieving independence and self-respect. It is in this sense and spirit that *Poor Richard's* practical precepts were read:

"Light purse, heavy heart."[47]

"Where bread is wanting, all's to be sold."[48]

"God heals, and the doctor takes the fees."[49]

"A countryman between 2 lawyers, is like a fish between two cats."[50]

As "The Busy-Body" in an earlier impersonation, Franklin had written:

'Tis certain, that no country in the world produces naturally finer spirits than ours, men of genius for every kind of science, and capable of acquiring to perfection every qualification that is in esteem among mankind.[51]

But they were retarded in their development by lack of access to the means of education. Within the limited space and resources of the almanac, he would do what little he could to alleviate this condition, never forgetting that education was more than the mere acquisition of knowledge.

... [It] is certainly of more consequence to a man that he has learnt to govern his passions; in spite of temptation to be just in his dealings, to be temperate in his pleasures, to support himself with fortitude under his misfortunes, to behave with prudence in all affairs and in every circumstance of life; I say, it is of much more real advantage to him to be thus qualified, than to be a master of all the arts and sciences in the world beside.[52]

Imbued with this moral aim, Franklin shared with his readers the benefits of his reading and experience, including the method he had devised for himself to achieve a rational and virtuous way of life. He was guided in the selection of proverbs and rhymes, as the examples below indicate, by the thirteen "virtues" he had set up as his own targets, but adapted his program of working at one virtue a week to working at one virtue a year, in deference to the annual interval and other limitations of the almanac and its reader:

> Each year one vicious habit rooted out,
> In time might make the worst man good throughout.[53]

He assumed, since any other contemporary reading matter rarely competed with his almanac, that it would be read over and over again, year after year, until it was engraved on mind and heart.

Temperance   "To lengthen thy life, lessen thy meals."[54]
"Nothing more like a fool, than a drunken man."[55]
Silence   "The heart of a fool is in his mouth, but the mouth of a wise man is in his heart."[56]
Order   "If you have time don't wait for time."[57]
Resolution   "No resolution of repenting hereafter, can be sincere."[58]
Frugality   ". . . In 100 acres are 4356000 square feet; twenty pounds will buy 100 acres. . . . In £20 are 4800 pence; by which divide the number of feet in 100 acres; and you will find that one penny will buy 907 square feet; or a lot of 30 feet square.—*Save your pence.*"[59]
Industry   "*All* things are easy to industry,
All things difficult to *sloth.*"[60]
Sincerity   "There is much difference between imitating a good man, and counterfeiting him."[61]
Justice   "It is better to take many injuries than to give one."[62]
Moderation   "Nothing brings more pain than too much pleasure; nothing more bondage than too much liberty. . . "[63]
Cleanliness   "Wife, from thy spouse each blemish hide
More than from all the world beside:
Let decency be all thy pride."[64]
Tranquillity   "He that can compose himself, is wiser than he that composes books."[65]
Chastity   "Old Socrates was obstinately good,
Virtuous by force, by inclination lewd.
When secret movements drew his soul aside,
He quell'd his lust, and stemm'd the swelling tide;
Sustain'd by reason still, unmov'd he stood,
And steady bore against th' opposing flood.
He durst correct what nature form'd amiss,
And forc'd unwilling virtue to be his."[66]
Humility   "To be humble to superiors is duty, to equals courtesy, to inferiors nobleness."[67]

Franklin was too wise and practical to make his moral aim obvious and exclusive, agreeing with Pope that "Men must be taught as if you taught them not."[68] Easy to say, hard to do—unless you have Franklin's inexhaustible zest for life, his irrepressible sense of humor, his passion for knowledge, and his great talent as a writer, all of which would now be mobilized for the entertainment and improvement of the common people of his "country."

It is amazing how much valuable knowledge, truth, understanding, and aspiration he was able to compress within the small compass of his almanacs, often with honesty and compassion of piercing simplicity:

> Death takes no bribes.[69]
> Sorrow is dry.[70]

Though he did not gloss over the great and little faults of men and women, he gave the impression that he was no better than his readers. There was no need, he implied, to despair, for the recognition of these faults could be the beginning of the desire to replace them by the opposite virtues. The task of self-improvement was difficult, but one that offered great rewards—in this life.

Franklin also touched on those aspects of the human scene that he thought would be interesting and useful to his readers: the nature of men and women, marriage, health, medicine, law, astrology, astronomy, history, and religion. He varied subjects and moods. Nothing was cut-and-dried, and surprises abounded. Even a catalog of the principal kings and princes of Europe, with the date of birth and the age of each, suddenly came to life in the last listing: *"Poor Richard,* an American prince, without subjects, his wife being viceroy over him, born 23 Oct. 1684, age 49!"[71] Readers turned expectantly to the next page or the next year's issue, never able to predict what it might reveal, and they were rarely disappointed. Some samples are taken at random:

After 3 days men grow weary, of a wench, a guest, and weather rainy.[72]

One good husband is worth two good wives; for the scarcer things are the more they're valued.[73]

Sin is not hurtful because it is forbidden but it is forbidden because it's hurtful.[74]

I foresee an universal droughth this year thro' all the Northern Colonies . . . and, in New-England, *dry* fish and *dry* doctrine. . . . [75]

The ancients tell us what is best; but we must learn of the moderns what is fittest.[76]

The sun never repents of the good he does, nor does he ever demand a recompence.[77]

Honour thy father and mother, i.e. Live so as to be an honour to them tho' they are dead.[78]

Observe all men; thy self most.[79]

The almanac as conceived and used by Franklin was a kind of one-way, ongoing correspondence course for the common people, included as a free supplement for the purchaser without risk or obligation on his part. Though the reader was generally unschooled, he had fortunately been taught or had taught himself as his Christian duty to read the Bible—an excellent primer—but he rarely owned any other books and was ignorant of the changes—scientific, philosophical, religious, and political—that had taken place in the modern world. To these secular changes Franklin, confident of the interest and ability of his readers, proposed to introduce them through his almanac, as a service to God and his country. He was well aware of the limitations; he could do little more than to start them thinking, to add a new dimension to their outlook, and trust to their native intelligence to go on from there.

This early experiment in free democratic education was a resounding success. It was free in a double sense: it did not cost any money, and it was not compulsory. Learning went on because the learner wanted to learn and the teacher wanted to teach. The almanac happened to be a convenient instrument for mass instruction on an individual basis. The student could advance at his own pace, could concentrate on the things that were most interesting to him, had as much time as he needed for review and reflection, and did not have to please the teacher or impress the other students.

It also helped greatly to have a teacher like Franklin, who had clear-cut principles, goals, and values. Whether one agreed with them or not, one knew what he stood for. He had considerable knowledge, but best of all he knew people. Although he had no illusions about them, he knew what their needs and ambitions and dreams were and gave practical advice on how to realize them. He was obviously a man of superior ability and knowlege; yet people felt at ease with him. He treated people like equals and did not talk down to them and make them feel inferior. There was nothing of the stuffed shirt in his manner.

He made learning easy and pleasant. His sayings were so apt and true that they stuck in people's memory, and his verses and essays were so funny or lifelike or inspiring that people wanted to memorize them. In time they began to feel that they were not altogether cut off from what was going on and being talked about in the great world faraway. Though now and then he would shake people up when he wrote about the new discoveries about the solar system and the distant stars or poked fun at the belief in the old science of astrology, or when he dared to question the things that had always been taken for granted in old-time religion, yet somehow he never got people's hackles up, and he made them think. Above all, he understood the grinding poverty, the daily struggle to keep oneself and one's family afloat. He understood how hard it was to do what was right when one was hungry or in debt. "An empty sack cannot stand upright." There spoke a man who was familiar with being poor, and yet he had found a way to educate himself and be somebody. The thing that was different about Poor Richard was that he made one laugh and feel better—and want to be and do better.

II Man of Expanding Interests and Influences

The dual success of *Poor Richard* as a profitable business venture and as a subliterary medium of self-education for the common people of the Philadelphia region prefigured the bifocal career of Franklin for many years to come. On the one hand, he was the prudent tradesman and family man of Philadelphia, quietly expanding his connections as a printer, merchant, investor, and officeholder on an intercolonial scale; and on the other hand, the student of man and nature, the public benefactor and champion of the common interest teaching his philosophy of community service, and the experimenter unobtrusively forging links with "ingenious men" in the American Colonies and England. Yet all these *personae* lived and worked harmoniously with each other and with him for a common purpose—to serve his interest and happiness by serving others. As Poor Richard (1737) remarked, "The master piece of man, is to live to the purpose."

The independence that Franklin required to release his manifold powers was now in the making. The *Gazette* was prospering, *Poor Richard* had got off to a good start, his printing contracts with the government seemed secure, the subscription library was firmly established, and his wife was a great helpmate. She had given birth to a boy, Francis Folger, a month before *Poor Richard* was born. For the first time in nearly ten years, "having become more easy in . . . [his] circumstances," he was able to visit his father and mother in Boston. On the way home he stopped off in Newport to see his brother James, who was in poor health. Their meeting was "very cordial and affectionate . . . former differences . . . forgotten." He promised his ailing brother that he "would take home his son, then but ten years of age, and bring him up to the printing business." After James's death two years later, he kept his promise generously, glad that he could make amends for his earlier "erratum" in breaking his contract of apprenticeship, morally, if not legally.

Franklin had already pushed the frontier of his interests beyond the horizons of Pennsylvania and the other Colonies soon after his marriage, when he recorded some critical "observations on . . . reading history":

> That the great affairs of the world, the wars, revolutions, &c. are carried on and effected by parties. . . .
> That as soon as a party has gain'd its general point, each member becomes intent upon his particular interest. . . .
> That few in public affairs act from a meer view of the good of their country, whatever they may pretend. . . .
> That fewer still in public affairs act with a view to the good of mankind.[80]

These conclusions, expressed with the clarity of a mathematical truth, set in motion the threefold moral imperative that had become a habitual part of Franklin's character—education, planning, and action. In practice this meant that, once he was convinced that a serious human need existed, and that he had worked out a practicable plan or project to meet that need, he should try to put it into effect by educating those concerned regarding its advantages to them and others. The need in this instance was worldwide, and in 1731 would seem beyond remedy, but not to Franklin, whose imagination, intellect, and benevolence easily embraced the human race. In his mind Philadelphia was a microcosm of the world, and what had been done successfully there could be done in the same way everywhere. To him it was a natural and simple step to extend the idea of the Junto to all countries, together with its "influence in public affairs and . . . power of doing good."

He accordingly envisioned "forming the virtuous and good men of all nations into a regular body, to be govern'd by suitable good and wise rules," a world society that at first would enroll "young and single men only" and remain secret until it had grown to be "considerable" in numbers.[81]

He was never able to find sufficient time for this project, but he observed many years afterward—and Franklin was no Utopian—that

I was not discourag'd by the seeming magnitude of the undertaking, as I have always thought that one man of tolerable abilities may work great changes, and accomplish great affairs among mankind, if he first forms a good plan, and cutting off all amusements or other employments that would divert his attention, makes the execution of that same plan his sole study and business.[82]

In the meantime he satisfied his international aspirations by studying French, Italian, and Spanish, and after these Latin, in the course of which he hit upon two important principles of learning: motivation through play (in rudimentary form) and progress from the less to the more difficult. He discovered the first while studying Italian. A friend of his who was engaged in the same study often tempted him to play chess and neglect the Italian. To reconcile duty and pleasure, he persuaded his friend to accept as a condition of each game that the winner would assign homework to the loser to be done "upon honour" before the next game. "As we play'd pretty equally," he added, "we thus beat one another into that language."[83]

Later, coming to the study of Latin after the modern languages, he was surprised to find he "met with the more success as those preceding languages had greatly smooth'd . . . [his] way." He therefore came to the conclusion that ". . . if you can clamber and get to the top of a stair-case without using the steps, you will more easily gain them in descending: but certainly if you begin with the lowest you will with more ease ascend to the top. . . ." There was an additional consideration. Should the students never reach the study of Latin, ". . . they would however have acquir'd another tongue or two that being in modern use might be serviceable to them in common life."[84]

While dreaming of a secret international league of benevolent young men and getting ready to overcome the barriers that separated him from these young men of other nations, Franklin went about the practical business of making enough money to gain the independence and leisure he craved. As opportunities opened up, he became a silent partner in printing and newspaper ventures in other colonies and the West Indies, usually in partnership with former employees or relatives. In these undertakings, as in the formation of the Junto and the Library Company, he chose his associates carefully, anticipated the possibilities of friction due to human weakness, and provided equitably for the interest of both parties.

Having more capital, he opened a stationer's store in the printing shop, where he sold a great variety of educational and professional books and books in the arts and sciences, some of which he printed himself. Many of the books were directed to the self-educational needs and conditions of the frontier, such as *"Every Man his own Lawyer, Every Man his own Doctor,* (Note, in a short time will be published, *Every Man his own Priest).* . . ."[85] In 1744 he issued a catalog of nearly 600 titles of books for sale in his shop. Over the years it had become a trading post where he stocked at one time or another items as disparate as spectacles, cheese, maps, codfish, prints, patent medicines, hose, and lumber.

Competition for the limited amount of business available was intense, and Franklin, who was playing for high stakes, played to win, but almost always in accordance with the principles of truth, sincerity, and honesty by which he had chosen to live. In the heat of the struggle, he occasionally slipped, but he was quick to acknowledge his error to himself and vigilant to avoid it in the future. Nor did he justify his own wrongdoing because others played the game unfairly. When, for example, Andrew Bradford as postmaster forbade his riders to carry the *Gazette,* Franklin bribed them to ignore the injunction, but remarked: "I thought so meanly of him for it, that when I afterwards came into his situation, I took care never to imitate it."[86] Franklin often succeeded in making friends of his enemies, winning them over by his generosity and intelligence, but Andrew Bradford remained implacable to the end, using every chance that offered itself to malign or injure him. The obituary notice that Franklin published in the *Gazette* the day after Bradford died in 1742 was as cold as the remains: "Last night died, after a lingering illness, Mr. Andrew Bradford, printer; one of the Common Council of this city."[87] It was one of the few times Franklin failed to live up to one of the most admirable of his moral precepts: "Forbear resenting injuries as much as you think they deserve."[88]

His preoccupation with affairs of personal business did not preclude his involvement with the demands of his social conscience. Two papers that he read to the Junto in 1735 led by way of his moral imperative to the founding of the Union Fire Company of Philadelphia and, after many delays, to a municipal police force. In 1736 he was elected clerk of the Pennsylvania Assembly and a year later postmaster of the city. Though he was enchanted by the eloquence of evangelist George Whitefield, who first came to Philadelphia in 1739, Franklin did not

Independence and Expansion: Manhood, 1727–1746

become one of his converts, still preferring the humanistic personal religion and morality he had worked out for himself. Franklin printed Whitefield's journals and sermons and participated in the construction of a nonsectarian building intended to accommodate unorthodox preachers like Whitefield who were usually excluded from the pulpits of the established clergy. Franklin was expressing his own brand of tolerance rather than that of the contributors when he described the purpose of the new building:

Both house and ground were vested in trustees, expressly for the use of any preacher of any religious persuasion who might desire to say something to the people of Philadelphia, the design in building not being to accommodate any particular sect, but the inhabitants in general, so that even if the Mufti of Constantinople were to send a missionary to preach Mahometanism to us, he would find a pulpit at his service.[89]

Fortunate as he was during these years, Franklin was not spared his portion of afflictions. A cruel practical joke involving a mock Masonic initiation, which had ended in the accidental death of the poor dupe, was seized upon by Andrew Bradford to print "some very false and scandalous aspersions" on Franklin in the *Mercury*. The facts, promptly set forth and attested in the *Gazette,* cleared him of the damaging allegations, but he was undoubtedly hurt by them. A few years later he failed in his attempt to launch the first magazine "for all the British Plantations in America," partly because, as once before, he made the mistake of talking over his plan in confidence with the prospective editor, who thought he could make a better deal with Franklin's rival. Andrew Bradford's *American Magazine* appeared in 1741, three days before Franklin's *General Magazine,* and was discontinued after three monthly issues; the latter ceased publication after its sixth.

But these reverses were trivial compared to the untimely death by smallpox in 1736 of his son Frankie, whose epitaph read: "The DELIGHT of all that knew him." Franklin never quite got over his loss. It was little consolation that he had intended to have him inoculated but had postponed it because the child was suffering at the time from a serious intestinal ailment. Near the end of his life he wrote:

I long regretted bitterly and still regret that I had not given . . . him . . . inoculation; this I mention for the sake of parents, who omit that operation on the supposition that they should never forgive themselves if a child died under it; my example showing that the regret may be the same either way, and that therefore the safer should be chosen.[90]

Characteristically he had translated his regret into constructive action. For many years he carried on an educational campaign for smallpox inoculation through articles and advertisements in the *Pennsylvania Gazette,* and later in the other colonies, arranging, in line with the idea of *Every Man his own Doctor,* for the free distribution of a pamphlet prepared by his friend, the distinguished London physician Dr. William Heberden, giving simple instructions that would enable any person to inoculate and treat himself and his family.

Franklin's lifelong interest in problems of health had begun, he said, at the age of sixteen when he happened to pick up a book recommending a vegetable diet, *The Way to Health, Long Life and Happiness,* by Thomas Tryon. It appealed to him because it would enable him to improve his health by temperance in eating and drinking and at the same time help him to save money for buying books. To be "healthy, wealthy, and wise" represented goals that he set for himself and his fellowmen, and he made frequent use of his *Gazette* and *Poor Richard* to teach them "the way to health, long life and happiness," the last-named being attainable, as he believed, only through achieving economic independence and having the wisdom to live according to universally recognized moral principles. One of the most serious hazards to health in his experience was the inefficient and expensive method of heating houses. He therefore applied himself to learning as much as he could about the subject of heat and methods of heating. He was particularly impressed by an ingenious but very costly fireplace invented early in the century by Nicolas Gauger in France. Franklin simplified and improved the Gauger fireplace and had his friend and former benefactor, Robert Grace, one of the original members of the Junto, and the owner of an iron furnace, make the plates for his first model, which Franklin assembled and installed in his own home. It exceeded his expectations. He found that, using a quarter of the wood consumed by his old fireplace, it kept the room twice as warm as before and the air fresh, eliminated drafts, and circulated the heat evenly through all parts of the room.

The news quickly got around among his friends, many of whom ordered the new "Franklin stoves" and likewise found them better and cheaper than their former fireplaces. After they were advertised in the

Gazette in December, 1741, orders multiplied, and by 1744 their superiority had been so convincingly demonstrated that Franklin decided to make their benefits known to a wider public. Toward the end of the year he wrote and printed *An Account of the New Invented Pennsylvanian Fire-Places*,[91] which were now available also in New York and Boston. It is a masterpiece of popular technical exposition, clear and often colloquial in its language, lucidly organized, and amply furnished with drawings and diagrams and precisely labeled instructions for assembling, installing, and using the stove. But it is also an expression of Franklin's moral and educational purpose—doing good to his fellowmen by contributing to their comfort and health and teaching them to take advantage of the opportunities for improving their condition. In conclusion, as he anticipated the social benefits that would accrue from the general use of his improved fireplace, he revealed a remarkable apprehension of the future problems of air pollution in cities:

We leave it . . . to physicians to say, how much healthier thick-built towns and cities will be, now half suffocated with sulphury smoke, when so much less of that smoke shall be made, and the air breath'd by the inhabitants be consequently so much purer.[92]

Even more remarkable was the response of the man who has been regarded by some as obsessed by love of money when the governor of Pennsylvania, after reading the pamphlet, offered to give him by patent the exclusive right to sell his invention:

. . . I declin'd it from a principle which has ever weigh'd with me on such occasions, viz. *That as we enjoy great advantages from the inventions of others, we should be glad of an opportunity to serve others by any invention of ours, and this we should do freely and generously.*[93]

Franklin mailed copies of the pamphlet to his friends, and they passed it on to their friends. One copy, for example, reached the noted Professor Gronovius of Leyden, who reported back that it was so popular that he could not prevent its translation into Dutch. The new fireplace may not have made a fortune for Franklin, but it made a reputation for him on both sides of the Atlantic that was worth much more to him over the long pull.

As an indefatigable newspaper editor, library founder, bookseller and book publisher, partner of printers from South Carolina to New

York, postmaster of Philadelphia, "dabbler" in the sciences (his word), inventor, and maker and keeper of friends, Franklin was becoming the key figure in a growing intercolonial junto of "ingenious" correspondents working more or less independently in the arts and sciences.

In scientific inquiry Franklin was truly humble, extremely cautious, quite skeptical, and completely honest with himself and his material. This may be seen in a letter written to a friend on the subject of waterspouts:

Here you have my method of accounting for the principal phaenomena, which I submit to your candid examination. If my hypothesis is not the truth itself, it is least as naked: For I have not with some of our learned moderns disguis'd my nonsense in Greek, cloth'd it in algebra, or adorn'd it with fluxions.[94]

Franklin's increasing involvement in scientific correspondence and studies, joined with the lessening demands of business on his time, set in motion again his complementary impulsions toward education and doing good. For example, he played a leading part in organizing "a course of philosophical lectures and experiments" to be given by Isaac Greenwood, formerly professor of mathematics at Harvard College, making available to him a room next to the library for his lectures and the library's scientific apparatus for his experiments.[95] The invention and publicizing of the Franklin stove occurred at this period in his life. He was also concerned that there was "no provision . . . for a compleat education for youth" in Pennsylvania. In 1743 he tried to establish an "academy" but dropped the plan when he was unable to find a qualified educator to head the school.

Encouraged by the success of the Junto, the Library Company, the *Gazette,* and *Poor Richard* as agencies of education and public improvement, he was strongly receptive to an idea that had been broached in 1739 by his friend John Bartram, the great botanist of Philadelphia—the formation of an association of scientists and scholars for the interchange of information about new developments and discoveries in the arts and sciences that were taking place in the Colonies. But Bartram, being an experimentalist rather than an organizer, had done little more than talk and write about his idea for an association, which was obviously not enough. It needed a Franklin to convert the idea into a reality.

Franklin's philanthropic and practical imagination, while fired by Bartram's idea, went beyond it and saw an opportunity now to enroll men of learning in the service of science and their fellowmen. Whether he realized it or not, he was setting up a variation of the international society of men of good will that he had dreamed of twelve years before. Franklin never wasted a good idea but would keep reverting to it until he succeeded in putting it into practice in one form or another. His activities as an editor of Colonial and foreign news and his acquaintance with men of science and learning in the Colonies and England had deepened his inclination to think as an American and a citizen of the world as well as a Philadelphian and Pennsylvanian. So it came about that in the spring of 1743 he drafted and printed a circular letter, entitled *A Proposal for Promoting Useful Knowledge among the British Plantations in America*, which embodied Bartram's and his own thinking, and mailed it to his circle of "ingenious" friends.

It bears what may now be regarded assuredly as the Franklin hallmark: a unique combination of careful planning, sense of timing, capacity for hard work, social and scientific imagination, journalistic genius, appeal to enlightened self-interest, organizational ability, American and international outlook without dilution of local loyalties, and the constants of altruistic and educational motivations.

To overcome the previous resistance of many in America and England who felt that the Colonies did not yet have the means and the men to support an American institution similar to the Royal Society of London, he explained:

The English are possess'd of a long tract of continent, from Nova Scotia to Georgia, extending north and south thro' different climates, having different soils, producing different plants, mines and minerals, and capable of different improvements, manufactures, &c.

The first drudgery of settling new colonies, which confines the attention of people to mere necessaries, is now pretty well over; and there are many in every province in circumstances that set them at ease, and afford leisure to cultivate the finer arts, and improve the common stock of knowledge. To such of these who are men of speculation, many hints must from time to time arise, many observations occur, which if well-examined, pursued and improved, might produce discoveries to the advantage of some or all of the British Plantations, or to the benefit of mankind in general.

But as from the extent of the country such persons are widely separated, and seldom can see and converse or be acquainted with each other, so that many useful particulars remain uncommunicated, die with the discoverers, and are lost to mankind; it is, to remedy this inconvenience for the future, proposed,

That one society be formed of virtuosi [i.e., scientist-scholars] or ingenious men residing in the several Colonies, to be called *The American Philosophical Society;* who are to maintain a constant correspondence.[96]

And emphasizing his conviction that the arts and sciences and the welfare of mankind recognize no Colonial or national or continental boundaries, he also recommended "that a correspondence already begun by some intended members, shall be kept up by this Society with the Royal Society of London, and with the Dublin Society."[97]

Since the society, unlike the Junto and the library, was not a local organization in which the details could conveniently be worked out in advance under his personal guidance and with prior consultation of all the members, he did not draw up the rules in complete detail, but stipulated

> that at the first meetings of the members . . . such rules be formed for regulating their meetings and transactions for the general benefit, as shall be convenient and necessary; to be afterwards changed and improv'd as there shall be occasion, wherein due regard is to be had to the advice of distant members.[98]

But the basic organization had to be outlined. He proposed that the headquarters be located in Philadelphia, because it was "nearest the centre of the Continent-Colonies" and had "the advantage of a good growing library," and that, in addition to the president, treasurer, and secretary, at least seven members living in or near Philadelphia serve as a committee representing the main branches of science—"a physician, a botanist, a mathematician, a chemist, a mechanician [mechanical engineer], a geographer, and a general natural philosopher." Quarterly and annual reports would be sent to members on proceedings, transactions, and valuable contributions. He devoted a paragraph to "the business and duty" of the secretary, the officer who he anticipated would bear the responsibility of making the society work. That may be the reason he volunteered "to serve the Society as their secretary, 'till they shall be provided with one more capable."

It would not be easy, Franklin recognized, to get independent students of nature and the arts who did not know each other to work together, to pool their resources and discoveries, to understand that in helping each other they would be helping themselves, but he hoped to succeed by appealing to the higher self-interest of each as he had done in establishing the Junto and the Library Company. Franklin informed a friend in the spring of 1744 that "the Society, as far as relates to Philadelphia, is actually formed, and has had several meetings." Officers had been chosen, with Franklin as secretary. Three members of the Junto were represented on the committee for the sciences, filling the positions for mathematician, "mechanician," and geographer. John Bartram was the botanist on the committee. Other notable scientists and men of learning in New Jersey, New York, Virginia, Maryland, Carolina, and New England had either joined the society or were about to become members.[99] Papers were being promised by members, and Franklin's pamphlet on the "Pennsylvanian fire-places" may have been regarded in his mind as a contribution to the society and "the conveniencies or pleasures of life," which he had announced as one of the goals of the society.

After the first wave of enthusiasm receded, it became evident that Franklin had misjudged the temper and need of the intellectual community. They still preferred, as Bartram wrote,[100] "the club, chess and coffee-house" to "the curious amusements of natural observations." It would appear that Franklin had also underestimated the problems of communication certain to be encountered at that time by an intercolonial society, as in his project to publish an intercolonial magazine. Whatever the reasons, the society sank into a state of suspended animation. But it did not die, and when it came to life again twenty-five years later, Franklin was elected president and continued to hold that office by annual election for the rest of his life.

When Franklin visited Boston early in the summer of 1743, he met Dr. Archibald Spencer, a physician who had recently arrived from England and had advertised a course in "experimental philosophy." He showed Franklin some experiments in electricity, which was a great novelty at the time and "a subject quite new" to him, and though the experiments were "imperfectly perform'd . . . they equally surpris'd and pleas'd . . . [him]."[101] This was the first fateful event of that summer, the second being the birth of his daughter Sarah. Dr. Spencer came to Philadelphia in 1744, perhaps at Franklin's invitation, where his course proved to be so popular that it was repeated at least twice.[102]

Franklin, impatient to conduct his own experiments, persuaded Dr. Spencer to sell him the electrical apparatus, which was supplemented not long after by a gift of an electrical glass tube from Peter Collinson to the library. He became absorbed for a time in these experiments to the exclusion of other interests. Electricity, that mysterious force, invisible and visible, on the borderline seemingly between the material and the immaterial, between man and God, seized upon his mind and imagination with an attraction he had never felt before. He wrote to Collinson in March, 1747:

I never was before engaged in any study that so totally engrossed my attention and my time as this has lately done; for what with making experiments when I can be alone, and repeating them to my friends and acquaintance, who, from the novelty of the thing, come continually in crouds to see them, I have, during some months past, had little leisure for any thing else.[103]

He acquired great proficiency in repeating the experiments of Dr. Spencer and "in performing those also which . . . [he] had an account of from England, adding a number of new ones." Never one to keep his enthusiasms to himself, he found that his "house was continually full for some time, with people who came to see these new wonders."[104] The irrepressible teacher and sharer then had a number of glass tubes made similar to the Collinson original, which he taught several friends to use for their own experiments.

In the aforementioned letter to Collinson, Franklin informed him that he and his colleagues in the experiments ". . . have observed some particular phaenomena that we look upon to be new. I shall, therefore communicate them to you in my next, though possibly they may not be new to you." As he made this promise Franklin unknowingly committed himself to an action that would give his life a new dimension and free him for services to his fellowmen on an international scale.

CHAPTER 3

Emancipation: Middle Years, 1746–1764

I *Pioneer in Education: The English School*

AS Franklin's printing business and partnerships and his other investments prospered and provided him with the means and the leisure for improving himself and others on a larger scale, his tremendous energies were released in new directions and channels—invention, education, and science. But, after the exertions of the day, he gave himself now and then to the convivial aspects of life—good wine, music, wit, and amusing trifles in verse and prose. Like his father, he also took pleasure in singing, though the songs were different. They were not "psalm tunes," but songs celebrating love, friendship, and wine.

Although he had long ago liberated himself from the orthodox Puritan mistrust of pleasure, provided of course that it was innocent and harmless to others, he was no libertine. A song, "The Old Man's Wish," that he said he had sung "a thousand times" when he was young, had as its refrain:

> May I govern my passions with absolute sway,
> Grow wiser and better as my strength wears away,
> Without gout or stone, by a gentle decay.[1]

And he composed a song to his wife, "my plain country Joan, . . . still the joy of my life," as a reasonable husband's protest against poems written by married men in praise of their imaginary mistresses, adding:

> Some faults have we all, and so has my Joan,
> But then they're exceedingly small;
> And now I'm grown used to them, so like my own,
> I scarcely can see them at all . . . .

He amused himself and others with greater originality and skill in prose, for which he was far better endowed by nature and practice. One of these compositions, commonly entitled "Advice to a Young Man on the Choice of a Mistress" and intended merely for the entertainment of a few discreet evening companions by way of the immemorial male sport of sexual fantasy, is not unworthy of Rabelais, though less exuberant in language. It was therefore copied and preserved as a subliterary masterpiece and passed on from generation to generation until it emerged soon after World War I from the once subterranean world of erotic literature into the unshaded glare of the twentieth century.

When, as sometimes happened, there was not enough news or other interesting matter to fill an issue of the *Gazette*, Franklin would make up a news story to take up the slack. In these cases he was inclined to indulge his fondness for poker-face satirical writing, by which he could satisfy what had become almost a compulsion to combine instruction and entertainment. In one of these fictitious stories, never used in his paper, whatever the reason, he reverted to playing a favorite role, that of the mature, independent woman, but this time with far greater authority of experience and art. It became known as "The Speech of Miss Polly Baker," which he pretended had been delivered ". . . before a Court of Judicature, at Connecticut, near Boston in New-England; where she was prosecuted the fifth time, for having a bastard child. . . ." "May it please the Honourable Bench," she began,

to indulge me in a few words: I am a poor unhappy woman, who have no money to fee lawyers to plead for me, being hard put to it to get a tolerable living. . . . This is the fifth time, Gentlemen, that I have been dragg'd before your Court on the same account; twice I have paid heavy fines, and twice have been brought to publick punishment, for want of money to pay those fines. This may have been agreeable to the laws, and I don't dispute it; but . . . I take the liberty to say, That I think this law, by which I am punished, is both unreasonable in itself, and particularly severe with regard to me, who have always lived an inoffensive life in the neighborhood where I was born, and defy my enemies (if I have any) to say I ever wrong'd man, woman, or child. . . . I have brought five fine children into the world, at the risque of my life; I have maintain'd them well by my own industry, without burthening the township, and would have done it better, if it had not been for the heavy charges and fines I have paid. . . . I have debauched no other woman's husband, nor enticed any youth; . . . I appeal to your Honours. You are pleased to allow I don't want sense; but I must be stupefied to the last degree, not to prefer the honourable state of wedlock, to the condition I have lived in. I always was, and still am willing to enter into it; and doubt not my behaving well in it, having all the industry, frugality, fertility, and skill in oeconomy [i.e., household management], appertaining to a good wife's character. . . . [3]

It might be said, she went on, that, even if her transgression were not unlawful, she should be punished for violating a religious injunction. "If mine, then, is a religious offence," she contended,

leave it to religious punishments. . . . You believe I have offended Heaven, and must suffer eternal fire: Will not that be sufficient? What need is there, then, of your additional fines and whipping? . . . But, how can it be believed, that Heaven is angry at my having children, when to the little done by me towards it, God has been pleased to add his divine skill and admirable workmanship in the formation of their bodies, and crown'd it, by furnishing them with rational and immortal souls. Forgive me, Gentlemen, . . . I am no divine, but if you . . . must be making laws, do not turn natural and useful actions into crimes, by your prohibitions. . . . What must poor young women do, whom custom have forbid to solicit the men, and who cannot force themselves upon husbands, when the laws take no care to provide them any; and yet severely punish them if they do their duty without them; the duty of the first and great command of Nature, and of Nature's God, *Encrease and multiply.* A duty, from the steady performance of which, nothing has been able to deter me; but for its sake, I have hazarded the loss of the publick esteem, and have frequently endured publick disgrace and punishment; and therefore ought, in my humble opinion, instead of a whipping, to have a statue erected to my memory.[4]

A copy of this roguish invention somehow crossed the Atlantic and surfaced in a London newspaper in the spring of 1747 as the bona fide speech of a defendant in an actual trial. The deadpan frontier humor got lost on the long sea voyage to the Old World, but the dramatic and timely social criticism, universal in its appeal, came through. The speech, its genuineness eagerly embraced, became an international sensation, reprinted in other London papers and in provincial newspapers, in magazines in London, Edinburgh, and Dublin, and, recrossing the Atlantic, in Boston, New York, and Annapolis newspapers. During the social and political ferment of the next forty years, it appeared in the works of several English and French reformers as an inspiring historical example of the untutored power of reason in overcoming the injustices and abuses of society.[5]

Many years later, during his mission to France, the secret of his authorship was disclosed privately by Franklin himself to his friend Abbé Reynal, the popular French historian and philosopher, who had been taken in like thousands of others. Undaunted, Reynal had graciously responded, with as much perception as courtesy, that for him Franklin's "tales" were still preferable to "many other men's truths."[6] Polly Baker, raising plain-spoken questions about the established systems of marriage, law, morality, and nature and widely acclaimed as a symbol of the new age of reason and the common man, revealed how clearly, though yet unconsciously, Franklin already reflected the new age, and how close he was to becoming its truest spokesman and teacher.

For Franklin the 1740s—a decade of war with France and Spain—were years of increasing leisure and declining interest in business and making money, of growing preoccupation with the welfare both of his city and colony and of the other English colonies. These interests stirred in him closer attention to the study of nature and the advancement of science, the cooperation among the insulated colonies, the promotion of the health and safety of the people, and the proper education of the younger generation in preparation for the great tasks that lay ahead.

He thought more and more of retiring from the active management of his printing and bookselling business to gain the full-time leisure needed for these interests, which he felt it was his duty and pleasure to cultivate. He was ready for this step, but watched and waited for the right concurrence of circumstances, and in 1748 it happened—when electricity and David Hall came together. He had become profoundly absorbed in electrical experiments, and in David Hall, the new foreman of his printing shop, he decided he had found an able and responsible partner. The articles of partnership, drawn up with the fairness and foresight that were characteristic of Franklin's business relations, were set for a term of eighteen years—a reasonable life expectancy for a man at the age of forty-two in those years—after which Hall had the option to buy the business for what it had been worth in 1748. The partnership lasted the full term to the satisfaction of both parties.

In the fall of that year Franklin informed his friend Cadwallader Colden that he had taken the fateful step. The tradesman had achieved the independence and leisure that had long been regarded as the exclusive property of the gentleman. But, as Poor Richard had observed in 1746, "A life of leisure and a life of laziness are two things."

He looked forward to enjoying life and his friends more than heretofore, being the master of his own time, visiting his most distant friends in America and England, and escaping the entanglements of politics. He wrote Colden:

> Thus you see I am in a fair way of having no other tasks than such as I shall like to give my self, and of enjoying what I look upon as a great happiness, leisure to read, study, make experiments, and converse at large with such ingenious and worthy men as are pleas'd to honour me with their friendship or acquaintance, on such points as may produce something for the common benefit of mankind. . . .[7]

Mankind had other plans for Franklin. For a very short time it let him do what he pleased, but then, since it had an inexhaustible need for him, and, since he, unlike most others, had time, inclination, and incomparable ability, it called on him more and more, though it could never quite possess him. That was reserved for nature and nature's God.

Among the first fruits of his retirement were the enlargement and improvement of his almanac, renamed *Poor Richard Improved*, which first appeared in 1748 and continued under his personal supervision for eleven more years. The education of the common people was an activity that he did not intend to relinquish to anyone else but planned rather to expand in the years to come. He had a calling and a unique gift that could be transferred neither to David Hall nor to any other. He therefore doubled the space in the almanac reserved for instruction, thereby converting the almanac to a minimagazine for the masses. He devoted the extra space to history, science, rational religion, education, health, geography, or demography, the condensed material being written or selected by him to make sure that learning would be pleasurable. A favorite device of his was to use the anniversaries of important events and the birthdays of famous men as points of reference for the concise, lucid paragraphs that he wrote himself to convey useful information incorporating the lessons of experience and the moral principles essential to the welfare of society and the individual. They are models of the art of popular writing and teaching, as a selection from *Poor Richard Improved* for 1748 will show.

Paragraph on the Copernican theory (January):

> On the 19th of this month, Anno 1493, was born the famous astronomer Copernicus, to whom we owe the invention, or rather the revival (it being

taught by Pythagoras near 2000 years before) of that now generally receiv'd system of the world which bears his name, and supposes the sun in the center, this earth a planet revolving around it in 365 days, 6 hours, &c. and that day and night are caused by the turning of the earth on its own axis once round in 24 h. &c. The Ptolomean system, which prevail'd before Copernicus, suppos'd the earth to be fix'd, and that the sun went round it daily. Mr. Whiston, a modern astronomer, says, the sun is 230,000 times bigger than the earth, and 81 millions of miles distant from it: That vast body must then have mov'd more than 480 millions of miles in 24 h. A prodigious journey round this little spot! How much more natural in Copernicus's scheme! Ptolomy is compar'd to a whimsical cook, who, instead of turning his meat in roasting, should fix that, and contrive to have his whole fire, kitchen and all, whirling continually round it.[8]

The verses on the heads of the months were also enlisted for instruction, as illustrated by the following selection on school and parents in April:

> On EDUCATION all our lives depend;
> And few to that, too few, with care attend:
> Soon as Mamma permits her darling joy
> To quit her knee, and trusts at school her boy,
> O, touch him not, whate'er he does is right,
> His spirit's tender, tho' his parts are bright.
> Thus all the bad he can, he learns at school,
> Does what he will, and grows a lusty fool.[9]

The war with France and Spain having been suspended soon after Franklin's retirement, the tradesman who had turned gentleman of leisure was freer in 1749 to pursue a project "of common benefit" to the people of Pennsylvania that had been on his mind for many years, a public academy for the proper education of its youth. He had begun working on it in 1743, but had put it aside for the time because he could not interest the one man he thought qualified to be the headmaster of the kind of school he envisioned.

He was not thinking of a Latin and Greek grammar school that prepared the sons of the well-born and the wealthy for college and a career in one of the professions, but of an English grammar school that was founded on the principles enunciated by Locke in his essay on education and adapted by Franklin for the sons of tradesmen, farmers, and a growing number of non-English immigrants in Pennsylvania, who could not aspire to a profession. Having been guided by Locke in educating himself, he was convinced that a school organized on the basis of Locke's principles and his own successful experience would produce graduates

> . . . fitted for learning any business, calling or profession, except such wherein languages are required; and tho' unaquainted with any antient or foreign tongue, they will be masters of their own, which is of more immediate and general use; . . . laying such a foundation of knowledge and ability, as, properly improv'd, may qualify them to pass thro' and execute the several offices [i.e., duties] of civil life, with advantage and reputation to themselves and country.[10]

In addition, he anticipated that they would also help to alleviate the critical shortage of rural magistrates and schoolmasters in the colony.

Fired by these aims, which seemed reasonable and practicable to him, he set about putting them into effect in accordance with the procedure he had perfected, using the *Gazette* to focus attention,[11] the Junto to serve as catalyst, and his formidable physical and mental powers to overcome inertia and resistance.

> The first step I took was to associate in the design a number of active friends, of whom the Junto furnished a good part: the next was to write and publish a pamphlet [in early fall of 1749] intitled, *Proposals relating to the Education of Youth in Pennsylvania.* This I distributed among the principal inhabitants gratis; and as soon as I could suppose their minds a little prepared by the perusal of it, I set on foot a subscription for opening and supporting an academy. . . . In the introduction to these proposals, I stated their publication not as an act of mine, but of some *publick-spirited gentlemen;* avoiding as much as I could, according to my usual rule, the presenting myself to the publick as the author of any scheme for their benefit.[12]

Twenty-four trustees, most of them the principal and richest men in the colony, were quickly chosen and elected Franklin as the president of the board. The greater part of the subscribers were attracted by the plan for an English school, but the greater part of the money came from men who believed in the traditional study of Latin and Greek and who insisted at once that a Latin and Greek school, as well as an English school, be established in the proposed academy. To get the English school, he reluctantly accepted their condition,

> . . . retaining however a strong prepossession in favour of . . . [his] first plan, and resolving to preserve as much of it as . . . [he] could, and to nourish the English School by every means in . . . [his] power.[13]

As a self-educated tradesman, however influential and brilliant, he had not yet attained the intellectual authority needed to override the educational prejudices of the conventionally educated trustees. To buttress his position, he therefore cited many distinguished educational authorities of his day, such as Milton, Locke, Charles Rollin, and George Turnbull. In fact, the buttresses were much larger than the building itself—635 lines of footnotes for 240 lines of text!

He was aware that placing English, "the vulgar tongue," on a par with Latin and Greek, the long-venerated languages of scholars and gentlemen, was as revolutionary as the translation of the Bible into the language of the people. It would in time cause the aristocracy of the professions and the gentry to lose their monopoly of education and power and compel them to share it with the talented sons of tradesmen and farmers, a prospect of which Franklin himself was a disturbing portent. Thomas Penn, who was astutely class-conscious, had written to the secretary of the province (and later one of the trustees of the Academy) a year before the Academy was projected, that Franklin ". . . is a dangerous man and I should be very glad he inhabited any other country. . . . However, as he is a sort of tribune of the people, he must be treated with regard."[14]

Within a short time the conservative majority of the trustees put the English School in its place and made certain that it would stay there by requiring, among other impediments, that the English headmaster teach twice as many students as the Latin and Greek headmaster for one-half the salary. In 1756, after the two schools had been incorporated as the College, Academy, and Charitable School, Franklin was eased out as president of the trustees and Richard Peters, the Proprietor's man, who had acknowledged that Franklin was "the soul" of the project,[15] was elected in his place. In a rare expression of bitterness at man's ingratitude, Franklin some years later wrote to a friend:

. . . The trustees had reap'd the full advantage of my head, hands, heart and purse, in getting through the first difficulties of the design, and when they thought they could do without me, they laid me aside.[16]

Nevertheless, he continued as a member of the board until his death.

Having determined to salvage as much as he could of his original plan, Franklin had to be satisfied with the organization of the English School as a separate entity within the Academy under its own headmaster. In partial compensation he was able to institute "a Free School for the instruction of poor children" as an adjunct of the Academy, offering reading, writing, and arithmetic and a full scholarship to the Academy, awarded annually to the most promising pupil. The Academy was opened in January, 1751, and the Free School in September of the same year.

To Locke, writing late in the seventeenth century, education had meant the education of gentlemen, but Franklin had found Locke's reforms equally applicable, and easily adaptable, to the sons of settlers in America, who could look ahead only to careers available in the New World—farming, trades, business, teaching, and local government. The fundamental principle of utility in education advocated by Locke, of relevance to the conditions under which the young could be expected to live and work, is one that can be applied to any kind of society at a given time, and Franklin undertook to apply it to Pennsylvania at the midpoint of the eighteenth century.

For Franklin in Philadelphia in 1750, as for Locke in London in 1690, the foundation of a good education must be sound training, first, in reading, speaking, and writing the mother tongue, using its literary classics as models; second, in arithmetic, keeping accounts, and elementary geometry; and, third, in history and geography, especially Greek and Roman, English, and American history. These were to be supplemented for practical reasons by courses in agriculture and mechanics, a program of regular physical exercise, including swimming, and practice in handwriting and drawing, to which he added, because of his own deep-seated interest in the subject and on the recommendation of "the much admired Mons. Rollin," the study of nature, and as a further original contribution of his own, the history of commerce, which Franklin thought had considerable local value.[17]

Neither Franklin nor Locke was opposed to the teaching of Latin and Greek and other foreign languages for those who would need them in divinity, medicine, law, or foreign trade, or even for those in the English School who had "an ardent desire to learn them." No advocate of the Latin School could have paid a more partisan tribute to the classical languages than Franklin when he wrote that

. . . the great men whose lives and actions they read in history, spoke two of the best languages that ever were, the most expressive, copious, beautiful; and . . . the finest writings, the most correct compositions, the most perfect productions of human wit and wisdom, are in those languages, which have endured ages, and will endure while there are men.[18]

But he had long believed with equal passion that they should not be compulsory for all.

The program of the English School, which Franklin had outlined for the trustees,[19] had six grades for boys between the ages of eight and sixteen and substantially the same course of study as that set forth in the *Proposals* for the Academy, with the time gained from the omission of foreign languages given to English and the English classics and to courses in ethics and logic. "It would be well," he wrote,

> if they could be taught *every thing* that is useful, and *every thing* that is ornamental: But art is long, and their time is short. It is therefore propos'd that they learn those things that are likely to be *most useful* and *most ornamental*, regard being had to the several professions for which they are intended.[20]

In all these studies, the teacher was to keep in mind at all times and actively pursue "the great aim and end of all learning," which, in Franklin's plain words, is the development of "an *inclination* join'd with an *ability* to serve mankind, one's country, friends and family," or, in Locke's less concrete expression, "virtue . . . the *solid* and *substantial* good. . . ." In the eighteenth century no one, however radical he might be in his views on politics, religion, or science, doubted that knowledge was secondary and auxiliary to character. In Franklin's Academy formal religion was relegated to an insignificant place in the scheme of education, but ethics still occupied a position of primacy.

Making allowances for the vast difference in times and circumstances, one still finds that Franklin's proposals for the Academy are uncannily modern in many respects: practice in letter writing and speaking, health education, field trips, the school library, provision for laboratory experiments, and the responsibility of the school for what is called guidance today. On the last point, he advised that the trustees (an echo of the spirit of the Junto)

> . . . look on the students as in some sort their children, treat them with familiarity and affection, and when they have behav'd well, and gone through their studies, and are to enter the world, zealously unite, and make all the interest that can be made [i.e., use all their means and influence] to establish them, whether in business, offices . . . or any other thing for their advantage. . . .[21]

He also anticipated the current stress in education on the importance of gifted teachers—to make learning pleasurable and purposeful, to develop the capacities of the students, and to imbue them with the best ideals of the community. He wrote to an admired friend and teacher:

I think ... that talents for the education of youth are the gift of God; and that he on whom they are bestowed, whenever a way is opened for the use of them, is as strongly *called* as if he heard a voice from heaven.[22]

But tradition and habit won out at the Academy, and the English School languished because of neglect and undernourishment. Commenting a year before his death on the failure of the trustees to carry out "the intentions of the original founders," Franklin observed with his customary acuteness and charity that

... there is in mankind an unaccountable prejudice in favour of ancient customs and habitudes, which inclines them to a continuance of them after the circumstances which formerly made them useful cease to exist.[23]

Yet in spite of the setback, he had set in motion forces that turned the Academy of Philadelphia part way toward the future and left a model for later generations to reexamine and improve. A student in an American high school in the year 1910 would have probably found himself in a school which merged the Latin-Greek and English Schools of the Academy, reluctantly accepted by Franklin for the proper education of youth in Pennsylvania in 1750, into an enlarged program of English, Latin, mathematics, Greek, modern foreign languages, and science as the basic offerings. But Franklin, while taking some satisfaction in the fact that most of his original proposals were ultimately accepted more than a century after his death, might have asked with a smile, "Do you think my Academy for the colony of Pennsylvania in 1750 an entirely proper and useful model for the education of youth in the United States in 1910?"

In retrospect the most significant feature of Franklin's original plan for an English school was that it introduced a radically new philosophy of education rooted in the then unique American experience of a people reshaping their environment, creating a society without precedent, governing themselves, and planning their own future. They were bound to the past by tradition and sentiment, but the present and the future were straining at the bonds. Clearly, the traditional aristocratic system of education was out of place and out of date in this open frontier society where *all* the people, eager to take full advantage of their opportunities and abilities, wished to have access to education conforming to their capacities and suited to the needs of Colonial America as well as to the traditions of England and Europe. Franklin's was and is a magnificent revolutionary concept whose challenge each generation of Americans since his time has had to face and has tried to realize in its own imperfect way.

II Scientist in the Service of Man: Electricity

One of the consequences of Franklin's first trip to London at the age of eighteen was that he acquired a taste for the strong wine of scientific research that was being fermented by the Royal Society. In the following years he sampled it in many varieties, and, after studying and practicing the experimental method as set forth in Newton's *Optics*,[24] he found that he had a talent for it and a matching desire and ability to make it serve men's needs and to overcome their resistance to its discoveries and applications.

He had gained a considerable amateur scientific reputation in a constantly widening circle of friends and correspondents well before he was introduced to electricity by Dr. Spencer in 1743 or began his own intensive experiments three years later with the encouragement of Peter Collinson, a fellow of the Royal Society. During the next five years, in spite of interruptions occasioned, at first, by the war with France and the threat of attack on Pennsylvania, and, later, by his commitment to the Academy, he persevered in carrying on these experiments, unencumbered by the ideas of other men and relying largely on the evidence of his experiments and the resources of his own intellect and imagination.

Collinson, responding to Franklin's selfless quest for the truth, sent him whatever material on electricity he could find, and Franklin in return gratefully transmitted by letter a full account of his experiments and observations as they progressed. Deeply impressed by the originality and "clear intelligent style" of these letters, Collinson shared them with other members of the Royal Society and finally decided to collect and publish the best letters in the belief that it would be "a great pitty that the publick should be deprived the benefits of so many curious [i.e., original *and* careful] experiments."[25]

The book, eighty-six pages in length, made its unheralded appearance in the spring of 1751, simply entitled, *Experiments and Observations on Electricity . . . by Mr. Benjamin Franklin*. It was original in several important respects:

1. Its language was simple, clear, and nontechnical, capable of being understood by any intelligent reader; and the letters often reflected the irrepressible humor and charm of their author.

2. Franklin presented experimental evidence for a radically new

theory of electricity. The prevalent theory of electricity at that time held that there were two kinds of electricity, *vitreous* (produced when glass is rubbed with silk), and *resinous* (produced when resin is rubbed with wool or fur). Franklin brilliantly deduced from his experiments that there is only one kind of "electrical matter," manifesting itself in two aspects, for which he invented the terms *positive*, or *plus*, instead of *vitreous*, and *negative*, or *minus*, instead of *resinous*.[26]

3. He disclosed the discovery of an electrical phenomenon, "the doctrine of points," never before observed: a long sharp pin, a pointed iron rod, or a *wet* pointed wooden rod has "the wonderful effect of . . . *drawing* off and *throwing* off the electrical fire."[27]

4. He offered considerable evidence that pointed to the identity of electricity and lightning. This was not a new hypothesis, but he dared for the first time to suggest and design an experiment to prove it. He proposed that it be tried "on the top of some high tower or steeple."[28] He did not try it himself, because he thought he needed a higher building than any then available in Philadelphia.[29]

5. He submitted that, if it were proved that electricity and lightning were the same, it followed from the doctrine of points that buildings and ships could be protected from lightning, and he showed how it could be done. In 1749, after three years of electrical experiments, he had expressed his disappointment to Collinson that he had "hitherto been able to discover nothing in the way of use to mankind,"[30] and it was gratifying to him at last that his doctrine of points was likely to benefit his fellowmen.

The dramatic novelty of the style and subject matter of the book, combined with its underlying philanthropic spirit, gave it a popular appeal outside the scientific fraternity that was unexpected. Sixteen years later the celebrated Joseph Priestley wrote that "nothing was ever written upon the subject of electricity which was more generally read, and admired in all parts of Europe than these letters."[31]

Less than a year after their publication they were translated into French by Thomas-François Dalibard and stirred such general interest that the king asked to have some of Franklin's experiments performed for him. The pleasure he expressed during and after the electrical show moved Dalibard and another French experimenter to risk making the experiment with lightning according to Franklin's specifications, except that they placed very long pointed iron rods in the ground instead of on a tower or steeple. Dalibard was the first to make the experiment successfully on May 10, 1752, and the other a week later. The epoch-

BENJAMIN FRANKLIN

.... was immediately conveyed to the Royal Society, where it produced a sensation—and some embarrassment, since they had failed to take up Franklin's challenge when they received it the year before.

Franklin himself, fortunately, did not know about the successful lightning experiments in France at the time that he, too, conceived of a simple, but dangerous, way to make the experiment without recourse to a high tower or steeple. He would use a kite, to which a pointed iron rod was attached at the top, during a thunderstorm, so that the wet string would serve as a conductor. He made the experiment successfully in Philadelphia in June, about a month after Dalibard's. More than thirty-five years later he still remembered "the infinite pleasure" he received in the success of his unpretentious experiment. A report on the kite experiment was read to the Royal Society in December of that year and received wide circulation in the *Gentleman's Magazine* and in the second edition of Franklin's book the following year. The image of a simple man, daring the lightning with a child's plaything, caught and gripped the imagination of men everywhere, from peasant to prince. Dalibard was forgotten, and Franklin became "the new Prometheus" and an inspiration to simple men the world over.

For a long time Franklin's enduring achievements in electricity were overshadowed by this popular image, but though electrical science has advanced far beyond his pioneer theories and discoveries—no man was more modest in assessing them than their author—they "laid the real foundation on which the whole superstructure of electrical theory and interpretation has been erected," in the opinion of Robert A. Millikan, Nobel Prize winner and one of the great physicists of our century.[32]

Franklin foresaw that electricity would ultimately be harnessed to become the servant of man. "There are no bounds," he wrote, "(but what expence and labour give) to the force man may raise and use in the electric way."[33] But as immediate gains his work taught men that lightning and nature were not to be superstitiously feared, but rationally studied and used for mankind's benefit, and his kite experiment and lightning rod helped to erase in the popular mind the myth of the scientist as a superman tampering with forbidden things and to substitute the image of Franklin as a very human benefactor of man taming the lightning.

His letters also performed a valuable service for science. Scientists in the eighteenth century were generally amateurs—doctors, lawyers, clergymen, government officials, merchants, farmers, teachers, shoemakers, or gentlemen with no occupation. In the absence of a professional code like the Hippocratic Oath, Franklin, practicing the moral principles of his private life in his scientific work, set an example of professional ethics—honesty, modesty, devotion to truth, and service to mankind—that had a great influence on scientists, especially the younger men, in this formative early period of scientific progress. It is evident in a comment made by Priestley, one of these younger scientists, on Franklin's letters on electricity:

> It is not easy to say, whether we are most pleased with the simplicity and perspicuity with which these letters are written, the modesty with which the author proposes every hypothesis of his own, or the noble frankness with which he relates his mistakes, when they were corrected by subsequent experiments.[34]

In science, as in business, journalism, philanthropy, education, and later in politics and diplomacy, Franklin's uncommon integrity was no less potent a factor than his exceptional abilities in raising him to a position of unparalleled influence over men's minds and actions. Unless we expose ourselves to his living words, it is difficult to have a full appreciation of the impact of his personality on his contemporaries. Let us cite just a few excerpts from his letters on electricity.

When he was asked by a correspondent to give the reason for a certain electrical phenomenon, he replied:

> You require the reason; I do not know it. Perhaps you may discover it, and then you will be so good as to communicate it to me. I find a frank acknowledgment of one's ignorance is not only the easiest way to get rid of a difficulty, but the likeliest way to obtain information.[35]

In the same spirit, he wrote to Collinson in September, 1753, after reporting additional electrical research:

> These thoughts, my dear friend, are many of them crude and hasty, and if I were merely ambitious of acquiring some reputation in [natural] philosophy, I ought to keep them by me, 'till corrected and improved by time and farther experience. But since even short hints, and imperfect experiments in any new branch of science, being communicated, have oftentimes a good effect, in exciting the attention of the ingenious to the subject, and so becoming the occasion of more exact disquisitions ... and more compleat discoveries, you are at liberty to communicate this paper to whom you please; it being of more importance that knowledge should increase, than that your friend should be thought an accurate [natural] philosopher.[36]

Even when he was nearly killed by an electric shock because of his carelessness during an experiment, he first noted the effect on himself in full detail in a letter to his brother John, and at the end ruefully compared himself to a clever fellow "who being about to steal powder, made a hole in the cask with a hott iron."[37]

Within a few years of publication of his *Experiments and Observations on Electricity* Franklin received honorary master of arts degrees from Harvard, Yale, and William and Mary and was elected a fellow of the Royal Society. He became a figure of unique significance among all classes of society in America and Europe, the first American to gain international fame, a self-made man of the people, and herald of a great shift, a new era, in human affairs—the age of science, technology, industry, and the common man.

III *Preacher of Union: Albany Plan*

The intellect and imagination that had unveiled some of the secrets of electricity and recognized the realities of education had long foreseen that the ties of common language, culture, trade, and interest would in time break down the geographical and political barriers separating the English Colonies in America. As a native son of one colony and the adopted son of another, linking New England and the middle colonies, Franklin started out early in life with an intercolonial outlook, and his choice of the printer's trade and subsequent affiliations with printers in the other colonies further enlarged it. Following the expansion of his scientific interests and correspondence, he initiated the first institutional project for the *cultural* union of the colonies by establishing the American Philosophical Society. Although it did not prosper at the outset, it survived—to extend a network of lines of communication across Colonial borders for the exchange of ideas, studies, and experiments by some of the best minds in America, with Franklin at the switchboard.

At the same time the war with France and Spain was demonstrating the urgent need for *military* cooperation and coordination between the colonies to protect themselves against the French in the north and the Spanish in the south. Pennsylvania, alone among the colonies, was totally unprepared for war because of Quaker doctrinal pacifism coupled with Quaker political control of the colony, and uninvolved in the war because of its position midway between the two distant war fronts. Unable to resolve the conflict between principle and self-preservation, it followed an uneasy policy of doing nothing and hoping for the best. But in the summer of 1747 the hope was suddenly shattered by probing raids from a French privateer along the Delaware River below Philadelphia and by ominous attacks on English and Colonial shipping in and near Delaware Bay. Franklin laid aside his electrical experiments for a while to lend his assistance in the emergency.

For three months the city council and a great number of the leading citizens, including more than a few Quakers, had vainly pleaded with the Quaker majority in the Assembly to take the necessary measures for the defense of the city and the colony.

There seemed to be no way to break out of this dangerous impasse until Franklin suggested a way around it, brilliantly adapting the method he had developed in creating the Junto, the Library Company, and the Philosophical Society—to unite people in a "voluntary association" arising from a common need and resulting in a common benefit. His projects always seemed simple and obvious after his genius as a writer and a teacher of men had explained them and after his phenomenal gift as a social engineer had created the appropriate instrument or form. He made his first move in this crisis on November 17, 1747, with the publication of an expository pamphlet, as was his practice in campaigns for the public good. The sober title, *Plain Truth*, and the unnamed (though not unknown) author, "a tradesman of Philadelphia," gave scarcely any intimation of the volcanic content. Citing the Bible, which the stubborn Quaker leaders revered, and Roman history, which they respected, and "speaking his mind" with an ardor that was unusual for him, Franklin recalled the dreadful fate suffered by those who in the past had neglected to be prepared in time of war, and painted in bold colors the present dangers—Indian attacks, economic disaster, and possible devastation by invaders—that the city and province invited by their defenseless condition.

Those who would pay the price of this folly would not be the rich, for "the means of speedy flight are ready in their hands,"[38] but the unarmed tradesmen, shopkeepers, and farmers. The Quakers, who controlled the assembly, did nothing. "Their religious prepossessions are unchangeable."[39] And the wealthy merchants who oppose the Quakers, rather than spend money and fight to defend the Quakers, say, "Let . . . the city burn." They reminded Franklin of the story of the man who refused to pump in a sinking ship "because one on board, whom he hated, would be saved by it as well as himself."[40]

"The way to secure peace," he concluded, "is to be prepared for war." To that end he proposed a plan to organize a voluntary private militia and to raise the money for it "without laying a burthen on any man."[41]

As to those "in the city, towns and plantations near the river," who were indifferent to the Indian threat on the frontiers, and to those "in the country," who paid little heed to the danger faced by the city, he made this appeal:

Is not the whole province one body, united by living under the same laws, and enjoying the same priviledges? Are not the people of city and country connected as relations both by blood and marriage, and in friendships equally dear? Are they not likewise united in interest, and mutually useful and necessary to each other? When the feet are wounded, shall the head say, *It is not me; I will not trouble myself to contrive relief!* Or if the head is in danger, shall the hands say, *We are not affected, and therefore will lend no assistance!* . . . so would the body be . . . destroyed: But when all parts join their endeavours for its security, it is often preserved. And such should be the union between the country and the town; and such their mutual endeavours for the safety of the whole.[42]

The fervor of the popular response surprised even Franklin and the friends associated with him in this audacious project for a voluntary, private, and independent military association for the defense of Philadelphia and Pennsylvania. What followed was like a blitzkrieg. He quickly prepared, with the help of a few friends, and printed the final draft of the "Form of Association" to be presented at a public meeting set for November 21, four days after the announcement in *Plain Truth*. Within two weeks the public meeting considered and agreed to the plan; "a great meeting of the principal gentlemen, merchants and others" unanimously approved it; "upwards of five hundred men of all ranks subscribed their names," as reported in the *Gazette*;[43] and the "Form of Association" was reprinted in the *Gazette*, with Franklin's comments on the several articles of the agreement. Soon afterward he initiated a lottery to pay for fortifications at key points around Philadelphia. At these batteries Franklin recalled that ". . . the Associators kept a nightly guard while the war lasted: and among the rest I regularly took my turn of duty . . . as a common soldier."[44]

Appeals were sent to Thomas Penn for cannon and to the admiralty for a warship to be stationed in Delaware Bay, but to meet the immediate emergency, small cannon were purchased in Boston and a number of "spare cannon" were borrowed from Governor Clinton of New York. Franklin, who was chosen as a member of the delegation appointed to negotiate with Governor Clinton, told how they got the cannon:

He at first refus'd us peremptorily: but at a dinner with his Council where there was great drinking of Madeira wine, as the custom at that place then was, he soften'd by degrees, and said he would lend us six. After a few more bumpers he advanc'd to ten. And at length he very good-naturedly conceded eighteen.[45]

By the time the war ended in 1748, the association had ten companies of about one hundred men each in Philadelphia and more than one hundred companies in the province under arms, trained and self-equipped. And in this amazing demonstration lesson of the resources of leadership and self-direction discovered in the common people of Pennsylvania in this emergency, Franklin was, as his friend James Logan later reported to Thomas Penn, "the principal mover and very soul of the whole . . . and all this without much appearing in any part of it himself."[46]

The "Form of Association" was clearly a revolutionary instrument designed by Franklin for a people whose political traditions were rooted in respect for law and legitimacy, but whose frontier experience had conditioned them to depend on themselves, except in a general emergency, when they expected the government to provide for their safety. Franklin now advanced the congenial American doctrine that, if the government failed in time of war to take measures for their defense, it was legitimate for them to depend on themselves in self-defense. The preamble to the agreement proclaimed:

That being . . . unprotected by the government under which we live, against our foreign enemies that may come to invade us, . . . we do hereby, for our mutual defence and security, and for the security of our wives, children and estates, and . . . the preservation of the persons and estates of others, our neighbours and fellow subjects, form ourselves into an association, and . . . do agree *solemnly* with each other in manner following. . . . [47]

The eight articles that ensued are startling in their originality and daring. They created a democratic "army of freemen," led by officers elected by their men for a term of only one year. The officers elected their regimental commanders. The soldiers and officers met once a year in their respective counties "for a general exercise and review" and to elect delegates from each county to a General Military Council, which drew up the necessary regulations for training, planning, and management of the citizen army, these regulations "to have the force of laws with us, and we promise to pay them all the obedience in our power."[48]

It is no wonder that the Proprietor, Thomas Penn, regarded the association as the equivalent of "a military common wealth" independent of the government of the province, "acting a part little less than treason," and considered its author "a dangerous man."[49] But Franklin, anticipating this reaction, had inserted moderating controls in the plan. The officers were to receive their commissions from the governor or, in his absence, from the Common Council. The General Military Council was not allowed to impose fines, "corporal penalties," or taxes. Finally, the eighth article stated that the association would continue only "until peace shall be established . . . and no longer."[50] In this and other respects, as Franklin blandly remarked, the association expressed "a dutiful regard to the government."[51]

The miracle is that the association *worked*, the first popular insurrection in the colonies that succeeded, and without violence, without civil strife. Yet it has received less than the attention it deserves as a historic lesson in the education of the American people, a lesson that signalized the political genius and maturity which would culminate in our Constitution forty years later. That anyone but Franklin could have carried it off is more than doubtful, for in the labyrinth of hostilities that had been built up in the city and domain of brotherly love only a leader of his integrity, common sense, political acumen, eloquence, modesty, wisdom, and faith in people could have inspired the trust of all factions in the doctrine of self-reliance and solidarity that he counseled. He could trust people, as they could trust him, because he knew his own defects and merits almost as well as he knew theirs and therefore could protect himself against himself, and them against themselves. Sensible of the human temptations that the association would evoke, he therefore cautioned the members in these sagacious words:

'Tis hoped this whole affair will be conducted with *good order* and *sobriety*, and that no *ill-natured* reflections, no *injuries* or *insults* will be offered our *peaceable friends*, *neighbours* and *fellow-subjects*, who, from their religious scruples, cannot allow themselves to join us.[52]

So when the war was ended, the association was disbanded as pledged, the great political power Franklin had acquired was given up without regret, and he went back gladly to his electrical experiments seeking a higher power, the knowledge of nature's mysterious ways, with which he hoped to make man's condition on earth a little less onerous. But what the people had learned in the association that he had shaped was not forgotten, and in Pennsylvania and the other colonies where the remarkable story was known his influence over men's minds and hearts increased and spread.

The half-dozen years following the "peace" of 1748 were a time of escalation in the life of Franklin and in the global conflict between England and France. He was elected to the city council and the assembly, he founded the Academy, he finessed the assembly into serving as midwife at the birth of the Philadelphia Hospital, he called together the fire companies of the city to form a mutual fire company, and in his spare time he made the experiments and observations in electricity that brought him worldwide fame and honors.

The peace treaty that had terminated the war was in reality merely a cease-fire agreement, as both sides recognized by accelerating their preparations for the resumption of the titanic struggle. The colonies, separated by geographical and political barriers, were painfully conscious of their unpreparedness and disunity, in which their inefficient intercolonial postal system was a considerable factor. Therefore, when it appeared in 1751 that the office of postmaster general for the colonies would soon become vacant, Franklin, seizing the opportunity to strengthen intercolonial relations, enlisted his friends on both sides of the Atlantic to advance his candidacy. He succeeded in getting the appointment in the summer of 1753, though jointly with William Hunter, printer of Williamsburg in Virginia and publisher of *The Virginia Gazette*, to whom the southern colonies were assigned, while the northern colonies were placed under Franklin. The two men worked well together, but, owing to the poor health of Hunter, Franklin became the more active and visible partner.

Though personal ambition had been a consideration in his seeking the office, Franklin's concern for the safety of the colonies was probably a motive of equal weight. His experience in trying to organize the American Philosophical Society had convinced him that without an effective postal service any plan for united action by the colonies, whether cultural, military, or political, would be seriously handicapped.

Intercolonial cooperation had been very much on his mind during these years of imminent war. To friends in New York, who shared his concern and solicited his advice, he had outlined a voluntary plan of military union published anonymously in 1751. He could not conceal a note of impatience as he contemplated the continued resistance of the colonies to forming a union for their urgent self-protection:

It would be a very strange thing, if six nations of ignorant savages [Iroquois Indian Confederacy] should be capable of forming a scheme for such an union, and be able to execute it in such a manner, as that it has existed ages, and appears indissoluble; and yet that a like union should be impracticable for ten or a dozen English colonies, to whom it is more necessary, and must be more advantageous; and who cannot be supposed to want [i.e., lack] an equal understanding of their interests.[53]

But nothing came of the plan—the danger was not yet great or close enough.

A paper that was written the same year, but was not published by him until 1754, his famous *Observations concerning the Increase of Mankind . . .* , revealed among other things that he was dreaming loyally of an American union within the British Empire that would in a hundred years be more populous and wealthy than the mother country.

For the present, drawing on his experience as postmaster of Philadelphia and comptroller of the Colonial postal system, he did his best with Hunter to make it an efficient instrument of communication between the colonies that would be available to serve them when they were ready for union. With the French openly preparing to build forts on the Ohio River, and the frontier settlements in Virginia and Pennsylvania in a state of alarm, the newly appointed postmasters general quickly prepared and sent out before the end of 1753 new regulations to all local postmasters designed to improve mail service and deliveries and set up a uniform system of accounting. Franklin then visited nearly every colony to make sure that the new regulations had been put into effect. The reforms were so successful that within a short time one of the major roadblocks to an effective military union for self-defense had been removed.

In the meantime the French moved ahead almost unopposed in the execution of their plans for the continental defense of their colonies in Canada and Louisiana, while the English colonies, unable to work out similar unified plans, failed to act decisively for their own protection and that of their Indian allies, the "Six Nations," who were reported to be wavering therefore in their loyalty to the English cause. The British government, disturbed by the reports of these developments, issued instructions early in 1754 for a Colonial congress to be held in Albany, New York, to repair the damage to the morale of the Iroquois by drafting a new treaty. Six northern colonies and Maryland sent commissioners; Virginia and New Jersey chose not to take part in the Albany Congress, which was to meet in June.

Franklin was an inevitable choice as one of the four commissioners from Pennsylvania. He had been beating the drum for a Colonial union of defense for several years and had sketched out a tentative plan of union in 1751. In May, 1754, one month before the Albany Congress, upon receiving news of the capture by the French of the small Virginia fort at the forks of the Ohio, he sounded the alarm in the *Gazette*, a common tactic of his, as we have seen, in the education of the public.

At the end of the article he summed up his message by printing a drawing of a snake cut into pieces that represented the divided colonies, with the motto "JOIN, or DIE" below. The "Snake Cartoon," the first and perhaps the most influential political cartoon published in an American newspaper, was a new weapon in Franklin's educational armory, a precursor of the visual journalism and education of today. The effect of this novel mode of expression and instruction was incalculable and was felt immediately in Boston, New York, Williamsburg, and Charleston, and, when the conflict between England and the colonies erupted a decade later, the motto was revived as a popular slogan to rally the advocates of American union.

On his way to Albany, Franklin said, he "projected and drew up a plan for the union of all the colonies, under one government so far as might be necessary for defence, and other important general purposes." This plan was similar to his 1751 plan, providing for "a president general appointed and supported by the Crown, and a grand council to be chosen by the representatives of the people of the several colonies met in their respective assemblies,"[54] but it was different in two critical points: it had been broadened to include general purposes other than defense, and it provided that the union be established by act of Parliament and not, as he had previously recommended, by voluntary action of the colonies, which he foresaw would be extremely difficult to accomplish.

The grand council would act for all the colonies in Indian affairs, defense matters, and the building of forts and new settlements, and would have the power to impose taxes for these purposes. The president general would have the right of veto over all acts of the council and the duty of executing them after they had been mutually agreed upon.[55]

Franklin had observed in the introduction to his 1751 plan

> ... that securing the friendship of the Indians is of the greatest consequence to these Colonies; and that the surest means of doing it, are, to regulate the Indian trade ... and to unite the several governments. ...[56]

He was still of the same opinion, and the Albany commissioners concurred.

With these basic considerations settled, they appointed a committee, of which Franklin was made a member, to examine and report on the various plans for union, written and oral, that were expected to be submitted by the delegations. Franklin's plan was preferred by the committee and, after much debate, by the congress in its essential features, with some minor modifications and additions.

There were four "generals" or principles that Franklin had incorporated in the Albany Plan: (1) the necessity of union, (2) fair treatment of the Indians, (3) democratic representation, and (4) no taxation without representation. These were the basic ingredients of the medicine prescribed by Franklin and most of the other commissioners to alleviate the disorders from which the colonies were suffering. It was soon apparent that the medicine was too strong and quite unpalatable, for the Colonial assemblies, without exception, refused to take it. Perhaps, if Franklin had been in a position, as in Philadelphia, to mount one of his characteristic educational campaigns in each colony, the plan would have had a greater success, but the time for union was not yet ripe, and the leaders were a little too far ahead of the people.

However, the Albany Congress and Franklin accomplished more than appeared on the surface. They called attention to the neglect and mistreatment of the Indian allies, indicated the direction in which political thinking in the colonies was moving, made the idea of union respectable, alerted the colonies and the British government to the danger of French expansion along the western frontier, brought together the leaders in the colonies who were America-minded, and outlined a structure of federal government that was available over thirty years later when the need for a central authority in an independent, but divided, American nation was again recognized. Franklin emerged from the congress as one of the acknowledged American political leaders rather than a noted Pennsylvania inventor, organizer, educator, and scientist. He had acquired an American constituency among the best political minds in the colonies.

Looking back on the stillbirth of the Albany Plan near the end of his life, after American independence and union had been definitely won, Franklin, who loved England and hated war and revolution, even when they were necessary, remarked sadly:

On reflection it now seems probable, that if the foregoing Plan or something like it, had been adopted and carried into execution, the subsequent separation of the Colonies from the mother country might not so soon have happened, nor the mischiefs suffered on both sides have occurred, perhaps during [i.e., until] another century . . . [and] the different parts of the Empire might still have remained in peace and union.[57]

A few months later in 1754, when Governor William Shirley of Massachusetts, a staunch advocate of concerted action by the colonies, sounded him out on an alternative plan for an intercolonial council of governors, with the costs to be defrayed by a Colonial tax levied by Parliament, Franklin objected that "excluding the people of the Colonies from all share in the choice of the grand council, would probably give extreme dissatisfaction, as well as the taxing them by act of Parliament, where they have no representative."[58] In reply to Shirley's suggestion of a closer union with Great Britain, including representation in Parliament, he fervently endorsed the idea, which he had long hoped to see realized, provided, he added astutely and wisely, that

. . . they had a reasonable number of representatives allowed them; and that all the old Acts of Parliament restraining the trade or cramping the manufactures of the Colonies, be at the same time repealed. . . . 'till the new Parliament, representing the whole, shall think it for the interest of the whole to re-enact some or all of them. . . . I should hope too, that by such an union, the people of Great Britain and the people of the Colonies would learn to consider themselves, not as belonging to different communities with different interests, but to one community with one interest, which I imagine would contribute to strengthen the whole, and—[confiding a sense almost of foreboding] greatly lessen the danger of future separations.[59]

This vision of a larger union than that of the colonies also proved to be premature, and, to fill the vacuum created by the rejection of both plans, General Edward Braddock was sent with two regiments of regulars to recapture the fort at the forks of the Ohio from the French. The regiments were "two of the worst" in the British army[60]—an indication of the ignorance of the government in London regarding conditions in the colonies. Braddock met with the governors of the five colonies endangered by the French advance in the west.

As postmaster general Franklin was responsible for communications between the general and the governors. In addition, he recruited wagons, horses, and pack animals in Pennsylvania, risking financial ruin by guaranteeing payment to their owners. He also tried in vain to alert Braddock to the dangers of the Indian method of warfare.

After Braddock's defeat, the Pennsylvania Assembly, under Franklin's guidance, reluctantly authorized the organization of a volunteer army modeled after the former democratic association militia. Franklin was promptly appointed by the governor to build a line of small forts on the northwestern frontier of the colony, which he completed in a week in spite of his age, confirming his view that Colonials served best under men they knew and respected.

The ill-fated Braddock expedition and the measures for defense arising from it in Pennsylvania resulted in unforeseen by-products. The Braddock "transaction," Franklin noted, "gave us Americans the first suspicion that our exalted ideas of the prowess of British regulars had not been well founded,"[61] and the wrangles in the assembly made him sick of politics. "If," he confided to Collinson, "my being able now and then to influence a good measure did not keep up my spirits, I should be ready to swear never to serve again as an Assembly-man. . . . "[62] And again, two months later, he wrote; "I abhor these altercations; and if I did not love the country and the people, would remove immediately into a more quiet government, Connecticut, where I am also happy enough to have many friends."[63]

IV Agent of the People versus the Proprietors: London

Disappointed in his hope of union for the colonies, harassed as leader of the popular party in the assembly because of his unyielding opposition to the Proprietors' claim of exemption from taxation, which he considered indefensible in principle and prejudicial to the best interest of the colony and the Penn family, and exposed to the cross fire of the opposing camps in his unsuccessful efforts to mediate the dispute, Franklin welcomed the decision of the assembly in 1757 "to petition the king" against the Proprietors and to appoint him as its London agent to seek redress. He certainly preferred this appointment to moving to Connecticut. But Deborah Franklin, dreading the long voyage across the Atlantic in wartime and probably fearing the perils of London society almost as much, chose to stay behind in the security of Philadelphia, and Franklin took his son William, now twenty-six, with him.

After waiting for a convoy in New York for more than two tedious months, they sailed late in June, leaving the convoy near Halifax. They made a swift passage of less than a month to Falmouth. They "were several times chas'd," he remembered, "but outsail'd every thing." As they approached Falmouth, they nearly struck some rocks on which a lighthouse was located. When they stepped ashore, he wrote to Deborah on the same day,

The bell ringing for church, we went thither immediately, and with hearts full of gratitude, returned sincere thanks to God for the mercies we had received: were I a Roman Catholic, perhaps I should on this occasion vow to build a chapel to some saint; but as I am not, if I were to vow at all, it should be to build a *lighthouse*.[64]

During the crossing, Franklin had completed his *Poor Richard* almanac for 1758, the last which he intended to prepare himself, composing a long "preface" for this farewell anniversary number that filled the usual space on the first page and all the pages opposite the twelve monthly calendars ordinarily reserved for his instructive miscellany. It was no less educational, being a collection of the best aphorisms on industry and frugality culled from the previous twenty-five issues, in each of which he had sought to reduce poverty and promote the independence and dignity of the individual. Determined as usual to be entertaining as well as instructive, he dramatized the collection and brought it up to date by presenting it as a speech by "Father Abraham"—"a plain clean old man with white locks," who had delivered it at a recent country sale in response to an inquiry about the heavy taxes occasioned by the war with France:

"How shall we be ever able to pay them? What would you advise us to?" he was asked.—Father Abraham stood up, and reply'd, "If you'd have my advice, I'll give it you in short, for a *word to the wise* is enough, and *many words won't fill a bushel*, as *Poor Richard* says."[65]

Then followed a chain of Poor Richard's sayings ingeniously tied together by the wise old man's comments. When his speech ended, Poor Richard remarked with his customary wry cnador:

The frequent mention he made of me must have tired any one else, but my vanity was wonderfully delighted with it, though I was conscious that not a tenth part of the wisdom was my own . . . but rather the *gleanings* I had made of the sense of all ages and nations . . . and though I had at first determined to buy stuff for a new coat, I went away resolved to wear my old one a little longer. *Reader*, if thou wilt do the same, thy profit will be as great as mine.[66]

Reprinted separately the same year in Boston, New London (Conn.), and twice in London, the preface gained steadily in popularity under the title of "Father Abraham's Speech," or more often, "The Way to Wealth." It has been published hundreds of times in one form or another since 1758, as pamphlet, chapbook, or broadside, in anthologies and school readers, and in translations into at least fifteen foreign languages, including Gaelic, Welsh, and Chinese,[67] carrying Franklin's practical message of self-help and hope to the poor throughout the world from his time to ours.

He was fifty-one years of age when he returned to London after an absence of over thirty years, bringing with him a distinguished reputation in science at home and abroad, an assorted baggage of large ideas and ideals, and a formidable gift as writer and publicist. He had preached and practiced—with reasonable tolerance for human weakness and error, not exempting his own—decency and responsibility in private and public life, cooperation for human betterment, the application of reason and science to human problems, a willingness to make personal sacrifice for the public good, devotion to human rights and liberties, faith in education based on knowledge, reason, and morality, and concern for mankind notwithstanding its discouraging imperfections—and all these ideals were enhanced by his extraordinary gift for making and keeping friends regardless of nationality, creed, race, color, or social class.

A half-serious letter that William Strahan, one of his previous correspondents and a prominent London printer, wrote to Deborah Franklin a few months after becoming acquainted with Franklin in person is a fair example of how he affected most of those who met him during this or any other period of his life: "For my own part," Strahan declared,

I never saw a man who was, in every respect, so perfectly agreeable to me. Some are amiable in one view, some in another, he in all. Now madam as I know the ladies here consider him in exactly the same light I do, upon my word I think you should come over, with all convenient speed to look after your interest; not but that I think him as faithful to his Joan, as any man breathing. . . . [68]

Not aware of her antipathy to William, Strahan also expressed his admiration of Franklin's relationship with his son, who had been enrolled in the Middle Temple to study law, and toward whom the father was "at the same time his friend, his brother, his intimate, and easy companion. . . . "[69] The widow, Mrs. Margaret Stevenson, in whose house on Craven Street near Charing Cross comfortable lodgings had been arranged for Franklin, and her daughter Polly became his lifelong friends. When he became very ill in the fall of 1757, Mrs. Stevenson attended him with such "assiduity," as Strahan reported in the same letter, that he recovered completely.

Franklin was advised by friends to try to negotiate a settlement of the taxation dispute with the Proprietors before entering a complaint against them with the government. He met with Thomas Penn a few weeks after his arrival in London and soon realized that, in spite of the politeness and professions of amenability, the Proprietor was largely responsible for the misinformation and disfavor with which the case of the assembly was viewed in government circles and even among friends of the colony. The situation was one quite familiar to Franklin, and the remedy he proposed to apply had been employed by him many times before—education of the public and of key individuals, primarily by skilful and persistent use of the press for the purpose of ". . . removing the prejudices that art and accident have spread among the people of this country against us, and obtaining for us the good opinion of the bulk of mankind. . . . "[70] To counteract "the prejudices . . . propagated by our enemies,"[71] he therefore sponsored a book on the history of the long conflict between the assembly and the Proprietors, *An Historical Review of the Constitution and Government of Pennsylvania*, published in 1759, with many of the materials supplied by Franklin, but with a frankly partisan point of view that was neither his style nor his feeling. The book was denounced by the Proprietors and their followers. Writing to Isaac Norris, the Speaker of the Assembly, Franklin mentioned the violent reaction of Thomas Penn and expressed his own opinion of the book:

The Proprietor is enrag'd. When I meet him any where there appears in his wretched countenance a strange mixture of hatred, anger, fear, and vexation. He supposes me the author, but is mistaken. I had no hand in it. It is wrote by a gentleman said to be one of the best pens in England, . . . who . . . will not be known [i.e., does not wish to be known]. . . . The old Proprietor and some others are set in a light I could have wish'd not to have seen them in; but the author contended for the sacredness of historical truth, which ought not to be violated in favour to one's friends . . . I look'd over the manuscript, but was not permitted to alter every thing I did not fully approve. And upon the whole, I think it a work that may be of good use here, by giving the Parliament and Ministry a clearer knowledge and truer notion of our disputes; and of lasting use in Pensylvania as it affords a close and connected view of our public affairs, and may spread and confirm among our people, and especially in the rising generation, those sentiments of liberty that one would wish always to prevail in Pensylvania.[72]

The chief figures in the private sector of Franklin's campaign were Collinson, Strahan, and the distinguished physicians, Dr. John Fothergill (who had written the preface to the first edition of Franklin's *Experiments and Observations*) and Dr. John Pringle (later president of the Royal Society). They were most helpful in introducing him to important men in the government and the opposition, many of whom were privately sympathetic to his liberal political philosophy, and to notable men of learning in the arts and sciences, among whom he was already celebrated for his achievements in electricity. Through these acquaintances, he sought to reinforce his counterattack against the Proprietors at every opportunity.

Franklin was a man of too many interests to confine himself entirely to the duties of his mission. He managed to find time for relaxation from business in a variety of experiments in electricity and the phenomena of heat and cold, performed usually in the morning, and often with curious friends in attendance; in the pleasures of music, having learned to play the violin, guitar, harp, and "harmonica" (musical glasses), which he had considerably improved as a musical instrument; in meetings at clubs, political and social; and best of all at home with his "family," his son Billy, Mrs. Stevenson, and Polly. When Polly went to live with an aunt in Essex, he undertook to give her a correspondence course in "moral as well as natural philosophy," remarking with habitual modesty:

I beg you would not in the least apprehend that I should think it a trouble to receive and answer your questions. It will be a pleasure, and no trouble. For tho' I may not be able, out of my own little stock of knowledge to afford you what you require, I can easily direct you to the books where it may most readily be found.[73]

Taking advantage also of the delays produced by the strategy of the Proprietors or by the bureaucratic process, he was able to enjoy health-restoring annual vacations from his London duties, traveling in successive years to the Midlands and the homes of his forebears, to the North of England and Scotland, to Wales and the western region of England, and to Belgium and Holland. Wherever he went he made new friends for himself and the cause of Pennsylvania and the colonies. The journey to Scotland in 1759 was most memorable. He received the degree of doctor of laws from the University of St. Andrews and added David Hume, historian and philosopher; William Robertson, historian; Lord Kames, judicial authority and versatile writer; and Sir Alexander Dick, president of the College of Physicians in Edinburgh, to his roll of friends. "I think the time . . . spent there," he wrote to Lord Kames, "six weeks of the *densest* happiness I have met with in any part of my life."[74]

As an American as well as a Pennsylvanian and a former New Englander, Franklin was inevitably drawn during these years of his mission into correcting the prejudices and misrepresentations regarding the American colonies that were prevalent in England, often writing letters to the press and speaking to friends and acquaintances. As the defeat of France became likely and peace terms began to be discussed, he considered it his duty to advance what he regarded as the long-range interest of the colonies and Great Britain by advocating the annexation of Canada. It was a logical extension of the grand imperial vision, which he had held for many years, of a united and glorious British Empire, with the colonies as equal partners represented in Parliament like the counties of Great Britain. He had expressed this view privately in his 1751 letter to James Parker and in his letters to Governor William Shirley in 1754, and publicly in his *Observations Concerning the Increase of Mankind* in 1754.

In a letter that he wrote to the *London Chronicle* in 1759, Franklin at first turned his talent for satire against those who in his opinion short-sightedly favored the return of Canada to France in exchange for the richer sugar colony of Guadeloupe, ironically citing eleven reasons for giving up Canada, of which the seventh is a sample:

Our colonies, 'tis true, have exerted themselves beyond their strength, on the expectations we gave them of driving the French from Canada; but tho' we ought to keep faith with our allies, it is not necessary with our children. That might teach them (against Scripture) to *put their trust in Princes:* Let 'em learn to trust in God.[75]

Then, the following year he published a sober, factual pamphlet in support of the retention of Canada, *The Interest of Great Britain Considered*, to which he appended his *Observations Concerning the Increase of Mankind* to reinforce his argument. It was his most ambitious attempt to influence British public opinion on a matter of vital interest to the American colonies and may have helped to tip the scale at the peace negotiations on the side of keeping Canada. The fear voiced by many that the rapid growth of the colonies might lead to their union and ultimately to separation Franklin answered somewhat ingenuously by declaring that this eventuality was "impossible . . . without the most grievous tyranny and oppression. . . . The waves do not rise, but when the winds blow."[76]

At that time he had faith in British fairness and good sense, which was confirmed later in the year when the Proprietors finally accepted in principle the right of the Pennsylvania Assembly to impose taxes on their properties in the colony. Franklin's policy and strategy had been vindicated. He had met the dilatory and defamatory tactics of the Proprietors decently and rationally, relying on the power of truth and the force of his genius and personality, and when the battle was over, Thomas Penn had to admit that Franklin had won without recourse to dishonorable means. "I do not find," he confided to the governor of Pennsylvania, "that he has done me any prejudice with any party, having had conversations with all, in which I have studied to talk of these affairs."[77] No friend could have paid Franklin a more honest tribute than this enemy who feared and hated him.

He was as reluctant to leave his friends in 1762 as they were to see him go. Many of them pleaded with him to stay and make England his home. To Polly Stevenson he later wrote nostalgically:

Of all the enviable things England has, I envy it most its people. Why should that petty island, which compar'd to America is but like a stepping stone in a brook, scarce enough of it above water to keep one's shoes dry; why, I say, should that little island enjoy in almost every neighbourhood more sensible, virtuous and elegant minds, than we can collect in ranging 100 leagues of our vast forests.[78]

Strahan informed a friend in Philadelphia:

. . . I part with him with infinite regret and sorrow. I know not where to find his equal. . . . There is something in his leaving us even more cruel than a separation by death; it is like an *untimely death*, where we part with a friend to meet no more, *with a whole heart*, as we say in Scotland.[79]

And David Hume, author of the then standard *History of England*, seemed to be delivering the historical verdict on Franklin when he wrote an embarrassingly laudatory letter of farewell to him:

I am very sorry, that you intend soon to leave our hemisphere. America has sent us many good things, gold, silver, sugar, tobacco, indigo &c.: But you are the first philosopher, and indeed the first great man of letters for whom we are beholden to her: it is our own fault, that we have not kept him: Whence it appears, that we do not agree with Solomon, that wisdom is above gold: For we take care never to send back an ounce of the latter, which we once lay our fingers upon.[80]

To which Franklin replied with matchless grace and modesty:

Your compliment of gold and wisdom is very obliging to me, but a little injurious to your country. The various value of every thing in every part of the world, arises you know from the various proportions of the quantity to the demand. We are told that gold and silver in Solomon's time were so plenty as to be of no more value in his country than the stones in the street. You have here at present just such a plenty of wisdom. Your people are therefore not to be censur'd for desiring no more among them than they have; and if I have *any*, I should certainly carry it where from its scarcity it may probably come to a better market.[81]

V Spokesman for Indians and Blacks: Philadelphia

Franklin was acclaimed on his arrival home "by all ranks of people,"[82] and formally thanked by the assembly "for his many services not only to the Province of Pennsylvania, but to America in general, during his late agency at the Court of Great-Britain."[83] In the meantime William Franklin had been appointed governor of New Jersey (at the age of thirty-one) in the hope that his father might be more cooperative with the Proprietors. Eyebrows were raised, of course, because of the governor's illegitimate birth. During the following year Franklin started the building of a new house for his family and made tours of inspection of post offices from Virginia to New Hampshire to remove any laxity that might have developed in the course of his long absence.

The peace treaty between England and France signed in 1763 did not bring peace to the western frontier of the colonies. During the summer the Indians formerly allied with the French launched attacks against the English garrisons on the frontier, seized the forts on the Ohio, except Fort Pitt, and massacred their defenders, and then raided western Pennsylvania, killing many settlers and taking others captive. Angered by the inadequate provision made by the assembly for the defense of their homes and unable to retaliate against the marauding Indians, some of the western settlers, known as "the Paxton Boys," turned their rage and frustration on the friendly Indians living in the province, who, as might be expected, were rumored to be aiding the enemy.

In December, a company of the Paxton Boys attacked a peaceful Indian village near Lancaster and murdered six who happened to be at home. The fourteen Indian men, women, and children of the village who survived were quickly gathered together by friendly white neighbors and taken to Lancaster for safety. To no avail. Two days after Christmas a large party of Paxton Boys rode into Lancaster and exterminated all of them. At the invitation of the assembly, about 125 Indians under the protection of the Moravians around Bethlehem had been mercifully brought to Philadelphia and quartered on an island nearby. Amid these alarums and reports that the Paxton Boys and their allies were planning to march on Philadelphia and kill the Moravian Indians, Franklin stepped into the breach with a passionate appeal to reason and humanity, his *Narrative of the Late Massacres,* published early in 1764.

The pamphlet was a decidedly risky venture for Franklin, politically and personally, in the highly charged atmosphere of the time, but he was so shocked by these events that he forgot discretion and castigated the murderers without mercy. "The only crime of these poor wretches," he observed regarding the Indian victims,

seems to have been, that they had a reddish brown skin, and black hair; and some people of that sort, it seems, had murdered some of our relations. If it be right to kill men for such a reason, then should any man, with a freckled face and red hair, kill a wife or child of mine, it would be right for me to revenge it, by killing all the freckled red-haired men, women and children, I could afterwards any where meet with.[84]

In the election campaign for the assembly in the fall of the same year, Franklin, as the head of the popular antiproprietary party, was viciously attacked by his old enemies and by the new enemies he had made in pleading the cause of the hapless Indians, and when the election came, he was narrowly defeated, though winning a moral victory. It was the first and the last electoral defeat for him.

He was also involved at this time, but not politically, in helping the other exploited racial minority in the colonies—the blacks. Shortly after his arrival in England, he had been approached by the secretary of the Bray Associates, a British religious society devoted to encouraging the education of blacks in America. Knowing of Franklin's interest in education and philanthropy, he had sought his advice on "how and by what means those poor ignorant people may be most effectually instructed."[85] In his reply Franklin suggested a school for black children in Philadelphia to teach reading and practical arts. The school was opened in less than a year; Franklin was elected chairman of the Bray Associates, serving for two years, and he assisted in the opening of three other schools for blacks in New York, Williamsburg, Virginia, and Newport, Rhode Island.

He continued his connection with the Bray Associates after returning to Philadelphia, and while traveling to inspect the Colonial post offices, checked on these three schools. Toward the end of 1763, though immersed in the Indian crisis, he found time to visit the school for blacks in Philadelphia and to send a remarkable report to the Bray Associates:

I was on the whole much pleas'd and from what I then saw, have conceiv'd a higher opinion of the natural capacities of the black race, than I had ever before entertained. Their apprehension seems as quick, their memory as strong, and their docility [i.e., teachability] in every respect equal to that of white children. You will wonder perhaps that I should ever doubt it, and I will not undertake to justify all my prejudices, nor to account for them.[86]

It is a historic statement, probably the first made by an eminent white American—distinguished, incidentally, in politics *and* science—expressing the belief that the scholastic ability of black children was equal to that of white children, and it is the more remarkable because the belief was based on personal observation rather than faith and because the believer had until then shared the common prejudice of his time and place regarding the academic ability of blacks.

Under the strain of the near civil war between the western and eastern counties of the colony over the Indian attacks, the strife between the governor and the assembly was exacerbated to such an extent, especially after Franklin was elected Speaker, that the assembly decided to petition the king to assume control of the colony, provided the privileges enjoyed under the existing constitution remained in force. Franklin thereupon was named as coagent in London to work with the resident agent, Richard Jackson, toward that end. For the second time he had the good fortune to leave behind him the petty partisan squabbles of the colony and return to England, his second love, and again Deborah refused to exchange her nearly finished new house and her family for the uncertain perils of a vast ocean and a strange land.

Franklin left Philadelphia late in 1764, with these premonitory parting words (he was nearly fifty-nine, a very old man for those times):

I am now to take leave (perhaps a last leave) of the country I love, and in which I have spent the greatest part of my life. ESTO PERPETUA. I wish every kind of prosperity to my friends, and I forgive my enemies.[87]

Sixteen years had passed since he "retired," years of intense activity in which he had liberated himself from the time-consuming treadmill of routine work and by study and experience largely freed himself from parochial interests and prejudices. The leisure that he gained he had intended to devote to doing as he pleased, which in his case meant chiefly the pursuit of one negative pleasure and four positive pleasures: the first was extricating himself from the entanglements of politics, and the others were studying nature by reading and experiment, cultivating the friendship of congenial men and women, expanding his horizons by travel, and contributing to "the common benefit of mankind," the ultimate goal of all his activities.

Given his political genius and public spirit, he could not have expected to be allowed to retire from politics, and the fact that these were years of almost constant "hot" or "cold" war ensured his failure in this aim and would have threatened the accomplishment of his other aims had he not been endowed with extraordinary versatility and energy. Consequently, mobilizing Pennsylvania for its defense and serving actively in the city council and the provincial assembly did not prevent him from pursuing his searching and original experiments in electricity, or planning and establishing the Academy, or rescuing the project for the hospital from financial collapse, or founding the Philadelphia fire insurance company.

Though he hated the unenlightened self-interest and strife of politics, he was willing and able to endure it because it increased his power to do good, which in turn enhanced his political power. This often ignored interaction between the material and the ethical was exemplified in action by his postal reforms, the choice of his plan of union at the Albany Congress, his services in behalf of Pennsylvania, the

American colonies, and the British interests during his first mission to England, and his work for friendly Indians and the education of blacks after his return.

As Franklin entered upon his second mission to the mother country, he was no longer solely the Pennsylvania agent, but also the representative American, the practical idealist of the New World, who advocated education and science in the service of all people and projected a British Commonwealth based on the principles of popular representation and common interest and justice.

CHAPTER 4

World Influence: Later Years, 1764–1790

I Representative of America in England

UPON his arrival in London early in December, 1764, Franklin returned to his familiar lodgings with the Stevensons on Craven Street and promptly paid his customary respects to the London weather by catching a severe cold that plagued him for several weeks. Despite a persistent cough he began working on his Pennsylvania commission, but was soon drawn into the larger controversy over the proposed Stamp Act. With the other Colonial agents, he vigorously opposed the act, but without success. Since he believed that it would be repealed in time and that the British government could ultimately be persuaded by reason and self-interest to accept the plan of a British Commonwealth in which the colonies would have local autonomy and equitable representation in Parliament, he failed to gauge the unyielding temper of the Colonists on this issue.

To make matters worse, when Lord Grenville, the Prime Minister, shrewdly advised the Colonial agents that each should recommend a qualified American to serve as Stamp Act officer in his colony rather than that the government send British officers, Franklin committed the only serious mistake of his political career and went along with the proposal, making the nomination for Pennsylvania. The violent reaction to his nomination and moderation was quickly exploited by his political enemies, who, judging him by their own motivations, accused him of selling out the American cause on the promise of royal favor.

Though he deemed the reaction to the Stamp Act excessive and premature and therefore harmful to the American interest, he was fully in accord with the principle of local fiscal independence, in the absence of Parliamentary representation. He also approved the conciliatory resolutions and petitions of the extralegal Stamp Act Congress held in the fall of 1765, disagreeing with a great many Americans and Englishmen who regarded them as presumptuous and dangerous. To counteract this view, he wrote privately: "I was extreamly busy, attending members of both Houses, informing, explaining, consulting, disputing, in a continual hurry from morning to night. . . ."[1]

Besides striving to educate the members of Parliament by day and holding forth at night among friends and acquaintances at parties and clubs, he resorted once more to his favorite medium of instruction, the press. He wrote "anonymous" letters to the London papers arguing for repeal of the Stamp Act, stressing the damage to the economic interest of Great Britain inherent in the act; and he made public for the first time his farsighted letters written in 1754 to Governor Shirley on taxation and popular representation. But his trump card was the mobilization of the British merchants and manufacturers, who were very much worried about the beginning of a concerted boycott of British goods by the colonies.

The mounting pressure for repeal from the colonies and especially from within Great Britain reached a climax early in 1766, and in February the House of Commons sitting as a Committee of the Whole summoned for questioning an array of witnesses opposed to the Stamp Act. The star witness was Benjamin Franklin, representative of America, who was called on the last day of the hearings. He came well prepared to answer the questions of those members who favored repeal, many of whom had been converted by his writings or his personal contacts with them, or, in case he was questioned by those who opposed repeal, to draw upon the vast treasure of orderly knowledge and experience stored in his phenomenal memory.

To Edmund Burke, who had been recently elected to Parliament, the scene resembled a classroom in which the schoolmaster was to be questioned by his pupils. It was a role that suited the principal actor in the drama—though he had never before been called on to *speak* his part in public, and with all England and America outside the classroom waiting to hear what he would say. He preferred and was accustomed to act the schoolmaster in writing or friendly conversation, but, if he had to speak publicly, the question-and-answer format of the witness stand was the least restrictive for him.

Throughout the examination, during which he answered 174 questions, Franklin was equally in control of the situation whether he was questioned by "friends" or "enemies" of repeal, and his spoken answers, like his writings, were honest, simple, clear, modest, and tactful. Even those who could not agree with him admired his masterly presentation and his brilliant command of the subject. Reporting on the examination, the *Gentlemen's Magazine* said:

The questions in general are put with great subtilty and judgment, and they are answered with such deep and familiar knowledge of the subject, such precision and perspicuity, such temper [i.e., composure] and yet such spirit, as do the greatest honor to Dr. Franklin, and justify the general opinion of his character and abilities.[2]

For example, Lord Grenville, the author of the Stamp Act, asked him:

Do you think it right that America should be protected by this country and pay no part of the expense?

To which Franklin replied:

That is not the case. The Colonies raised, cloathed and paid, during the last war, near 25000 men, and spent many millions.

"Were you not reimbursed by parliament?" Grenville countered.

We were only reimbursed what, in your opinion, we had advanced beyond our proportion, or beyond what might be reasonably expected from us; and it was a very small part of what we spent. Pensylvania, in particular, disbursed about 500,000 pounds, and the reimbursements in the whole did not exceed 60,000 pounds.[3]

One of the members, referring to the record of frequent disputes between Colonial governors and assemblies over voting the expense budget, asked:

. . . In case a governor, acting by instruction, should call on an assembly to raise the necessary supplies, and the assembly should refuse to do it, do you not think it would then be for the good of the people of the colony, as well as necessary to the government, that the parliament should tax them?

"I do not think it would be necessary," Franklin answered.

If an assembly could possibly be so absurd as to refuse raising the supplies requisite for the maintenance of government among them, they could not long remain in such a situation; the disorders and confusion occasioned by it must soon bring them to reason.

"If it should not," the questioner persisted, "ought not the right to be in Great-Britain of applying a remedy?" The reply was circumspectly reasonable:

A right only to be used in such a case, I should have no objection to, supposing it to be used merely for the good of the people of the colony.

Then, the barbed question: "But who is to judge of that, Britain or the colony?" And the Delphic response: "Those that feel can best judge."[4]

As the examination proceeded, it was evident that Franklin was weaving a balanced design of constitutional principle—no taxation without representation, and national interest, that is, avoidance of political and economic disaster—in arguing for repeal. At the same time he was interweaving in the background an appealing image of America in support of his argument and in furtherance of his vision of a just and happy British Commonwealth united by allegiance to the Crown and by representation in Parliament.

Another well-disposed questioner obliged by asking ". . . if . . . [Parliament] should think fit to ascertain its right to lay taxes, by an act laying a small tax, contrary to their opinion, would they submit to pay the tax?" And Franklin replied with pacific frankness:

The ringleaders of riots they think ought to be punished. . . . But as to any internal tax, how small soever, laid by the legislature here on the people there, while they have no representatives in this legislature, I think it will never be submitted to. They will oppose it to the last.[5]

The lesson on America ended with these plain monitory answers:

What used to be the pride of the Americans?
To indulge in the fashions and manufactures of Great-Britain.
What is now their pride?
To wear their old cloaths over again, till they can make new ones.[6]

The examination of Franklin in the House of Commons made a profound impression on his hearers. They had been familiar with the scientific genius, the great philanthropist, the reforming educator, the guide to the way out of poverty, the brilliant pamphleteer, the indefatigable lobbyist, the incorrigible rebel, the good companion. This was a newly discovered Franklin—political scientist and American statesman. The legislators of England who had been present on this occasion realized that they had witnessed the unforgettable performance of a master at his best. The repeal of the Stamp Act that followed a month later *may* have been inevitable before Franklin's examination; it was no longer in doubt after it.

When the account of the examination and the news of the repeal reached the colonies, Franklin became the first authentic American civilian hero—a true hero by his own definition, who "fights to *preserve*, and not to *destroy*, the lives, liberties, and estates, of his people."[7] Even his enemies grudgingly acknowledged his merit and joined in the toasts to the champion of the rights of America. *The Examination* was published in England in 1767 and was reprinted frequently in the following years in America and Europe, where liberals hailed him as the voice of freedom-seeking people everywhere.

Franklin himself was less elated than his admirers over the repeal of the Stamp Act, for he knew that Parliament had not abandoned the right to tax the colonies, in fact, had confirmed that right in passing the repeal act, and showed no inclination to consider the principle of colonial representation. Writing to a friend not long after repeal, he observed uneasily:

The Parliament here do at present think too highly of themselves to admit representatives from us, if we should ask it; and, when they will be desirous of granting it, we shall think too highly of ourselves to accept of it.[8]

He was finally able to take a travel vacation that summer with his friend John Pringle, visiting Hanover and Göttingen in Germany and meeting Rudolph Erich Raspe, the future author of "Baron Munchausen," and other literary and scientific personages. The Royal Society of Sciences in Göttingen elected him to membership. He returned to England in August, refreshed as usual, to learn that the Pennsylvania Assembly had renewed his agency for another year. He stayed on in the Stevenson household, where Temple Franklin, the illegitimate son of William Franklin, often came to see his affectionate grandfather.

In 1767 relations between the home government and the colonies worsened again. Parliament laid new duties on glass, paper, and tea, which, though technically not taxes, were strongly resented because the revenue was to be used to pay the Colonial governors and judges, thereby making them independent of the assemblies and local interests. Franklin had foreseen this event at the time of the premature rejoicing over the repeal of the Stamp Act. Deeply troubled by the senseless drift of events, he wrote a long letter to Lord Kames expressing his anxieties and forebodings—which he hoped would reach the attention of the ministry:

> . . . It becomes a matter of great importance that clear ideas should be formed on solid principles, both in Britain and America, of the true political relation between them, and the mutual duties belonging to that relation. . . . I am fully persuaded with you, that a consolidating union, by a fair and equal representation of all the parts of this empire in Parliament, is the only firm basis on which its political grandeur and stability can be founded. . . . The Parliament cannot well and wisely make laws suited to the colonies, without being properly and truly informed of their circumstances, abilities, temper, &c. This it cannot be without representatives from thence. And yet it is fond of this power, and averse to the only means of duly acquiring the necessary knowledge for exercising it, which is desiring to be *omnipotent* without being *omniscient*. . . .
>
> Upon the whole, I have lived so great a part of my life in Britain, and have formed so many friendships in it, that I love it and wish its prosperity, and therefore wish to see that union on which alone I think it can be secur'd and establish'd. As to America, the advantages of such an union to her are not so apparent. She may suffer at present under the arbitrary power of this country; she may suffer for a while in a separation from it; but these are temporary evils that she will outgrow. . . . America, an immense territory, favour'd by nature with all advantages of climate, soil, great navigable rivers and lakes, &c. must become a great country, populous and mighty; and will in a less time than is generally conceiv'd be able to shake off any shackles that may be impos'd on her. . . . And yet there remains among that people so much respect, veneration and affection for Britain, that, if cultivated prudently, with kind usage and tenderness for their privileges, they might be easily govern'd still for ages, without force or any considerable expence. But I do not see here a sufficient quantity of the wisdom that is necessary to produce such a conduct, and I lament the want of it.[9]

The letter never reached its destination, having probably been picked up by the authorities. But if they read it, it apparently taught them nothing.

With Pringle accompanying him again, Franklin late in the summer of 1767 made his first visit to France, seeking relief from the disappointment and the pain he endured in observing the suicidal course of the British government which, with all his unceasing public and private efforts, he could not modify. He carried many letters of introduction from the French legation, where the minister had of late been extremely friendly to him. He suspected "that intriguing nation" of seeing a chance to "blow up the coals between Britain and her colonies" and trusted that she would be disappointed.[10]

However, the extraordinary welcome he received from the French scientific community was unmistakably genuine, as was the high regard shown him by leaders of the liberal new Physiocratic school of *économistes*, the first to attempt a science of economics. Franklin's position as the representative of an agricultural society, his study of the growth of population, his interest in free trade, and his views on the relation between colonies and home country seemed to bear a sufficient resemblance to some features of the Physiocratic doctrine as to encourage their hope that they could convert the world-famous American.[11] They were not entirely mistaken, for he found the doctrine so congenial that he wrote to du Pont, one of its most ardent adherents:

. . . There is such a freedom from local and national prejudices and partialities, so much benevolence to mankind in general, so much goodness mixt with the wisdom, in the principles of your new philosophy, that I am perfectly charmed with them . . . [and hope that] it becomes the governing philosophy of the human species.[12]

The summer of 1767 revealed that Franklin at sixty-one was still capable of change and growth. Travel always made him feel young in mind and heart, stimulating his curiosity and power of observation in small and large matters. During these hospitable months the teacher became a student again, consolidated old epistolary friendships, made new friends, and gradually shed one of his few remaining Colonial prejudices—his British chauvinism with reference to the French. One of his disciples, who called themselves *franklinistes*, is quoted by Carl Van Doren as declaring that "France was as much Franklin's country as England: a father was in his own country when his children lived there."[13] Franklin later wrote his friend Dalibard:

The time I spent in Paris, and in the improving conversation and agreable society of so many *learned* and *ingenious* men, seems now to me like a pleasing dream, from which I was sorry to be awaked by finding my self in London.[14]

Above all, his becoming acquainted with the agrarian philosophy of the Physiocrats at a time when he was growing more and more disillusioned with the political and economic system of Great Britain subtly influenced his thinking and feeling about the conflict with the colonies. After his return to London, a new Physiocratic note can be detected in his writing. He observed in one letter that England ". . . is fond of manufactures beyond their real value; for the true source of riches is husbandry. Agriculture is truly *productive* of *new wealth;* manufactures only change forms. . . ."[15] And a year later, as the confrontation between commercial and manufacturing Britain and agricultural America became increasingly rigid, he listed in a private memorandum the following "position" as the last of twelve that should be considered more carefully:

. . . there seem to be but three ways for a nation to acquire wealth. The first is by *war* as the Romans did in plundering their conquered neighbours. This is *robbery.* The second by commerce, which is generally *cheating.* The third by *agriculture* the only honest way; wherein man receives real increase of the seed thrown into the ground, in a kind of continual miracle. . . .[16]

It is obvious which role England plays in this black-and-white contrast, and which America.

Nevertheless, though he was almost convinced in his own mind by 1768 that a break between Britain and the American colonies was approaching, he continued to labor constantly for a reconciliation between the two parties in private gatherings and anonymously in the press. One of the most famous of his easily identifiable "anonymous" letters to the press was his *Causes of the American Discontents before 1768,* which appeared in the *London Chronicle* early in the year under the signature of "F + S."[17]

The letter reiterated the familiar arguments tactfully, as if it were an impersonal report by "an impartial historian of American facts and opinions," but it did not "undertake . . . to support these opinions of the Americans."[18] The restraints on trade, the taxes disguised by the Townshend ministry as "duties" on imports to the colonies, and the infringements on the time-honored rights of the Colonial assemblies were cited again as the major causes of the disaffection of the Americans, who still remained loyal to the Crown in the face of the numerous provocations committed by the Parliament, and the warning of a united Colonial boycott of British manufactures was repeated. "We were separated too far from Britain by the ocean," he reported the Americans as saying ominously in conclusion, but we were united to it by respect and love, so that we could at any time freely have spent our lives and little fortunes in its cause. But this unhappy new system of politics tends to dissolve those bands of union and to sever us for ever. . . .[19]

As is often the fate of reconcilers, Franklin was regarded by the British as too American and by the Americans as too British, although he was at this time more advanced than the most militant Colonial leaders in his *thinking*.[20]

The response of the ministry was to dangle before him alternately the prospect of a higher royal post than the Colonial post office and the imminence of dismissal from the postmastership. He was well aware of the game that the government was playing with him. Knowing that his letters were being opened and read by the authorities, he confided defiantly to his son that he was tired of presenting his views "to so many different inattentive heads," though he must continue to go on doing it as long as he remained in England.[21] As for his postal office, he would not be very sorry, he said:

. . . if they take that from me too on account of my zeal for America, in which some of my friends have hinted to me I have been too open. . . . I am myself grown so old as to feel much less than formerly the spur of ambition. . . . [22]

The honest homespun American was an old master at the game of diplomacy, and in this cat-and-mouse charade he may have pretended to be the mouse. But who was really the cat and who the mouse? The fact is that for several years he went on nibbling at the cheese without springing the trap—defending American interests without getting fired.

The recognition in the colonies of Franklin's invaluable services in the ongoing crisis led to his appointment as London agent for Georgia and his native Massachusetts. He now had official as well as de facto status as the informal ambassador of America, representing the interests of its three major regions from New England to the South, and symbol in his own person of the emerging unity of the American colonies.

Yet by a miracle of metabolism and talent the mounting burdens of his public duties did not seem noticeably to contract the area of his private concerns and pleasures. He maintained an intimate correspondence with his family in America and a constant flow of letters to his personal and scientific friends everywhere; he took an active part in the everyday affairs of his loved and loving adopted family on Craven Street; he supervised the greatly enlarged fourth and fifth editions of *Experiments and Observations on Electricity*, adding papers on a great variety of other scientific topics; he got involved in a huge private colonization project for the Ohio Valley; he made a second trip to France and a long tour through Ireland and Scotland; he began writing a long autobiographical letter to his son, which he hoped would be instructive as well as interesting to him; and he did not altogether neglect his favorite pursuits—friendship and scientific research. During these busy years of political activity, he took time off to study lead poisoning, common colds, sun spots, and the phenomena of heat, cold, and magnetism.

He was often homesick, but events and responsibilities kept him far from home. The house he had planned was finished. His daughter Sally was married and the mother of a boy, Benjamin Franklin Bache, whom Deborah doted on, filling her letters to Franklin with stories describing the unique achievements and exploits of their grandson. "It makes me long to be at home and to play with Ben," he wrote to her after telling her about Polly's cute son, and his godson. Undoubtedly the agitation and violence arising from the resistance to the Townshend duties in the Massachusetts and Virginia Assemblies, attended by the despatch of naval and military forces to Boston and the consequent "Massacre" of several residents, intensified his longing to return home. He had always been deeply disturbed by the irrationality of violence and killing, especially between those who should be or had been friends.

After his tour of Ireland and Scotland in 1771, the distant land of America—the Puritan colony he had run away from, the unspoiled Indians who had attacked the settlements on the frontier—glowed in his imagination and memory as in the light of the Promised Land:

In those countries a small part of the society are landlords, great noblemen, and gentlemen, extreamly opulent, living in the highest affluence and magnificence: the bulk of the people tenants, extreamly poor, living in the most sordid wretchedness, in dirty hovels of mud and straw, and cloathed only in rags. . . .

I thought often of the happiness of New England, where every man is a freeholder, has a vote in publick affairs, lives in a tidy, warm house, has plenty of good food and fewel, with whole cloaths from head to foot, the manufacture perhaps of his own family. . . .

Had I never been in the American Colonies, but was to form my judgment of civil society by what I have lately seen, I should never advise a nation of savages to admit of civilization: For I assume that in the possession & enjoyment of the various comforts of life, compar'd to these people every Indian is a gentleman; and the effect of this kind of civil society seems only to be, the depressing multitudes below the savage state that a few may be rais'd above it.[23]

Britain's problems were compounded by the frequent changes of the ministry, which left the government without a consistent policy of either accommodation or repression. As a result the government moved ineffectively from half-measure to half-measure. Parliament passed the Stamp Act, it repealed the Stamp Act, but declared its right to tax the colonies; it imposed the Townshend duties, it removed the Townshend duties, but retained the duty on tea and gave the East India Company a monopoly of the tea trade, which united the Colonial merchants and militants and culminated in the Boston Tea Party and the closing of the port of Boston.

However discouraged by the excesses on both sides and wearied by the interminable alternation of blunder and reaction to blunder, Franklin postponed his return to America from year to year, always hoping that the men of reason and good will in the government and the nation would gain the ascendancy and establish the union of Britain and the colonies that alone could end the escalating discord. A continuing stream of letters, essays, satires, and fables aimed at the education of the British public flowed from his desk to the press in reply to constant attacks on American political principles and acts. The best known and most effective of these, his *Rules by Which a Great Empire May Be Reduced to a Small One* (September, 1773) and *An Edict by the King of Prussia* (October, 1773), were satirical pieces intended to cool emotions, restore a measure of reason, and warn the British government and people of the dire consequences of the official policy toward the colonies.

The *Rules* listed twenty prescriptions that were certain to accomplish the indicated result. "In the first place," he advised,

. . . you are to consider, that a great empire, like a great cake, is most easily diminished at the edges. Turn your attention, therefore, first to your remotest provinces; that, as you get rid of them, the next may follow in order.[24]

Make sure these provinces are treated as inferiors.

If they happen to be zealous whigs, friends of liberty, nurtured in revolution principles [i.e., those of the Revolution of 1688], *remember all that* to their prejudice, and resolve to punish it; for such principles, after a revolution is thoroughly established, are of *no more use*. . . .[25]

Send them corrupt and incompetent governors and judges, and when they complain, treat their grievances with contempt. Have the Parliament, in which they have no representatives to voice their views, also impose taxes on them; if they protest these taxes, dissolve their assemblies.

Finally, send armies into these colonies "under pretence of protecting the inhabitants," but do not employ the soldiers to defend the frontiers—quarter them in "the heart of the country," where they can be protected by the inhabitants. "This will seem," he concludes, "to proceed from your ill will or your ignorance, and contribute farther to produce and strengthen an opinion among them, that you are no longer fit to govern them."[26]

The second satire, a legal hoax like *Polly Baker* on a national scale, is a royal "edict" that considers England, which was settled by Germans from Saxony, as a colony "under the protection" of Prussia. Prussia's treatment of its English "colony" is an ironic duplicate of England's treatment of its American colonies. For example, having helped England in its recent war with France, Prussia claims the right to declare duties on English imports and exports as a means of raising revenue to compensate it for all it has done for its colony. Moreover, the edict forbids the manufacture of woolen goods, iron or steel, or products made of iron or steel, and, for the benefit of its English colony, authorizes the sending of its criminals to England instead of to jail. As precedents for these measures, the proclamation cites specific acts of the English Parliament, or "other equitable laws" observed by the English, or "instructions given by their princes," or "resolutions of both Houses, entered into for the good government of their own colonies in Ireland and America."[27]

Those who were well disposed to the American cause were regaled by these delectable political ironies, but the government and its supporters were too keenly stung by the barbs to appreciate the humor or the message. Though Franklin's satires were directed against policies and not personalities, the ministers, being incapable of retaliating in kind, looked about for an opportunity to strike back at the author himself, who some believed was also the author of the American resistance rather than its agent and advocate.

They found the opportunity at hand in a petition of the Massachusetts Assembly calling for the dismissal of Governor Thomas

Hutchinson and his lieutenant governor, Andrew Oliver, on the ground that they had in secret correspondence with ministers of the Grenville administration advised that repressive measures be taken against the refractory colony. The letters in evidence had been confidentially conveyed to Franklin, the assembly agent, and, by agreement with the transmitter, forwarded to a few specified leaders of the assembly, with instructions that they were not to be made public in Boston. It was the transmitter's and Franklin's hope that the letters would persuade these leaders that the British government, in its ignorance of American conditions, had been misled into a policy of coercion by highly placed Americans and might therefore reverse its policy if these Americans were discredited.

As Franklin should or might have expected, the Hutchinson-Oliver letters were published, and, to protect his associates, he publicly acknowledged that he had received and sent the letters to Boston. Writing to his son on January 5, 1774, he observed: "This has drawn some censure upon myself, but as I grow old I grow less concerned about censure when I am satisfied I act rightly."[28]

The "administration" struck quickly, setting January 29 as the day for the hearing on the petition before the Privy Council for Plantation Affairs. Since Franklin assumed full responsibility and refused to reveal how he had obtained the letters, he would be defenseless against whatever attack the government planned to make against him. That it would be vicious could be foreseen when it became known that Alexander Wedderburn, the ministry's most brilliant and unprincipled prosecutor, was to represent Hutchinson and Oliver at the hearing. The word went around beforehand that the petition was certain to be rejected, the writers of the letters to be honored, and Franklin to be removed from the postmastership after the hearing. "I suppose," he divined, "because I was there to be so blackened that nobody should think it injustice."[29]

The hearing, held in the Cockpit, was the bitterest political experience of his life, and it was made worse by the news of the Boston Tea Party, which reached London a day or two before the hearing. Bound in honor to conceal the truth that could exonerate him, he had no choice but to place himself at the mercy of those who had been unequal to answering his slashing criticisms of their American policy and at long last could watch their master inquisitor humiliate and scourge this American tradesman and through him all those presumptuous Colonials who defied the rightful authority of their Parliament and king.

World Influence: Later Years, 1764–1790

The chamber was packed—there were seats only for the Committee of the Council—with standing courtiers, members of the ministry and the opposition, and as many other spectators as had enough influence to gain admission to the show. Wedderburn lived up to his promise, entertaining the audience for nearly an hour. During all this time, Franklin had remained standing, alone, silent, his face an expressionless mask, as he heard himself charged with being a fraud, a thief, an enemy of peace, and a conspirator seeking to become governor of Massachusetts! He remarked later that

. . . not one of their lordships checked and recalled the orator to the business before them, but on the contrary, a very few excepted, they seemed to enjoy highly the entertainment, and frequently broke out in loud applauses.[30]

The very next day, which was Sunday, he was notified by letter that he had been dismissed from his post. Soon after, the petition that had been used as an excuse to crucify him was rejected. For a few weeks he was very angry and planned to publish a reply, but wisely refrained.

The king and his Tory henchmen, who could not understand that Franklin was the best American friend Great Britain had, were not to be dissuaded from taking the road to disaster either by the weak, divided Whig opposition or by the wiser heads in the Tory party. Though Franklin had terminated all official contacts with the ministry after the Cockpit hearing, he cooperated with these two groups in a last desperate attempt to prevent the imminent breach. The first Continental Congress met and remonstrated in moderate terms with no effect on the ministry, now headed by Lord North. Lord Chatham, the greatest and wisest British prime minister of the century, with Franklin present as his guest, vainly pleaded in the House of Lords for withdrawal of the troops from Boston and for recognition of the just grievances of the colonies, and, when one of the lords, looking at Franklin, insinuated that Chatham's suggestions for ending the conflict had been prepared by "one of the bitterest and most mischievous enemies this country had ever known," the ailing statesman answered bluntly and magnanimously:

. . . that if he were the first minister of this country and had the care of settling this momentous business, he should not be asham'd of publickly calling to his assistance a person so perfectly acquainted with the whole of American affairs as the gentleman alluded to, and so injuriously reflected on; one, he was pleas'd to say, whom all Europe held in high estimation for his knowledge and wisdom, and rank'd with our Boyles and Newtons; who was an honour, not to the English nation only, but to human nature.[31]

Late in 1774, Franklin was secretly approached by mediators for the more temperate ministers in the government, who greatly exaggerated even the considerable influence he had in the Continental Congress, apologizing for the unscrupulous personal attack on him by the Privy Council and hinting at dazzling royal rewards that he could expect if he succeeded in effecting a reconciliation with the colonies. When it was proposed by one of the mediators that the first step toward reconciliation on the part of the government must be payment for the tea destroyed in Boston Harbor, Franklin said he would pay for it himself, though he had no instuctions to make the offer nor any assurance that he would be reimbursed and was therefore risking his entire fortune to prove his good faith. There was only one condition attached to his offer: the Coercive Acts of Parliament against Massachusetts must first be repealed.

The ministers, of course, could not believe that he meant what he said and assumed that he was engaged in the immemorial practice of diplomatic bargaining, while secretly empowered by the Congress to accept less than he was asking. It took them a long time to realize that he did not control the Congress as the king controlled Parliament.

In the midst of these political futilities, Franklin heard of the death of his wife, his "plain country Joan," and informed one of the mediators that he must return to Philadelphia by the first ship, unless he could truly serve the cause of peace. When he was advised to call once more on the key negotiator, it was still thought that he was using his wife's death as a pawn in the diplomatic match, and he was met again with apologies for the Wedderburn tirade and the intimation of future honors if he accomplished a settlement "on terms suitable to the dignity of government." This time he answered in unmistakably clear, undiplomatic language, which ended the secret negotiations:

That in truth private resentments had no weight with me in publick business.... That I was certainly willing to do every thing that could reasonably be expected of me. But if any supposed I could prevail with my countrymen to take black for white, and wrong for right, it was not knowing them or me; they were not capable of being so impos'd on, nor was I capable of attempting it.[32]

A few weeks later Franklin sailed from Postsmouth with his grandson Temple, mourning the death of his faithful Deborah and the end of his dream of a mutually beneficial union of America and Britain. On his first day at sea he started setting down, for his son and the record, a detailed and documented account of the fruitless secret negotiations that had ended his mission in England, and when that task was finished, he turned for relief from a grieving heart and mind to "useful" experiments and observations on the Gulf Stream, often from early morning to late at night.

Franklin's mission abroad had been a liberal education for him and for the people of England. The concerns of Pennsylvania had been merged into the concerns of America, and his more intimate knowledge of the corruption of British politics and the wretched life of most of the people of Great Britain had burned away the remains of his provincial and English prejudices in a passionate love of what America was and could be.

He had worked tirelessly and with some success to overcome the misconceptions and ignorance of the British government and public about America—not overlooking at the same time every opportunity to make Americans aware of the serious private and political opposition to the extreme actions of the government. He still loved the best in English life and tradition, personified in his host of British friends of every class and party, and he prayed, though with little hope, that the best would rise to the challenge, as often before, and avert the horror of civil war.

But when he stepped ashore in Philadelphia on May 5, 1775, he learned about the bloody fighting at Lexington and Concord. The next morning the assembly hastened to elect the first citizen of Pennsylvania and America as one of its delegates to the second Continental Congress, and he attended the opening session on May 10.

II *World Revolutionary: America and France*

A few months later, in a letter to his English friend Bishop Shipley, Franklin described the state of affairs in the colonies at the time of his arrival:

I found at my arrival all America from one end . . . to the other busily employed in learning the use of arms. The attack upon the country people near Boston by the army had rous'd every body and exasperated the whole continent; The tradesmen of this city were in the field twice a day, at 5 in the morning, and six in the afternoon, disciplining [i.e., drilling] with the utmost diligence, all being volunteers. . . . The same spirit appears everywhere and the unanimity is amazing.[33]

This was information given gratefully in return for the news he had received about the latest developments in Parliament, but, since he knew that it would be shared with other friends of America and ultimately would find its way to the ministry, it was also a continuation *in absentia* of the campaign of education about America that he had waged in England for ten years and would carry on as long as there was the slightest chance of averting full-scale war.

With the same intent and using the argument by arithmetic that he had often employed in *Poor Richard,* he wrote to Joseph Priestley that fall, projecting the future cost of the war to Great Britain:

Britain at the expense of three millions, has killed one hundred and fifty Yankees this campaign, which is twenty thousand pounds a head. . . . During the same time sixty thousand children have been born in America. From these *data* . . . [one can] easily calculate the time and expense necessary to kill us all.[34]

His letters made a strong impression on his friends in England, if not on the government, for he received one hundred pounds collected by them for the relief of Americans wounded at Lexington and Concord or of the widows and orphans of those killed. He had less influence with his own son, whom he could not persuade to join him in the struggle for the present and future of a free America. It was a profound disappointment to him, for he loved his only son deeply and had always treated him not only as a son, but as a younger and intimate friend. ". . . Nothing has ever hurt me so much," he confessed long after,

. . . as to find myself deserted in my old age by my only son; and not only deserted, but to find him taking up arms against me in a cause, wherein my good fame, fortune, and life, were all at stake. . . . [35]

The second Continental Congress included an extraordinary number of extraordinary men—John Adams, Thomas Jefferson, Patrick Henry, Samuel Adams, John Jay, Robert Livingston, and Robert Morris, to name a few—but Franklin was the most extraordinary of them and the only one with the great experience, statesmanship, and reputation needed to guide his associates in the multifarious civil and military tasks confronting this unprecedented assemblage of representatives from twelve proud and independent revolutionary constituencies.

It was fortunate for the inexperienced delegates that they had a mentor whom nearly all revered and trusted, for the centrifugal forces in the Congress were in uneasy balance with the centripetal, and it needed a proven stabilizer like Franklin to keep it from flying in all directions. The young men in particular looked up to this friendly septuagenarian who could think younger and work harder than most of them. Youthful General Nathanael Greene of Rhode Island met him late in 1775 and wrote:

I had the honour to be introduced to that very great man, Dr. Franklin, whom I viewed with silent admiration the whole evening. Attention watched his lips, and conviction closed his periods.[36]

The young women were no less adoring. Abigail Adams, writing to her husband after meeting Franklin at a dinner in Boston, recalled that from infancy she had been taught to venerate Franklin's character and observed:

I found him social but not talkative, and when he spoke something useful dropped from his tongue. He was grave, yet pleasant and affable. . . . I thought I could read in his countenance the virtues of his heart.[37]

Every problem in the informal Congress, whether large or small, had to be handled by committees, and the immensely versatile Franklin, who got things done, was naturally called on to serve on a great many of them, including committees dealing with the importation of munitions, an American postal system, printing money, relations with Indians, the Continental army, the French Canadians, treaties with foreign countries, the seal of the United States, and many others.

His own colony of Pennsylvania also made many demands on him, electing him a member of the assembly, chairman of the extremely busy Committee of Safety (Defense), and president, after independence, of the state constitutional convention, which adopted his two basic recommendations, a plural executive and a unicameral legislature.

Any man of uncommon energy who was half his age would have taxed his strength to the limit under this burden, but Franklin, after many years of arduous public service, had of necessity learned how to husband his energy by not wasting it on nonessentials. He would sit in the Congress, John Adams remarked, day after day without saying a word, "a great part of the time fast asleep in his chair."[38] Still, after many months of uninterrupted activity, often extending into the evening for writing and other public chores, his eyes were so strained that he could not write, and his weakened condition brought on a rash of boils and an attack of gout.

Franklin understood better than the other delegates that there was very little chance of a reversal of British policy, and this could occur, in his opinion, only if the colonies now adopted an aggressive, united stance. He therefore boldly submitted to Congress, about a year before the Declaration of Independence, a modified version of his Albany Plan of 1754, entitled *Articles of Confederation* for "The United Colonies of North America." The revised plan stopped short of independence, stating that the union of the colonies was to "remain firm" until their grievances were completely removed and reparation made, but it warned that "on failure thereof, this confederation is to be perpetual."[39] The wise old campaigner was still too far ahead of his younger compatriots, however, and his tactical proposal was shelved for the time.

His most important assignment came toward the end of 1775, when he was named to the secret committee of foreign correspondence, an area in which he had no peer. Soon after, he was approached by a secret agent of the able foreign minister of France, the Comte de Vergennes, who was seeking assurance that the colonies would declare their independence and thereby weaken the British Empire. After several clandestine meetings with Franklin and the committee, the agent went back to France six months before the Declaration of Independence, convinced that independence would come in the near future. But until independence was formally enacted, it was understood that France could not risk war with Great Britain on a promise, even though it was backed by *"le grand* Franklin."

In the months following, Franklin secretly wrote to his influential friends and acquaintances in France, Spain, and Holland, as if he were the foreign minister of an already independent American government. To take a typical example, he informed an eminent correspondent in Spain of the proceedings of the "American Congress," reported some American military successes to him, and held out to his government the bait of profitable future trade and relations with ". . . a powerful dominion growing up here, . . . [which] being united, will be able not only to preserve their own people in peace but to repel the force of all the other powers in Europe."[40] Astonishingly audacious and prophetic words at the time, but convincing, not only because they were plausible, but even more because Franklin believed them himself.

The two sides moved rapidly closer to an open break early in 1776 as Parliament imposed a complete blockade on the colonies and Tom Paine's *Common Sense* (which had been prompted by Franklin and to whom the first copy off the press was sent by the author in appreciation) swept through the colonies, raising the fever of independence to an unprecedented level. In June, Franklin was still suffering from the gout and was absent from the momentous sessions of the Congress, though he was appointed with Jefferson, John Adams, Sherman, and Livingston to the committee for preparing a formal declaration of independence. It was a month of great pain for him for another reason. On the day he was appointed to this committee, his son, Governor William Franklin, was ordered arrested by the New Jersey Assembly and two weeks later was imprisoned by the Congress. The shock to Franklin and his friends is reflected in a simple comment on the event made by a newspaper at the time: "He is son to Dr. Benjamin Franklin, the genius of the day and the great patron of American Liberty."[41]

The committee draft of the Declaration of Independence, written by Jefferson and amended in some details by the other members of the committee and by the Congress, was finally approved on July 4—the resolution on independence having been passed two days earlier—and the engrossed copy was signed on August 2. On July 30, in reply to a conciliatory letter from Lord Howe, who had participated in the secret negotiations in London, and was now in command of the large English fleet near New York, Franklin wrote wistfully, but conclusively:

Long did I endeavour with unfeigned and unwearied zeal to preserve from breaking that fine and noble china vase the British Empire; for I knew that, once being broken, the separate parts could not retain even their shares of the strength and value that existed in the whole, and that a perfect reunion of those parts could scarce ever be hoped for.[42]

In September, the Congress elected Franklin one of three commissioners—first among equals—to the court of France, to follow through on the secret overtures made by Vergennes, for without substantial help from France the Declaration of Independence was no more than a worthless scrap of paper. When the election of Franklin was announced, he remarked wryly: "I am old and good for nothing, but, as the storekeepers say of their remnants of cloth, 'I am but a fag end, and you may have me for what you please.' "[43] By present-day longevity standards he was not seventy, but eighty, and he was not joking. Knowing better than anyone else what lay ahead, he could not reasonably have expected to see the end of his mission, and, if he were captured at sea, as was not unlikely, there would not be even a beginning.

He prepared for departure as if it were his last. With no wife to provide for and a son who had chosen a separate and apparently safer course, he gave "all the money he could raise, between three and four thousand pounds" (the equivalent today of perhaps $150–200,000) as a "loan" to the Congress,[44] to demonstrate his faith in the American cause and to encourage others to do the same. A trunk containing the sole manuscript copy of the first part of his *Autobiography* and all his "correspondence, when in England, for near twenty years,"[45] he left with his Loyalist friend, Joseph Galloway, for safekeeping, and made him one of his executors (again a case of misplaced trust). Carefully weighing the risks and odds, he divided his family in two parts, taking with him two of his grandsons, Temple and Benjamin, aged sixteen and seven, and leaving behind his daughter Sarah and his three-year-old grandson Will in the care of his son-in-law, Richard Bache, whom he appointed deputy postmaster general to run the postal system in his absence.

He embarked secretly on October 26 on the warship *Reprisal*, and, after a swift but rough passage, which did not prevent him from resuming his study of the Gulf Stream, he landed in France early in December, quite exhausted. But two days later the old "remnant" of a man wrote in his journal:

On the road yesterday, we met six or seven country women in company, on horseback and astride; they were all of fair white and red complexions but one among them was the fairest woman I ever beheld.[46]

As always, the indomitable lover of life was quickly revived by the pleasurable variety of travel.

Cordial as had been his reception during the two previous visits to France, Franklin was unprepared for the public homage and honor accorded to him on this journey to Paris. As a result of a remarkable series of fortuitous events in his life and the phenomenal responsiveness of his talents and character to the social forces of his time, the commoner who had braved the lightning, the poor boy who had raised himself to wealth and greatness, the homespun philosopher of the bright New World, educator of the uneducated, defender of the rights of the common people, champion of liberty, and now the David of the American Republic challenging the hated British Goliath—this modest American genius had drawn to himself, like the pointed rod of his invention, the fiery passions and aspirations of all classes of the French nation. Franklin and France were ripe for each other.

He was quick to sense this compatability and engage it on behalf of his mission. When he realized that the French identified "Benjamin Franklin of Philadelphia" with the uncorrupted Quaker sect which had founded the city of brotherly love, he acted the part of a New World Quaker, wearing a plain brown coat and appearing without a wig even at formal court functions. The people of France took the captivating American whom they yearned to love to their heart. Within a few weeks of his arrival his picture adorned innumerable mantelpieces and in the following years was reproduced on countless snuffboxes, rings, watches, clocks, vases, dishes, handkerchiefs, pocketknives, and even on an elegant porcelain chamber pot presented out of envy by the king to a lady at court! His likeness could also be seen everywhere in portraits, prints, busts, medallions, and statuettes.[47] When John Adams, whose temperament would clash sharply with Franklin's, replaced Silas Deane as commissioner in Paris, he observed:

. . . [Franklin's] reputation was more universal than that of Leibnitz or Newton, Frederick [the Great] or Voltaire, and his character more beloved and esteemed than any or all of them. . . . His name was familiar to government and people, to kings, courtiers, nobility, clergy, and philosophers, as well as plebeians, to such a degree that there was scarcely a peasant or a citizen, a *valet de chambre*, coachman or footman, a lady's chambermaid or a scullion in a kitchen, who was not familiar with it, and who did not consider him as a friend to human kind.[48]

Though this unprecedented popularity was overwhelming, it did not upset Franklin's equilibrium or raise his previous opinion of himself. Combined with his diplomatic experience and genius, Vergennes's anti-British strategy, and the providential surrender of General Burgoyne, it enabled him to win the financial and military support of the most glamorous monarchy in Europe for a republican revolution that, if successful, could set off a chain reaction against the monarchical institution in France and other countries. But France was so intent on weakening the too powerful British Empire that she chose to close her eyes to this danger. Even after recognizing the United States of

America and going to war with England, she was haunted, in spite of Franklin's sincere assurances to the contrary, by the fear of a separate peace between the American states and the mother country that would keep them in the empire. After the defeat of Burgoyne, the British government naturally sought by every means at its disposal to accomplish this end.

During the first year of his mission, when his position was unofficial and ambiguous, Franklin retired to Passy, a peaceful village not far, but removed, from the spotlight of Paris, from which he could inconspicuously avail himself of the lines of communication that he had promptly after his arrival laid down with Vergennes and old and new friends—a fundamental tactic in Franklin's brand of personal diplomacy. He was, of course, under the constant surveillance of British spies, but he refused to waste his time and energy worrying about them. Besides, Franklin's policy of telling the truth confounded the spies as much as it had formerly misled his political enemies, and his friends in France and in England kept him better informed than any spies of his own could.

After the American commissioners received official recognition from the French government, Franklin continued to operate quietly from his headquarters in Passy, where he enjoyed the convenience of easy access to Paris essential to his work and of friendly neighbors equally essential to his health—the parish priest, the tradesmen, and several resident families as warm-hearted as the Stevensons in London (the Chaimonts, the LeVeillards, the Brillons, and Mme. Helvétius and her satellites)whom he visited regularly and where he was refreshed after the debilitating business of the day by good food, conversation, music, chess, and the company of charming and affectionate women. He set up a private press in Passy, on which he printed materials needed in his work and light essays, *bagatelles,* in English and French, for the amusement and edification of his intimate friends.

In 1778, Congress, wisely disregarding the attacks and insinuations of his enemies at home and abroad, appointed him as its sole envoy to France. This action enabled him to pursue a consistent policy in all his dealings and freed him from the harassment he had endured from Arthur Lee, one of the other commissioners, a man so obsessed by suspicion and resentment that he finally drove Franklin to write one of the very few harsh personal letters of his life. Having purged himself of his own anger, he felt better and apparently refrained from sending the letter and compounding his associate's miseries.

The load of work that Congress placed on the old shoulders of Franklin seems inhuman to us today. With a staff of two, consisting of his grandson Temple as secretary and one clerk, he performed the duties of ambassador, consul, banker, merchant, naval secretary, admiralty judge, and director of information and propaganda! Above all, during the seven long years of uncertain war, whenever defeat and despondency threatened to undermine the resolution of America and her friends, he maintained an appearance of serene confidence and unshakable conviction of ultimate victory. His solo performance remained unmatched in spirit and effect for 150 years, until an indomitable Englishman again sustained a nation during its days and months of terrible adversity.

In propaganda, as in education and science, Franklin practiced the principles of utility and truth that had always served him well. *In his hands*, education was propaganda, and propaganda education, both sharing the same objective—to influence people to live rightly and rationally. Though he often used satire to get attention as a necessary aid to instruction, he did not doubt that any form of propaganda that was designed to misinform and mislead would sooner or later be unmasked to the permanent detriment of the interest it represented.

Soon after he came to Paris, he began to contribute propaganda items to a periodical publication in Paris that backed the American cause.[49] The most important of these were the constitutions of the various American states, which appeared separately at first, and had a profound effect on political thought in France. Franklin's *Examination* before the House of Commons, his masterly lecture on America, and his jugular satires, *Rules* for reducing a great empire and *Edict* of the King of Prussia, were also reprinted in this periodical with good effect.[50]

One of the main centers of Franklinist influence in Paris was the Masonic lodge of the Nine Sisters, whose membership belonged on any honor roll of the liberal arts and sciences in France. Franklin was made a member soon after his arrival in Paris and signally honored by being elected Grand Master two years later. The members of the lodge were constitutionalists who hoped that France would some day become a constitutional monarchy, and one of the members, the young Duc de La Rochefoucauld d'Enville, at Franklin's suggestion, undertook to translate the constitutions of the American states a month after Franklin reached Paris.[51]

Other works of his published during this period enhanced his influence among the people and intellectuals of France (and England). The *Way to Wealth*, which was published in Paris in 1777 under the title *La Science du Bonhomme Richard*, was immensely popular, going through five issues in one year. And in spite of the war, Benjamin Vaughan in 1779 published the *Political, Miscellaneous, and Philosophical Pieces* of Franklin in London, identifying him as "Minister Plenipotentiary at the Court of Paris for the United States of America,"[52] whose existence was not yet recognized by the British government. Father Abraham was also working subversively for the American rebels in these critical years through printings in London, Dublin, Canterbury, and Edinburgh, and translations of Vaughan's collection of Franklin papers gained politically valuable adherents for Franklin and the fledgling American nation in Germany and Italy.

But in many ways the best propaganda weapon of Franklin was Franklin himself, his character and his personality. It was not only what he said and wrote, but what he was, that influenced men's minds. This was the catalytic factor that dispelled the suspicion of strangers, the distrust of cynics, the contention between the sexes, and the antagonism of enemies. Since very few Europeans knew America, he was America. Admiring and loving him, they admired and loved America.

This steadfast interplay in Franklin of character and propaganda, of morality and politics, was exemplified in his memorable reaction to the report he received in 1779 that Captain Cook would be returning soon to England from his third voyage of exploration—it was not yet known that he had been killed in Hawaii. Franklin issued instructions to the commanders of all armed American ships that, if Cook's ship were captured,

. . . you would not consider her as an enemy, nor suffer any plunder to be made of the effects contain'd in her, nor obstruct her immediate return to England, by detaining her or sending her into any other part of Europe or to America, but that you would treat the said Captain Cook and his people with all civility and kindness, affording them, as common friends to mankind, all the assistance in your power, which they may happen to stand in need of.[53]

The impact of this humane act in time of war may be gauged by the fact that the British Admiralty later sent him a copy of Captain Cook's *Voyage to the Pacific Ocean*, and the Royal Society presented him with one of its medals commemorating the great navigator.

With the surrender of Cornwallis at Yorktown, which practically

World Influence: Later Years, 1764-1790

ensured the military and moral defeat of England, the jockeying by England, France, and Spain began in earnest, with dubious assists by Russia and Austria, each pursuing what it considered its own national interest in the changed and unstable state of international affairs. The only thing that was not up for bargaining, it turned out, was the friendship and trust between Franklin and Vergennes. The British, who tried to break it up, and the other American peace commissioners, John Adams and John Jay, who misjudged it, failed to understand that neither man expected the other to be less devoted to his country's best interest because of it. Except for one misunderstanding, which was cleared up, they remained faithful to their duty and friendship all the way through the murky labyrinth of negotiations that ended in peace in 1784. Against this background of duplicity and betrayal, a letter sent by Franklin to an English friend glows with the indignation and integrity of a true statesman. The letter was in reply to a semiofficial proposal of a ten-year truce made in response to a report that the American government was interested in making a separate peace. "The Congress," he wrote,

will never instruct their commissioners to obtain a peace on such ignominious terms; and tho' there can be but few things in which I should venture to disobey their orders, yet if it were possible for them to give me such an order as this, I should certainly refuse to act, I should instantly renounce their commission, and banish myself for ever from so infamous a country.[54]

The American peace commissioners, notwithstanding differences of temperament, experience, outlook, and method, were equally patriotic and generally in agreement on what was good for the American nation. Franklin kept a steady hand on the wheel and an alert eye on wind and weather, steering the negotiations unerringly toward the "essential" [i.e., non-negotiable] terms he had laid down in his first informal contacts with British emissaries—acknowledgment of independence, withdrawal of all British forces from the United States, retention of the prewar boundaries between Canada and the former American colonies, and fishing rights for Americans on the Newfoundland banks. Being a trader of long standing, he made these basic terms more attractive by adding several negotiable conditions, for instance, the ceding of the whole of Canada to the United States!

The inordinate strains of the years of war and negotiation, relieved only by social and literary pleasures among his devoted friends in

Passy, together with his sedentary life and the toll of old age, gradually impaired Franklin's health. He suffered more and more often from attacks of the gout compounded by a painful kidney stone. In public he maintained his legendary good humor and unruffled demeanor, but in private, when the pressures and pains kept beneath the surface became intolerable, he would now and then lay aside his iron tranquillity and let the miseries boil over. At one time, for example, after another of the many disputes inflicted on him by Arthur Lee, he wrote in confidence to his grandnephew, Jonathan Williams: ". . . I have been too long in hot water, plagu'd almost to death with the passions, vagaries, and ill humours and madnesses of other people. I must have a little repose."[55]

Passy was the only repose he found, and the refreshment it gave him is evident in his *bagatelles,* as light and nourishing as a French omelet. Even in these playthings, as in everything Franklin wrote, entertainment and instruction were inseparable and compulsive for him. The tragicomedy of the human scene evoked in him both compassion and laughter, and sometimes rage, especially against "man's inhumanity to man." His love for benevolent and talented men, for children not yet hardened by the knowledge of evil, and for women beautiful of body and soul, a love which he retained to the end of his long life, lightened the burdens that he carried and gave him the will and the strength to bear the calumny, deceit, ingratitude, and pain that could not be avoided in his position.

With the formal ratification of the treaty of peace in 1784, the grand task, which Franklin had not expected to see brought to a successful conclusion in his lifetime, had been accomplished. Neither age nor intrigue nor dissension nor mischance had been able to prevail over his invincible resolution, and among all the masters of diplomacy with whom he had had to contend none could outplay or corrupt him. Rarely had one man achieved so much with so little help from any source other than his own talents and character. Thanks largely to him, Great Britain emerged from the long struggle diminished, France weakened, and only the incredible United States of America stronger than ever before.

In the years of respite following the signing of the preliminary articles of peace in late 1782, Franklin had somewhat more leisure for the constructive scientific, political, and personal activities that he had had to subordinate to his prodigious ministerial responsibilities. He had never entirely neglected these activities even during the most difficult years, somehow finding time, for example, to attend scientific meetings, visit laboratories, keep up with scientific advances, write scientific papers and letters, and help friends.

In the same year, with the approval of Congress, he sponsored the publication in French of the constitutions of the American states and gave two copies of the book to each ambassador in Paris, besides sending copies to friends all over Europe. The missionary aim of distributing these working models of government and law in this time of American triumph was as practical as it was obvious. They were time bombs that would explode later in the countries where they had been dropped.

Franklin's private press in Passy was so active during these years that at one time he employed a printer full time for five months to assist him. The year 1784 was particularly productive. He printed two engaging and instructive pamphlets in English and French, wrote the second part of his autobiography, and sent a long letter to his daughter regarding the Society of the Cincinnati, which was fated to have a great influence.

Dazzled by the miraculous victory of the young American republic, great numbers of Europeans of all classes were prompted to consider emigrating to the United States and wrote, of course, to Franklin for advice and assistance. Many of them were gentlemen, scholars, and artists without money—as well as ordinary poor people—who entertained wildly utopian expectations, imagining that Americans were so rich and so eager to encourage the immigration of Europeans of good family, education, and talents that they offered free passage, land, slaves, tools, and cattle! To prevent them from making a disastrous mistake, he printed *Information to Those Who Would Remove to America,* a useful and honest account of the prospects for those who wished to leave their homes. While he pulled no punches, he could not hide the love and pride he felt for his unspoiled country, "where people,"he said,

do not inquire concerning a stranger, *What is he?* but *What can he do?* . . . The husbandman [i.e., farmer] is in honor there, and even the mechanic, because their employments are useful. The people have a saying, that God Almighty is himself a mechanic, the greatest in the univers; and he is respected and admired more for the variety, ingenuity, and utility of his handyworks, than for the antiquity of his family. . . . "[56]

Land was cheap, and wages high enough for money to be saved with which to buy land; the air and the climate were healthful; and food was plentiful.

In short, America is the land of labour, and by no means what . . . the French [call] *Pays de Cocagne,* where the streets are pav'd with half-peck loaves, the houses til'd with pancakes, and where the fowls fly about ready roasted, crying, *Come eat me! . . .* "[57]

Frequently questioned about the American Indians, he decided to print a second pamphlet, *Remarks Concerning the Savages of North America,* in which he gathered together the stories he had been telling friends about the American Indians for years to illustrate the anthropological theme that

. . . if we could examine the manners of different nations with impartiality, we should find no people so rude, as to be without any rules of politeness; nor any so polite, as not to have some remains of rudeness.[58]

Both pamphlets were widely popular, published together in London and Dublin in 1784 as *Two Tracts* and in Italian translations in 1785, and the *Information* separately in France (1784) and Germany (1786).

The letter to Sarah was written in criticism and ridicule of the undemocratic Society of the Cincinnati, recently formed in the United States by former officers of the American army and headed by George Washington. Membership was to be hereditary, descending from generation to generation through the oldest son, like a European title of nobility. ". . . Honour," Franklin declared,

worthily obtain'd (as for example that of our officers), is in its nature a *personal* thing, and incommunicable to any but those who had some share in obtaining it. Thus among the Chinese, the most ancient, and from long experience the wisest of nations, honour does not *descend,* but *ascends.* If a man. . . is promoted by the Emperor to the rank of Mandarin, his parents are immediately entitled to all the same ceremonies of respect from the people, that are establish'd as due to the Mandarin himself; on the supposition that it must have been owing to the education, instruction, and good example afforded him by his parents, that he was rendered capable of serving the public. . . .

I wish, therefore, that the Cincinnati, if they must go on with their project, would direct the badge of their order to be worn by their parents, instead of handing them down to their children. . . .[59]

Though Franklin, because of his official position, was dissuaded by friends from publishing the letter himself, as he was at first moved to do, his revolutionary ideas found their way into a French brochure on the Cincinnati by the younger Mirabeau and an associate, both of them known to friends of Franklin. Ostensibly a translation of a paper on the same subject by an American, Aedanus Burke, it was intended by the translators as a veiled attack on the system of nobility in France and the rest of Europe. Printed in London in 1785, on Franklin's recommendation, and soon after in English translation, and a year later in Philadelphia, it had an unexpected success and a far-reaching effect.[60]

Franklin's last months in France were a grateful harvest time for the venerable minister. Passy was regarded by the young idealists of France and other European countries as a shrine, the seat of the philosopher-statesman who had performed the miracle of making a republican revolution without malevolence and unreason. For example, young English reformers like William Wilberforce (antislavery) and Samuel Romilly (penal reform) made pilgrimages to Passy to receive inspiration and guidance from him for the future. When Jefferson arrived in Paris in August, 1784, he observed that ". . . more respect and veneration attached to the character of Doctor Franklin in France, than to that of any other person, . . . foreign or native."[61]

In December, the widowed Polly (Stevenson) Hewson came at his invitation to spend the winter with him in Passy, bringing into his household cherished filial love and the laughter of children. And in the spring Congress finally gave him permission to return home, appointing Jefferson to succeed him—for no one could replace him, his great admirer was fond of saying. His intimate friends, unwilling to let go of him and fearing that the long and hazardous Atlantic crossing would be too much for him at his age and in his uncertain state of health, entreated him to stay with them for the rest of his life. But the pull of home, from which he had been away for nearly a decade, was stronger than the risk of death and even than his love for his adoring friends and France, and he did not wish to die and be buried in a foreign land.

Franklin himself doubted whether he would even reach Havre or Southampton, from which he had arranged to sail. For his comfort he traveled in a litter that belonged to the queen and was borne smoothly by two tall mules. On the road for the first time in many years, he immediately felt revived, reinvigorated. Making twenty to thirty miles a day with very little fatigue, and entertained royally every evening, he reached Havre in six days. Crossing the Channel in two days, he was the only one in his party who was not seasick! Friends came down to Southampton to see him off, among them his son William, with whom he went through a perfunctory reconciliation. The love he had felt for his only son was gone, the void now filled by his grandsons, who were returning with him. They sailed on July 28.

On the second day at sea, he began to take daily recordings of the temperature of the air and water. Instead of resuming his autobiography, as his friends had entreated him to do, he zestfully summarized his nautical studies in his valuable *Maritime Observations* and wrote two other scientific papers. Nearly eighty, he found his health improved and his intellectual acuity undimmed. For the second time in his life he looked forward happily to retiring from politics and devoting himself to his beloved science. The busy days passed quickly, and on September 14 he came "in full view of dear Philadelphia."

When he stepped ashore at the Market Street wharf, where he had landed long ago, an unknown and friendless runaway of seventeen, bells pealed, cannons puffed, and a large crowd shouted—Welcome!—to the legendary hero who had returned miraculously alive and well and smiling benignly. They followed and cheered him all the way home to his family and the four grandchildren he had never seen. Home. "God be praised and thanked for all His mercies!" he wrote at the end of the journal of his last voyage.[62]

III *Founding Father of the American Union*

Franklin's hope of retiring from politics and resuming scientific investigation was quickly dissipated. During the first two weeks after his arrival, he listened to a long succession of welcoming addresses from representatives of the State Assembly, the University of Pennsylvania, the State Militia, the American Philosophical Society, and others. The following month he was unanimously elected president (governor, with limited powers) of the Council of Pennsylvania, which had a plural executive.

He seemed to have found his second wind in the journey from Paris. Though he was in constant discomfort on account of the kidney stone, it was bearable, and he was buoyed up by his official work, his family, and his friends at home and abroad. In 1786 his beloved Polly Hewson moved with her family to Philadelphia to be near him. He knew how to husband his remaining strength, but he sometimes wished, as he wrote to a friend, that

I had brought with me from France a balloon sufficiently large to raise me from the ground. In my malady it would have been the most easy carriage for me, being led by a string held by a man walking on the ground.[63]

Lacking the balloon, he usually used a sedan chair as a substitute.

After an absence of nine years, he was astonished by the general economic vitality and prosperity of the country. His own properties had tripled in value since 1776. The farmers, he said,

who are the bulk of the nation, have had plentiful crops, their produce sells at high prices and for ready, hard money. . . . Our working-people are all employed and get high wages, are well fed and well clad. . . . In short, all among us may be happy, who have happy dispositions; such being necessary to happiness even in paradise.[64]

Partly because he enjoyed construction, he built several houses and an addition to his own house for his large library and a state dining room. He sponsored the election of ten French and English friends—and William Temple Franklin—to the American Philosophical Society. He served as president of the Pennsylvania society for the abolition of slavery. And he founded another institution for the education of his fellow Americans—the Society for Political Enquiries, in the conviction that the "arduous and complicated science of government" should not be "left to the care of practical politicians or the speculations of individual theorists."[65]

Whether because of his age or his apparent acceptance of conditions in the country under the Articles of Confederation, Franklin was not involved in the strategy that culminated in the Constitutional Convention during his second term as president of Pennsylvania, but he was added as a member of the Pennsylvania delegation three months after it had been chosen by the assembly. In spite of his failing health and the increasing distress from his ailments, he attended every session for five hours a day for nearly four months.

During these four months he rarely spoke, as was his habit. Whenever he intended to present his views on important issues in the debates, he wrote them out beforehand and had them read for him since it was very painful for him to stand. Having seen at close hand the abuses and corruptions of monarchical and aristocratic governments in Europe, he advocated limiting the power of the presidency and increasing the power of the representatives of the people, specifically a plural executive, as in the constitution of Pennsylvania, and a single-chamber legislature, like the Pennsylvania legislature and the former Colonial assemblies; and, to reduce corruption in government—unsalaried officials! (He had chosen not to use his salary as president of Pennsylvania for himself.) These major proposals, which seemed quite visionary at that time, were respectfully rejected by the delegates.

In accordance with his political principles, he opposed giving the president the right of absolute veto over Congress and setting up a property qualification for voting or holding office, and he favored making the president impeachable. The historical alternative to impeachment was assassination, in which the chief magistrate, he asserted,

> . . . was not only deprived of his life but of the opportunity of vindicating his character. It would be the best way therefore to provide in the Constitution for the regular punishment of the executive when his misconduct should deserve it and for his honourable acquittal when he should be unjustly accused.[66]

The virulent anti-Jewish speech that Franklin was "discovered" in 1934 to have made at the convention proved on investigation to have been a palpable Fascist forgery, which could have been invented only by a mind cancerous with malice and profoundly ignorant of the character, literary style, and life of Franklin.[67]

His greatest contribution to the convention was not in specifics, but in the moderating and conciliatory influence that he exercised throughout the long summer when tempers or conflicts flared up, threatening to wreck this second, but nonviolent, American Revolution. After one of these clashes, he lectured them, like a class of unruly pupils:

> . . . we are sent here to *consult* not to *contend* with each other; and declarations of a fixed opinion, and of determined resolution, never to change it . . . tend to create and augment discord & division in a great concern, wherein harmony and union are extremely necessary . . . in promoting & securing the common good.[68]

And, as he was by far the oldest, wisest, and most venerable delegate, they listened to him.

The chief obstacle to completing the task of framing a viable Constitution was the apparently irreconcilable conflict of interest between the more populous and the less populous states over the principle of representation in Congress. When it seemed that the latter were ready to walk out on this issue and break up the convention, the worldly veteran in the art of diplomacy promptly introduced a motion to open all future sessions with a prayer for divine guidance! Though the motion was defeated, the discussion that was occasioned by it produced a tranquillizing effect, as he had intended.

Several days later, at a meeting of the special committee representing all the states, which had been charged to work out and report a compromise to break the deadlock, Franklin moved the great compromise that saved the convention and the Constitution—unequal representation by population and control of appropriations in the House of Representatives, and equal representation by states in the Senate.

On the final day of the convention he performed his last great service to his country, pleading with equal modesty and wisdom for unanimous approval of the unique document, as he sat quietly in pain while James Wilson of Pennsylvania read his speech to the assembled delegates:

I confess that there are several parts of this constitution which I do not at present approve, but I am not sure I shall never approve them: . . . the older I grow, the more apt I am to doubt my own judgment, and to pay more respect to the judgment of others. . . .

I think . . . that this [government] is likely to be well administered for a course of years, and can only end in despotism, as other forms have done before it, when the people shall become so corrupted as to need despotic government, being incapable of any other. . . . I consent . . . to this Constitution because I expect no better, and because I am not sure, that it is not the best. . . . On the whole, . . . I cannot help expressing a wish that every member of the Convention who may still have objections to it, would, with me, on this occasion doubt a little of his own infallibility, and, to make manifest our unanimity, put his name to this instrument.[69]

Copies of Franklin's eloquent address, which proved completely effective in the convention, except for three uncompromising delegates, were soon widely circulated by delegates in their own states, contrary to the rule of secrecy, and it was finally published in December in the *American Museum*. Coming from the trusted leader who had been not unhappy with the national government under the less confining *Articles of Confederation*, it won over great numbers of citizens who feared a strong national government and was decisive in ensuring ratification of the new Constitution.

His last great undertaking in political guidance accomplished, Franklin's thoughts, rising above the "excruciating pain" that now was his almost constant companion, turned naturally to the time when only his words would survive to entertain and instruct. To his fellow delegates at the convention he may have appeared a glorious figure out of the past, but in his writings of these terminal years he belonged to the future.

To a European friend he sent a copy of the Constitution, which had fired his imagination and reawakened his youthful dream of a union of nations joined in peace. "I was engag'd," he wrote, as hopeful at eighty-one as at twenty-one,

4 months of the last summer in the Convention that form'd it. It is now sent by Congress to the several states for their confirmation. If it succeeds, I do not see why you might not in Europe carry the project . . . into execution, by forming a federal union and one grand republick of all its different states & kingdoms; by means of a like Convention; for we had many interests to reconcile.[70]

He made his last will and testament in 1788 and soon after started working on the third part of his autobiography, which he brought to a close with his arrival in London in July, 1757, at the beginning of an unimaginable new career of extraordinary national and international consequence. A very short supplement (Part IV) continued the autobiography to 1760.

Education and the disinherited were very much on Franklin's mind—as clear and incisive as ever—in the last year of his life. He prepared for the record his indictment of the trustees of the Academy, entitled *Observations Relative to the Intentions of the Original Founders of the Academy in Philadelphia,* and with barbed pen unblunted by age wrote the satire *On the Slave-Trade* in response to a speech delivered in Congress by one James Jackson of Georgia, which warned against "meddling with the affair of slavery, or attempting to mend the condition of the slaves."[71] He also wrote at about this time his *Plan for Improving the Condition of the Free Blacks* and probably his *Hints . . . Respecting the Orphan School-House in Philadelphia.*

After reviewing in detail the "shameful" history of the "constant disposition [of the trustees] to depress the English School in favour of the Latin," he called for a separation of the two schools and the execution of "the plan they have so long defeated," with restoration to the public of "the means of a compleat English education." "At this day," he concluded firmly,

the whole body of science, consisting not only of translations, from all the valuable ancients, but of all the new modern discoveries, is to be met with in . . . [the modern] languages, so that learning the ancient for the purpose of acquiring knowledge is become absolutely unnecessary. . . .

I am the only one of the original trustees now living, and I am just stepping into the grave myself. . . . I seize this opportunity, the last I may possibly have, of bearing testimony against those deviations. I seem here to be surrounded by the ghosts of my dear departed friends, beckoning and urging me to use the only tongue now left us, in demanding that justice to our grandchildren that our children has [sic] been denied.[72]

But time ran out for him, and the public had to wait until their great-grandchildren were born.

Ever since his connection with the Bray Associates during his first mission to England, Franklin had been deeply concerned with the problem of slavery in its various aspects—education, the free blacks, the slave trade, and abolition. As president of the Society for Promoting the Abolition of Slavery, he drew up an intelligent plan to provide free blacks with advice and protection, education, apprenticeships, and employment. When, therefore, James Jackson's speech on slavery appeared in the *Federal Gazette,* Franklin immediately composed and sent its editor (twenty-four days before his death!) his satire *On the Slave-Trade.*

It pretended to be the translation of a similar speech made by a governor of Algiers in opposition to a petition for the abolition of *Christian* slavery, which, he said with tongue in cheek,

. . . may be seen in Martin's account of his consulship, anno 1687. . . . Mr. Jackson does not quote it; perhaps he has not seen it. If, therefore, some of its reasonings are to be found in his eloquent speech, it may only show that men's interests and intellects operate and are operated on with surprising similarity in all countries and climates, when under similar circumstances.[73]

The fictitious governor cited the familiar arguments, *mutatis mutandis*—economic disaster; uncertainty of compensation; hardships of freed Christians ("Men long accustom'd to slavery will not work for a livelihood when not compell'd"); and the enslaved condition of "free" men in Christian countries: "Is their condition made worse," the governor asked,

by their falling into our hands? No; they have only exchanged one slavery for another, and I may say a better; for here they are brought into a land where the sun of Islamism gives forth its light, and shines in full splendor, and they have an opportunity of making themselves acquainted with the true doctrine, and thereby saving their immortal souls.[74]

In 1788 La Rochefoucauld d'Enville, one of Franklin's most devoted disciples and a leading spirit among those who hoped for a constitutional monarchy in France, informed his master that the tide of reform was rising in that country:

> . . . France, whom you left talking zealously of liberty for other nations, begins to think that a small portion of this same liberty would be a very good thing for herself. Good works for the last thirty years, and your good example for the last fourteen, have enlightened us much. . . .[75]

As the tide continued to swell and began to lash the shore and shatter the well-ordered communities that bordered it, Franklin's feelings were ambivalent. He was justly apprehensive for the safety of his friends amid the first signs of the approaching cataclysm. For example, he wrote anxiously in 1789 to another of the *franklinistes:*

> It is now more than a year, since I have heard from my dear friend Le Roy. . . . Are you still living? Or have the mob of Paris mistaken the head of a monopolizer of knowledge, for a monopolizer of corn, and paraded it about the streets upon a pole? . . .
> Great part of the news we have had from Paris, for near a year past, has been very afflicting. . . . The voice of *Philosophy* I apprehend can hardly be heard among those tumults. . . .
> Our new Constitution is now established, and has an appearance that promises permanency; but in this world nothing can be said to be certain, except death and taxes.[76]

But, viewing the upheaval impersonally as a student of political history and a believer in liberty under law, he wrote to his English friend, David Hartley, just three weeks later:

> The convulsions in France are attended with some disagreeable circumstances; but if by the struggle she obtains and secures for the nation its future liberty, and a good constitution, a few years' enjoyment of those blessings will amply repair all the damages their acquisition may have occasioned. God grant, that not only the love of liberty, but a thorough knowledge of the rights of man, may pervade all the nations of the earth. . . .[77]

Two months before, Franklin had written a warm farewell letter to "President" Washington, with whom he had enjoyed a lifelong friendship of mutual regard and affection unmarred on either side by the disease of envy. "For my own personal ease," he remarked,

I should have died two years ago; but, tho' those years have been spent in excruciating pain, I am pleas'd that I have liv'd them, since they have brought me to see our present situation. I am now finishing my 84th [year], and probably with it my career in this life; but in whatever state of existence I am plac'd hereafter, if I retain any memory of what has pass'd here, I shall with it retain the esteem, respect, and affection, with which I have long been, my dear friend, yours. . . .[78]

He died seven months later, as he had wished, in his own country, with family and friends near him, at peace with himself and the world, and was buried beside his wife.

IV *Envoi*

Benjamin Franklin had been a towering phenomenon for so long that it was hard to accept the fact that the most versatile and influential genius America had produced, probably the greatest American personality of his time, was gone. Yet, though Americans revered his genius and character, they were still too close to him to fully appreciate his qualities as a man and an American.

That Franklin was a great man in very many ways is remarkable enough, but less remarkable than that he was a truly self-made man, in character as well as in business, journalism, education, science, and politics. Starting with superior natural endowments and an apparently adverse environment, he conscientiously set out to mold his character in preparation for the major goals in life that he had chosen for himself—personal independence and service to his fellowmen. Books and life were his first teachers, and these taught him that character, rooted in sound moral principles, was the foundation of independence and happiness. He therefore studied his own weaknesses of character and then invented a program of self-examination and correction that enabled him in time to save himself from being a slave to them.

In everything that Franklin undertook, his integrity, his steadfast adherence to the principles of truth, sincerity, fairness, and altruism were the indispensable catalytic agents that inspired trust, overcame inertia, and reduced opposition. Combined with his superb intellect, his native humor and wit, his love of people, his indifference to distinctions of class and creed, his pacific and amiable disposition, his ingenuity, his genius as a writer of lucid, hearty English, and his propensity for teaching and helping others, these catalysts precipitated the exceptional number and diversity of his achievements—all characteristically American—notably, the promotion of voluntary associations, such as the Junto, the Library Company, the American Philosophical Society, the Academy, the Hospital, and the Society for Political Inquiries; the development of mass communication and education; his scientific discoveries; the invention of the Franklin stove and the lightning rod; and his contributions to the concept and realization of a federal American republic, finally institutionalized in the Constitution of 1787.

The goals that he had set for himself did not result in works of art intended to give pleasure, or systems of thought and belief meant to give consolation, to existing and future generations, useful as these accomplishments are, but rather in institutions and inventions designed to improve the quality of human living and make better and happier individual men and women. They were goals that called for imagination and talents of a very rare kind, capable of modifying reality and humanity.

In this lifelong quest, Franklin was compelled to exert all his powers, including his indubitable personal magnetism. And as the circumference of the circle that he sought to educate and enlighten grew from neighborhood to city, colony, continent, and ultimately the entire Western world, his character deepened and his resources expanded almost miraculously to meet the greater needs. Step by step the man who founded the Junto "for mutual improvement" devised larger and larger Juntos for the same purpose until his aim embraced America and the world. From this view, Franklin's life and his educational endeavors were inextricably intertwined, reinforcing each other and forming a single stout line of natural development.

Franklin did not, like Aristotle or Aquinas, create an all-embracing system of thought, in which the confusions of the human condition were reduced to a timely semblance of order and reason. He performed an equally uncommon miracle—he forged a teacher and a leader of men in whom the conflicts and complexities of the human personality were brought into harmony and coordinated with his great abilities to work for the welfare of his fellowmen. In the short range, this work required that he instruct them regarding their best interest in dealing with immediate problems. In the long range, he strove, first, to raise the level of knowledge and morality of the common people, who were generally poor and unschooled in his time, and, second, to recommend a different kind of school for the young based on a new philosophy of education.

The underlying principle of Franklin's philosophy is that education be "useful" to the individual and to society; disregarding either side of the scale unbalances both. Education should, therefore, aim to serve the needs and abilities of the individual and prepare him for the kind of society in which he is going to live and work, and it should try to anticipate what the needs of that society will be and what kind of society the people living in it would like it to be. The concept of "needs" as Franklin understood it was as broad and varied as people are. In his view, it embraced—with due recognition of the limitations of time, place, money, and culture—the material and the spiritual, the intellectual and the artistic; the practical and the moral; the past, present, and future; the rich, the middle class, and the poor; men and women; the young, the mature, and the old; the majority and the minorities. In essence, it is a dynamic concept, requiring that schools and other agencies of education be reexamined and revised whenever major changes occur in the needs of the individual and society.

Franklin's Academy represented in part the application of his philosophy to the needs and possibilities of the youth of Pennsylvania in 1750. The curriculum, in addition to meeting the special needs of preparation for the professions in the Latin and Greek School of the Academy and for other economic opportunities in the English School, provided for personal development by stressing the importance of achieving excellence in reading, writing, and speaking English with the help of the English literary classics, of studying ancient and modern history for better understanding of government and politics, and, above all, in all studies and activities, of inculcating moral ideals and encouraging the "inclination" and the "ability" of students "to serve" others.

Implicit in the planned program of the school was the society that Franklin saw about him and foresaw in the future—a free society whose people, guided by time-tested moral principles, were moving to take command and determine its shape and fate themselves. Though the actual school, as modified by the conservative trustees during Franklin's long absences from Philadelphia, was a betrayal of his original plan, his philosophy of education survived and lives on as a source of inspiration in the continuing American experiment in democratic government and education.

To the multitude of Franklin's friends and admirers on both sides of the Atlantic his death was an irreplaceable personal loss. In their eyes the man was larger than his works: a genius who felt at home with men, women, and children; a patriot who loved the country of his birth and any other land where freedom and justice were prized; a teacher whose instruction encompassed the concerns of every day as well as mankind and the universe; a mundane philosopher who was ravished by the mysterious forces of nature and life; a prospector ever searching for cosmos beneath the chaos.

CHAPTER 5

Inspiration to the Common Man

*P*oor *Richard* (1738) advised those who wished to be remembered after they died: "Either write things worth reading/Or do things worth the writing." Franklin himself succeeded brilliantly in doing both, and for good measure projected his personality into the future so vividly that he has made more friends after death than in life—and some enemies, too, especially among the followers of the Romantic revolution. For a long time neither his friends nor his enemies knew the whole polygonal man. He was loved by the common people and their leaders for his lifelong crusade against poverty and oppression, and disdained by many of the children of affluence and their literary mentors for his teaching of the way to economic independence and the everyday virtues. As the true dimensions of his life and character have become more familiar, his friends have increased and his detractors dwindled in number. The legendary Franklin has always been a potent figure in the world, but the true unvarnished Franklin continues to grow in stature and humanity.

In the year following his death the memorial honors and eulogies for Franklin, idol of the common people, were modulated by the political temper of the time and place—by the ascendancy of the conservatives in America and of the reformers in France. In Philadelphia, his inveterate enemy, William Smith, though assisted by Jefferson and other friends of Franklin, was chosen to deliver the eulogy before the American Philosophical Society. The populist House of Representatives, on the motion of Madison, unanimously voted to wear mourning for a month, but the more conservative Senate declined.

In France, on the other hand, where the tide of reform was rapidly rising, the National Assembly approved by acclamation the proposal of Mirabeau that the members

. . . during three days, shall wear mourning for Benjamin Franklin, . . . this mighty genius, who, to the advantage of mankind, compassing in his mind the

heavens and the earth, was able to restrain alike thunderbolts and tyrants
. . . [and was] one of the greatest men who have ever been engaged in the
service of philosophy and of liberty.[1]

Franklin's friend Condorcet, several months later, giving the Franklin
eulogy at the Royal Academy of Sciences, perceptively noted among
other things that Franklin ". . . did not want any class of citizen to
remain without instruction. . . . A common printer did for America
what the wisest governments have had the arrogance to neglect or the
weakness to fear."[2]

Within the year other generous eulogies were delivered in Paris by
his friends at memorial observances in the Society of 1789, the Masonic
Lodge of the Nine Sisters, the Commune of Paris, the Royal Society of
Medicine, and the Society of Journeymen Printers of Paris, all reflecting the admiration and love of the French people for him in this period
of liberal fervor.

The first publication anywhere of Franklin's *Autobiography*, in 1791,
was a French translation of Part One, which he had written in 1771,
covering the first twenty-five years of his life (1706–1731) and comprising less than half of the memoirs. The first two printings in English,
which appeared in London in 1793, were retranslations from this incomplete French version! The better of the retranslations was included
in a two-volume collection of Franklin's works published in the same
year and reprinted over 150 times during the following seventy years in
Great Britain, the United States, and Ireland, and in French, German,
Danish, Dutch, Polish, and Spanish translation.[3] The "complete" English text of Parts One, Two, and Three (1706–1757), edited from a
copy of the original manuscript by William Temple Franklin, his
grandson and the inheritor of his papers, was finally brought out in
London in 1818 and remained the standard text until 1868, when the
complete original manuscript in Franklin's hand, including Part Four
(1757–1760), was discovered and published by John Bigelow, the
American minister to France.

But for seventy-five years after its publication, the twice
homogenized Franklin of Part One who had appeared in the two-volume edition of 1793, often overlaid with the Poor Richard of *The
Way to Wealth*, was for most readers the only Franklin they knew—the
obscure, ambitious, self-taught youth scrambling to find an independent and respected place for himself in a harsh world. Although his
sharply competitive spirit had not yet been tamed by self-discipline

and success, there was already clear evidence, even in this partial reflection, of his intellectual and literary power, joined with a talent for making and keeping friends, a responsiveness to good influences, and a determination to improve the education and condition of the common people, from whom he had risen. This image was enlarged for them by the legend of the mature Franklin, inventor of *Poor Richard,* the lightning rod, and the free and independent American union (with the assistance of George Washington and a few other patriots!).

Franklin had never forgotten his lowly origins; indeed, he had employed his eminence and great abilities to help those born in similar circumstances. The story of his early life as he had told it, with its frank acknowledgment of youthful faults and follies and its accompanying guideposts showing the way to self-realization through education, rational morality, and liberation from poverty, though written for the benefit of his son, seemed equally valid for them. The example of his genuine dedication to the principles of decency that he preached, together with the reality of his dazzling achievements, was an inspiration to all those, wherever they might be, who were beginning life under the handicaps he had started with. Although it was uniquely American in spirit and style, his story was addressed to conditions and hopes not limited to any particular country or time and was expressed with a simplicity and liveliness universal in its appeal, especially to the young.

A poor boy who was born on a farm in Connecticut the year before Franklin died, and who had read the *Autobiography* at a very early age, wrote to a friend that it had delighted him so much that he read it several times over. "It was this book," he added,

which first roused my mental images . . . prompted me to resolutions, and gave me strength to adhere to them . . . inspired me with an ardor, which I had never felt before . . . taught me that circumstances have not a sovereign control over the mind.[4]

The boy was Jared Sparks, who grew up to be a distinguished historian, president of Harvard, and the first great editor of his teacher's works.

Another farm boy, Thomas Mellon, less poor, but avid for education and wealth, regarded his reading of the *Autobiography* in 1827 as "the turning point in my life," spurring him to leave the family farm in western Pennsylvania and seek his fortune in Pittsburgh, where he founded the Mellon banking dynasty. In his later years Judge Mellon had a thousand copies of the book printed privately to give to young men who came to him for advice or money.

In distant Florence in 1853, a middle-aged printer, Gaspero Barbéra, finding himself in a moral crisis that threatened to ruin him, turned for guidance to the *Autobiography*, which he had read with great pleasure several years before. "At the age of 35," he recalled, "I was a lost man. . . . I read again and again the Autobiography of Franklin, and became enamored of his ideas and principles to such a degree that to them I ascribe my moral regeneration."[5] He was also so profoundly impressed by Franklin's "ardent love for education, and especially for that kind of education which teaches one to know his brother and to discern in this world the true from the false,"[6] that he made the *Autobiography* a key element in a program of popular education he later initiated.[7]

And the Argentinian educator and statesman Domingo Sarmiento, when he read the *Autobiography* in his youth, was transported by the man and the story. "The Life of Franklin," he wrote,

was for me the same as Plutarch was for him. I felt myself to be a Franklin. . . . I was very poor, as he was, and by contriving to follow in his steps, I could some day succeed in forming myself in his image, to be, like him, an honorary doctor and to make a place for myself in American letters and political life.[8]

In later years Sarmiento was fond of referring to himself as "the Little Franklin."[9]

Like their teacher, these men were helped by their reading and in time felt impelled to use it to help others. The living words of the *Autobiography* had the power to perform the miracle that has always been the elusive goal of true education, to change men for the better, each according to his own nature. Franklin never sought to mold others in his own image, enjoying and appreciating the infinite richness of humanity and nature too deeply to think this was either desirable or possible. What he aimed at was releasing men—and women—from the personal prisons in which they were confined by birth, circumstance, ignorance, or error. For example, the trust funds left to the people of Boston and Philadelphia in Franklin's last will and testament were hopefully designed to project and expand this liberating power of his teaching for 200 years in the future! He wished, as he explained, "to be useful even after my death."[10]

Although the world has been changing spectacularly since 1790, nevertheless, wherever people, especially the young, have been poor and uneducated, the teaching and example of Franklin have continued to be "useful," giving encouragement to them and setting many of them free; and wherever governments have been callous to the condition of the common people, the legendary hero who taught them in his lifetime how to promote and defend their individual rights by voluntary association, to the point of risking everything, has also been "useful," giving inspiration to the oppressed and courage to those who would prompt them to liberate themselves.

In the young United States, with an advancing frontier and unprecedented opportunity, the "self-made" Franklin of the early *Autobiography* and *The Way to Wealth* was a potent influence for Abraham Lincoln[11] and Horace Greeley in their youth, as well as for Jared Sparks and Thomas Mellon and a multitude of lesser young men. Greeley placed Franklin above Washington as "the consummate type and flowering of human nature under the skies of colonial America," who had attained greatness "without the aid of inherited wealth, or family honors, or educational advantages."[12]

The dominance of Franklin as the archetype of the self-made American was fostered in numerous public lectures, popular biographies ("Parson" Weems), and schoolbooks. It was taken for granted that he was a great patriot and democrat, but it touched the hearts and hopes of ordinary Americans that he was also a self-made man. Ten years before the midcentury Horace Mann said that he was the "god of Americans."[13]

In the minds of most Americans this view of Franklin persisted into the twentieth century. After the Civil War, the immense expansion of industry and the sweep of population to the Pacific Coast carried the cult of the self-made man to its zenith. During this period more biographies were written about Franklin than about any other American. His *Autobiography* was a favorite in home and public libraries and was read in schools as an English literary classic for the guidance of youth.

One of the great American writers of the century, Mark Twain, self-educated and self-made too, found a proper subject for ridicule in this uncritical adulation of Franklin in an essay written in 1870, in which he acknowledged that

Benjamin Franklin did a great many notable things for his country, and made her young name to be honored in many lands as the mother of such a son. It is not the idea of this memoir to ignore that or cover it up. . . . I merely desired to do away with somewhat of the calamitous idea among heads of families that Franklin *acquired* his great genius by working for nothing, studying by moonlight, and getting up in the night instead of waiting till morning like a Christian . . . [and that this program] will make a Franklin of every father's fool.[14]

Franklin would have been the first to agree and applaud.

At about the same time an awareness of his phenomenal versatility and integrity was beginning to make its appearance alongside the popular one-dimensional likeness. James Parton had published in 1864 the first biography that did justice to the multifaceted greatness of Franklin, and John Bigelow four years later brought out the first edition of the *Autobiography* based on Franklin's complete manuscript. But among the common people of America Franklin remained the self-made hero whom they needed to guide them in the grand economic and political mission on which they had embarked—the subjugation of a continent. For this task they preferred Poor Richard and his progeny, like Horatio Alger's Ragged Dick (born 1867) and Dick's numerous siblings, to Parton's and Bigelow's truer Franklin, and they paid little attention to the literary dissenters, for example, Hawthorne, Lowell, and Melville, or the political dissenters in the rancorous tradition of the Adams family, all of whom suffered from an uninformed confusion of Franklin with Poor Richard, hero of *The Way to Wealth*. Had they known Franklin better, they might have been proud to be his friends, like so many of his "enemies" in life after they had discovered his benevolence and amplitude by intimate acquaintance.

In France, where the living Franklin had appeared to aristocrats and commoners alike as the gifted apostle of liberty, equality, and simplicity, this confusion worked in startling reverse. Poor Richard, their Bonhomme Richard, assumed the characteristics of the Franklin they remembered, while in his own country Franklin took on the qualities of Poor Richard—for better or worse. Consequently, in France for decades after his death, *The Way to Wealth* of Bonhomme Richard was regarded as a work of "sublime morality"[15] and the book in which it was included, together with a brief life of Franklin and his celebrated *Examination* before the House of Commons, was considered an ideal textbook for the education of the masses and of children in elementary schools.

The extraordinary influence of *Bonhomme Richard* and the *Autobiography* in France lasted well past the middle of the nineteenth century. Sainte-Beuve, in his brilliant essay on Franklin, offered an explanation of the phenomenon not only in France, but also in the entire world. "Franklin's *Memoirs*," he observed acutely,

are full of interest for all those who have had a toilsome early life, and have experienced the difficulties of existence and the lack of generosity in men, but who are, nevertheless, not embittered, . . . not spoiled either, nor fallen into the corruption and intrigues of self-interest; . . . to all such, and to all whom the same circumstances await, these *Memoirs* are a source of observation that will always be applicable, and of truth that will always be felt.[16]

This adaptability of the many-sided Franklin image is strikingly exemplified in his influence in Italy for the past 200 years.[17] He had been first introduced to Italian scientists and scholars by Giovanni Beccaria, one of his numerous scientific correspondents, soon after the publication of the *Experiments and Observations on Electricity*, on which Franklin's reputation largely rested during the next twenty-five years. Beccaria's great pupil, Alessandro Volta, was deeply impressed by Franklin's discoveries in electricity and visited him frequently in Paris in 1782, and Franklin was honored by election to membership in the learned societies of Padua (1781), Turin (1783), and Milan (1786). Though his hope of traveling to Italy was never fulfilled, Franklin contributed substantially to the development of electrical science in that country.[18]

Franklin's diplomatic role in France shifted the interest of Italians from his scientific to his political achievements. The example of the unification and victory of thirteen sovereign states, in which he was represented as the prime mover,[19] gave impetus once again among Italian thinkers and historians to the old dream of a united Italy, a modern Roman republic. His civic spirit, incorruptibility, statesmanship, and wisdom were compared to the ancient Roman virtues and cited as an inspiration to Italian patriots. But with the advent of Napoleon and, after his fall, of Metternich, neither of whom could tolerate Franklin's subversive common sense and hatred of arbitrary power, the adulation of his political disciples had to be muted. Under these circumstances malleable Poor Richard passed through an Italian assimilation. The frugality, industry, and self-discipline he preached were now needed to make Italy a modern nation. It is not surprising therefore that the printing of biographies of Franklin was forbidden by the Austrian censor.

It was safer, and perhaps just as effective, to convert Franklin, the political teacher, to Franklin, the "paragon of . . . patriotically inspired educators,"[20] for, in the words of an unknown patriot, "the beginning and base of every social improvement is popular education."[21] Nationalists, commenting on the place of Franklin in the history of the American people, pointedly observed that, through his newspaper and almanac, he "became one of their principal educators before being one of their most glorious liberators.[22]

In a beguiling effort to uplift the common people, *The Way to Wealth* was reprinted in Italy 100 times between 1815 and 1817 and during the next half-century was extensively used in popular and elementary education, often in conjunction with selections from his other writings and particularly his self-teaching moral project. In families as well as in schools, Franklin was regarded as an invaluable guide for parent and child. In presenting a Franklin miscellany as a gift to her son on his twelfth birthday, a devoted Italian mother wrote: "I have read repeatedly the little essays of the immortal Benjamin Franklin and tried to the best of my ability to absorb his every teaching, both for my own profit and in order better to educate you."[23]

The "Free Propaganda" society of Turin, organized in 1850 to distribute free books to workers and peasants in an ambitious program of mass education, included *The Way to Wealth* and a short life of Franklin in its list. Through school readers several generations of schoolchildren were nurtured on the precepts of Poor Richard and the example of the poor boy who was born like them in obscurity and rose by hard work, ability, and adherence to moral principles to gain a glorious name as "benefactor of his fellows, his country, and the whole human race."[24] He was extolled in similar vein in prose and verse and honored as one of the great "teachers of the people."[25]

As Risorgimento, the movement for Italian national independence, acquired momentum, the spirit of Franklin manifested itself again in high places and low. Cavour, whose resourceful diplomacy prepared the way for the unification of Italy, had been an ardent student and admirer of Franklin from the age of fourteen, and especially of his crucial diplomatic career in France. The wooden steamboat in which Garibaldi was carried across the Straight of Messina to open his campaign for the liberation of southern Italy was named the "Franklin," and the guerrilla leader who helped Garibaldi's Redshirts on their forced march to Naples used the alias of "Franklin."[26]

After unification and the end of the long period of repression, the Italians could give free rein to the adoration of their American idol. Streets were named in his honor, and children were saddled with appellations like Franklin Colamanico.[27] Books about Franklin were frequently given as school prizes. A translation of the new complete Bigelow text of the *Autobiography* went through ten editions from 1869 to 1903.

The rising workers' movement of these years found another facet of the Franklin image congenial. The story of the printer's apprentice and journeyman, presented in a new aspect as "the great American worker,"[28] was told in educational publications designed to inspire workers seeking to better their lot, whether in evening schools or self-study.

The influence of Franklin in Italy suffered a marked decline in the twentieth century prior to the Second World War. Franklin's open frontier society, untroubled by the insufficiency of natural resources, extreme class inequality, overpopulation, and unemployment of modern Italy, seemed utterly remote and his teachings quite inapplicable, with a few exceptions. His untarnished example was still invoked by those who called for a sense of responsibility in exercising the right of free speech and by those who believed that honesty and sincerity in the pursuit of the general welfare were in the long run "practical" assets in democratic politics.

During the Fascist period, Franklin again became a symbol of protest against a repressive regime. His *Autobiography* appeared in fresh translations in 1925 and 1938, and there was a surge of interest in original Franklin documents as well as in his contribution to the development of electrical science in Italy, his political relations with the Italian states, and his career as a man of letters. In the economic and moral disorder attending the collapse of fascism, many Italians turned back once more to the spirit of *Poor Richard* for the way to independence and self-respect,[29] like the one who wrote in a pamphlet on the life of Franklin:

Fellow worker: at this moment in which the world is so disturbed and upset, we offer you this humble but precious little book. Democracy, justice, liberty are ideals to which everyone aspires. But if you expect everything from outside, you will remain confused, you will understand little, construct little. Use your own forces, build yourself. Your future is in your hands, in what you do.[30]

As in Italy and France, Franklin's spectacular experiments in electricity, translated into German in 1758, first catapulted him to fame in Germany. Goethe remembered that he had learned about them as a child.[31] He was almost seventeen years old at the time of Franklin's visit to Germany in the summer of 1766 and may have been thinking of that time and event when he wrote in the autobiographical *Dichtung und Wahrheit (Poetry and Truth)* that in his youth he had been tremendously impressed by Franklin's "deep insight and emancipated outlook" and encouraged by his phenomenal career.[32]

In 1791, the year the French translation of the *Autobiography* was published, Goethe and his friends, Herder and Wieland, started their own Junto, which they named the "Friday Club" (The Junto met Friday evenings). At its first meeting the "Rules" Franklin had drawn up for the club were reverently read. But the Friday Club was largely a synthetic copy of the original model. Its founders were not poor young men, meeting to improve their limited education and harness it to the task of making their pioneer town a better place for its inhabitants, including themselves. They were highly educated middle-aged writers of great influence living under ducal patronage in Weimar, a town going back to medieval times. However, stirred by the recent death of Franklin, who had demonstrated what one man of genius and dedication could do for his country, these nationalist poets were also planning to do what they could to advance the cause of a united Germany. The Junto spirit and method seemed to be as universally adaptable as its creator. Herder sensed this gift of Franklin—"his sturdy understanding, his clear and beautiful spirit, . . . his humanitarian character."[33]

Franklin's teachings evoked a less popular and passionate response in Germany than in France or Italy, but their influence remained at a more constant level. In addition to biographies, at least eighty editions of his works, including nine editions of *The Way to Wealth,* were published in German between 1758 and 1900, both for the general public and for elementary and trade schools,[34] and, with rare exceptions, he was extolled by many poets, novelists, and historians.

The twentieth century brought little outward change in his reputation, but disclosed a fading of the familiar image in the new united industrial Germany. He was still regarded as one of the greatest founders of American freedom and literature and as the "teacher of mankind,"[35] but at the beginning of the century the cultural tide was running more often from the new dynamic nation on the North Sea toward the shores of the long-established United States.

In spite of the two great wars between the United States and Germany and the intervening Nazi blight, the indestructible Franklin influence survived as a bond between the two peoples. During the worldwide celebration of the 250th anniversary of his birth in 1956, the

West German government established a Benjamin Franklin Scholarship at Franklin and Marshall College in Pennsylvania for the education of the German youth of the state; as a citizen of the world, he was further honored by the building of the Benjamin Franklin Kongress Halle in Berlin for international conferences;[36] and he was widely commemorated in the press, in films, on radio, and in public addresses as "America's great scholar and statesman," the founder of the first German-language newspaper in the colonies, the champion of a free press, and a pioneer in politics as well as in science.[37]

The influence of Franklin likewise survived the bitter family quarrel of the American War of Independence. His friends and some of his adversaries in England, numbering among them many of the best men and women in the country, knew that he hated war and loved old England, the England of liberty under law, of Locke and Newton and Chatham. They regarded him therefore as a reluctant enemy who had done his utmost to avert the conflict, who had wept at the dreadful prospect of its imminence. They remembered his humane orders to American commanders at sea when Captain Cook's ship was known to be on its way home from the Pacific, and they recalled his efforts after the war to promote a spirit of reconciliation between the two English nations.

That memory remained fresh, with a few exceptions, during the century and a half after Franklin's death, manifesting itself in the popularity of his writings and the judgments of the most distinguished critics, scientists, historians, and diplomats.[38] His hope of reconciliation between the two peoples was gradually realized in a tacit alliance during the nineteenth century and in an open partnership in the two global wars of this century. The wisdom of his imperial policy was recognized and applied in the building of the second British Empire in the last century and in the dismantling of it in this century. Today the house on Craven Street in which Franklin lived and worked in London is a shrine for Americans and Englishmen alike. An occasional discordant note has been sounded, attracting widespread attention because it was so rare, as when the brilliant but unbalanced D. H. Lawrence, while confessing that he admired Franklin, attacked him with a virulence that bordered on hallucination and gave the impression that Franklin had become for him the embodiment of everything that he hated in himself, America, and the human race.[39]

One would expect that the upheaval set off by World War I and climaxed in World War II—the emergence of the United States as the strongest and richest nation in the world and of Soviet Russia as the dynamic center of the ideology of proletarianism, together with the explosion of science, technology, and population, and the revolution in religion and morals—would have overwhelmed Franklin, the apostle of reason, democracy, accommodation, Puritan morality, and the rising middle class, and reduced him to an irrelevant historical figure.

But this volcanic period has witnessed a great revival of interest in him. Scholars have studied more deeply special aspects of his multiple talents and achievements. A monumental definitive collection of all his works, letters, papers, and miscellaneous writings, meticulously edited and annotated, is in process of publication under the joint auspices of Yale University and the American Philosophical Society. Eighteen volumes have been published since 1959, and it is estimated that the complete edition will embrace about forty volumes! In the freer relations and perhaps better understanding between the sexes of our era, the reservation about his moral character which caused his Victorian admirers to misconstrue his unconventional friendships with women of charm and intelligence, and to censor his Rabelaisian literary trifles, has dissolved into another instance of his being far ahead of his time. In general, American biographers have placed a greater stress on his true character and personality, in that way restoring the man behind the myth, and yet the myth has not been diminished. As in life, the better one knew him, the more one loved him and the greater he appeared. It would be difficult to find in history another man of his genius and greatness who was as human and heart-winning as he.

In 1956 the celebration of the 250th anniversary of Franklin's birth dramatized the extraordinary depth and breadth of his influence on the minds and lives of men in his own country and the rest of the world. More than a thousand groups in seventy-two countries voluntarily joined in the tribute. In Europe, Asia, Africa, and South America there was an unprecedented spontaneous outpouring of veneration and affection. Argentina, Brazil, Peru, Chile, Yugoslavia, Rumania, Russia, Egypt, Morocco, Iran, China, Japan, Indonesia, and Pakistan were among the nations participating in the anniversary.

Franklin's humanity and religious tolerance, his faith in the common man, his love of scientific advancement, and his hatred of war were honored. Tributes were paid to him as an inspiration to those who fought for national independence and social reform. Everywhere, the teachings of Franklin on behalf of the poor, the disfranchised, and the disinherited were carried to the schools and the people by reprints of his writings, and by pamphlets, books, newspapers, magazines, lectures, films, and radio.

In the United States, the anniversary year was a time of reviewing and reassessing Franklin and America a century and a half after the death of one and the Constitutional birth of the other. Clearly he had entered into the history and spirit and character of this country as no other American. In the decade before the American Revolution the creator of *Poor Richard,* founder of the American Philosophical Society and the Academy, American scientist and inventor, defender of the people of Pennsylvania against the proprietors and the French, framer of the Albany Plan, reorganizer of the American postal system, agent of America in London, and witness for America at the examination on the Stamp Act in the House of Commons, who had been teaching the people of the colonies to think and act American for thirty years, was universally hailed as "the Father of His Country."

Fortunately, Franklin lived long enough to make an even greater contribution to the establishment of the United States. He was the wise old pilot in the activities of the second Continental Congress and the evolution of independence; his diplomacy and character provided the money, the guns, the ships, and the alliance with France that gave the weak Congress and its strong leaders the means to hold together in spite of inexperience and limited powers, and afforded Washington the opportunity to exercise his military genius and extraordinary force of character; the Albany Plan served as the prototype of a federal structure in the deliberations of the Constitutional Convention; and the wisdom and authority of Franklin kept the convention from breaking up at several points of crisis and helped to bring about the adoption of the Constitution.

Franklin, living on in the unparalleled story of his life told by himself and filled out by others, in the institutions he sponsored, and in the ideals and ideas he consistently promoted, has inspired and guided every generation of Americans ever since Poor Richard made his unheralded appearance in Philadelphia in 1733. He has lived on in the lives of countless Americans born in poverty who raised themselves by force of character, hard work, ability, and luck to independence and self-respect and in a great many cases, for example, Harry S Truman,[40] to positions of eminence and service. He has lived on in the lives of men who dedicated themselves to bettering the education of the young and the mature, to the advancement of science and invention for the benefit of mankind, to raising the political and economic status of the common people, to the abolition of slavery and the education of the former slaves, to the cause of tolerance and peace.

He has lived on in the standards he set for the freedom and responsibility of the press, in the high level of integrity that he exemplified in personal relations, business, and politics, in the sense of social responsibility of democratic American capitalism—"richesse oblige," and in the doctrine of self-reliance and free mutual association for worthy purposes as against complete dependence on government.

He has lived on in the innumerable offspring of the Junto, the Library Company, the Union Fire Company, the American Philosophical Society, and "the Association": in our service clubs, our chautauquas, our symphony orchestras, our opera companies, our museums, our learned societies, our "grass roots" organizations, our consumer groups, our tenant associations, our labor unions, our foundations, and the countless other popular institutions that share with government the vast and complex task of maintaining and improving the democratic American way of life.

Pervading the myriad patterns, forms, and activities which constituted the legacy of Franklin was a way of looking at life and education that he lived and taught. It had grown out of his American roots and was so sensitive to, and representative of, American life and character that its vitality shows hardly any signs of abatement after nearly two hundred years. It was an attitude and a faith compounded of many elements common to him and his fellow Americans: the Puritan heritage, the Quaker association, the pioneer experience, the best English political traditions, and the scientific and reforming spirit of the European Enlightenment, all enriched and transformed by his own gifts of mind and heart.

All these factors interacted and fused to create a new American man and society: committed to trying to live by God's commandments; self-reliant, but ready to engage in mutual help; valuing practical ability and dependable character regardless of creed, previous nationality, or social position; working hard to convert open opportunity to economic and personal independence and buoyed by numerous examples of success; accustomed to making personal decisions and participating in community decisions; taught by the challenges of nature and life, but recognizing the importance of training and knowledge and the new science in the struggle to make a better life for the individual and a better society; and over the years slowly learning to forge unity out of diversity.

The new man and the new society succeeded in founding the United States upon the revolutionary political ideal of government of the people, by the people, and for the people. Franklin, with the uncanny simplicity that concealed the subtlety and depth of his thought and action, foresaw that the political ideal was unrealizable without the sustaining revolutionary ideal of education also of, for, and by the people.

Generation after generation has labored to carry forward these mutually dependent ideals, both of which have had rough going at times. But still the basic ideals, principles, institutions, and methods of education advanced by Franklin and adapted to changing conditions, have been realized to an astonishing extent in the development of the vast and varied American educational enterprise, without parallel past or present, and are partly responsible for the vitality and greatness of the American people. The seeds that Franklin planted in the fertile American soil have proved to be hardy and adaptable to different conditions and have borne good fruit in each generation.

Last and not least, Franklin understood the part that public-spirited newspapers, magazines, and other journalistic publications can play in the education of the people. His *Gazette* and *Poor Richard's Almanack*, his letters to the press, and his timely pamphlets on current issues were potent instruments of popular education in his hands, and he would have been delighted as a teacher of the people to have had the additional use of the audiovisual tools that modern science has given us—recorder, film, radio, and television. He would have said that they should make it easier for us to to keep our republic and that therefore they impose a great responsibility on those who wield them.

A footnote may be added here to set forth another instance of the strange, almost fateful, identification of Franklin with the American people and vice versa: the observation that the life of Franklin seems to foreshadow their history, both falling naturally into four parts: the early years of exploration and discovery, the years of independence and expansion, the middle years of emancipation from parochial limitations, and the late years of world influence.

Confronted with the evidence of the immense impact of Franklin on the American character and way of life and on the lives of men on every continent striving to free themselves and their countrymen from poverty, ignorance, self-contempt, and tyranny, one is inescapably drawn to replace the title that was duly transferred from him to another great American, our first commander-in-chief and president, with an equally just title, MENTOR OF AMERICA AND MANKIND, which Benjamin Franklin still is and promises to be for a long time to come.

CHAPTER 6

Guide on Education and Other Problems Today: An Extrapolation

TO the extent that history is the record of man's frailties, it seems to repeat itself, as events of the last few years in the United States and the rest of the world have demonstrated. In such circumstances the wisdom and relevance of many of Franklin's teachings become remarkably manifest. He was a master in dealing with the events of his own time, and few men saw as clearly as he the universals which underlay them and which were therefore likely to appear again. Here are some examples whose recent topical reference is obvious.

Today we deeply feel his conviction that *"truth, sincerity and integrity* in dealings between man and man, were of the utmost importance to the felicity of life";[1] and also the analogy suggested by his description of the British government in 1758: "[The nation] . . . knows and feels itself so universally corrupt and rotten from head to foot that it has little confidence in any public men."[2] Again, we are closer to accepting his concern for the common man and his "dislike of everything that tended to debase the spirit of the common people."[3] Franklin was also aware of the potential peril in the rapid development of science without a parallel moral improvement of mankind: "It is impossible to imagine the height to which may be carried . . . the power of man over matter. . . . O that moral science were in as fair a way of improvement, . . . and that human beings would at length learn what they now improperly call humanity!"[4] He further observed that ". . . there are two passions which have a powerful influence on the affairs of men. They are ambition and avarice; the love of power and the love of money. Separately each of these has a great force in prompting men to action; but when united in view of the same object, they have in many minds the most violent effects."[5]

We can understand his warning concerning monarchy: ". . . there is a natural inclination in mankind to kingly government . . . I am apprehensive therefore, perhaps too apprehensive that the government of these States, may in future times, end in a monarchy."[6] And his opinion of unjustified war is a sore reminder: "A highwayman is as much a robber when he plunders in a gang as when single; and a nation that makes an unjust war is only a great gang."[7] Also, his appeal to common sense and to compassion in condemning war moves us more than ever: "What vast additions to the conveniences and comforts of living might mankind have acquired, if the money spent in wars had been employed in works of public utility . . . [instead of] destroying the lives of so many . . . working people, who might have performed . . . useful labour!"[8] Finally, his admonition to the people of the United States strikes a relevant note today: "Let us beware . . . of being both enervated and impoverished by luxury; of being weakened by internal contentions and divisions."[9]

Indeed, there is hardly a major problem today that Franklin did not anticipate in his writings by specific or implied reference, or that his wisdom cannot illuminate directly or indirectly. A city dweller himself, he was conscious of urban problems, of the need for city planning and the refreshment of nature. A student of medicine, he was concerned about the effects of air pollution on the health of the community in semirural Philadelphia as well as in industrial Manchester, England. A believer in the rights and responsibilities of man, he advocated justice for minorities and help for undeveloped countries. He supported a project to assist the natives of New Zealand in these plain words:

With all my heart I would subscribe to a voyage intended to communicate, in general, those benefits which we enjoy to countries destitute of them in the remote parts of the globe . . . Many voyages have been undertaken with views of profit or of plunder . . . But a voyage is now proposed, to visit a distant people on the other side [sic] the globe; not to cheat them, not to rob them, not to seize their lands, or enslave their persons; but merely to do them good, and make them, as far as in our power lies, to live as comfortably as ourselves.[10]

At the heart of Franklin's life and works is an article of faith that he extracted from the Puritan creed of his family in Boston and adapted for personal and secular purposes: "The most acceptable service of God . . . [is] the doing good to man."[11] From the time of his youth this deceptively simple credo permeated the many facets of his extraordinary personality and career. It both expanded and contracted the sphere of his thinking and acting. It led him to embrace all mankind and our "beautiful and admirable" planet in his outlook; but, by making the good of mankind the focus of his energies, it also restrained him from engaging in man's equally persistent quest for the "flaming ramparts" within himself and nature. It is one of the primary sources (with or without the approbation of God) of the immense influence that he exerted during his lifetime and that he has continued to have in all parts of the world. Let us sample some of its ramifications as they impinge on several present-day problems.

I *Welfare Projects*

Helping people is a difficult and complex matter, as leaders of philanthropic foundations and welfare societies can testify. Since resources are always limited, one must select projects that will do the most good and the least harm in the long run, or, to use Franklin's often repeated expression, that will be the "most useful." He was well aware of the problem. In a letter to Peter Collinson in 1753, he remarked: "To relieve the misfortunes of our fellow creatures is concurring with the Deity, 'tis God-like." But he cautioned against doing it in a way that might "provide encouragements for laziness and supports for folly. . . ."[12] He refused to support good projects that were poorly planned, as, for example, the orphanage that the evangelist George Whitefield proposed to establish in Georgia.[13] In other instances, such as the Pennsylvania Hospital, he rescued a sound project from failure with his "head, hands, heart, and purse," which represent essential factors in helping others—generosity, intelligence, hard work, and money, one's own, if available, as well as others'.

Intelligence is necessary not only in selecting and planning, but also in realizing the plan. For example, Franklin learned in organizing the Library Company of Philadelphia that it was inadvisable to present oneself as "the proposer of any useful project that might be suppos'd to raise one's reputation in the smallest degree above that of one's neighbours, when one has need of their assistance to accomplish that project."[14] Thereafter, he always kept himself out of sight as much as he could in such projects.

Another use of intelligence is convincing the beneficiary that the benefaction is in his best interest. This is not always self-evident. Therefore, when the project was a matter of public concern, as in the case of the Hospital, Franklin would first seek to educate the public "by writing on the subject in the newspapers, which was . . . his usual custom in such cases."[15]

II Aim of Education

The necessity of general as well as *ad hoc* education was a corollary of Franklin's basic credo. He wrote to Dr. Samuel Johnson, first president of Columbia College, when he was engaged in setting up the Academy in Philadelphia, ". . . that nothing is of more importance for the public weal [i.e., welfare], than to form and train up youth in wisdom and virtue. Wise and good men are, in my opinion, the strength of a state: much more so than riches or arms."[16] In his program for the Academy he declared: "The idea of what is *true merit*, should . . . be often presented to youth, explain'd and impress'd on their minds, as consisting in an *inclination* join'd with an *ability* to serve mankind, one's country, friends and family; which *ability* is . . . to be acquir'd or greatly encreas'd by *true learning;* and should indeed be the great *aim* and *end* of all learning."[17]

He believed that a "useful" education would appeal to the natural idealism of youth. Perhaps our educational programs have been more successful in this respect than we realize. A recent letter to the New York *Times* from the executive of a populous upstate New York county asserts that the desire of college youth today for "self-fulfillment" represents a desire to contribute to the welfare of their fellowmen as well as to help themselves.[18] Whether they know it or not, they may be confirming the truth of Poor Richard's observation: "When you're good to others, you are best to yourself."[19]

III Democracy—The Dignity of the Common Man

It was inevitable that Franklin's commitment to the welfare of mankind would entail his seeking to improve the condition of the common people, who were generally poor and without influence at that time. His concern for them was rooted not only in his article of faith, but also in the deeply felt personal experience of having been born one of them and subjected to the same disabilities. "Having been poor is no shame," Poor Richard observed, "but being ashamed of it, is."[20] Once he had found the way through self-education to raise himself to independence and self-respect, he felt compelled to help them as he had helped himself. He began locally with the Junto and continued with his newspaper, the subscription library, and his almanac.

Franklin's determination to promote "the general welfare" was bound to bring him into public service and politics. He was a refreshingly different kind of politician, for he had become convinced as a result of his youthful mistakes that he could not respect himself or win the respect of others unless he was able to act consistently in accordance with universally accepted ethical principles, among which he stressed "truth, sincerity and integrity." He once advised a young man who was preparing for a public career that "one who would persuade people to follow his advice . . . [must pursue] such a course of action in the conduct of life, as would impress them with an opinion of his integrity, as well as of his understanding; that, this opinion once established, all the difficulties, delays, and oppositions, usually occasioned by doubts and suspicions, were prevented."[21] He noted further that "A good example is the best sermon."[22]

Franklin remained in public service, though he disliked the contentious nature of politics, because it "would enlarge . . . [his] power of doing good," but he added frankly, "I would not however insinuate that my ambition was not flatter'd."[23] Being honest with himself as with others, he could draw a clear line between the public interest and his own—an uncommon occurrence in the political arena, he noted, where ". . . few . . . act from a meer view of the good of their country, whatever they may pretend; . . . men primarily consider'd that their own and their country's interest was united . . . [and] fewer still in public affairs act with a view to the good of mankind."[24]

In political, as in philanthropic, projects, Franklin used the press to educate the people on their "true interest," identifying himself with "the common people in general" against the power centers of Pennsylvania as early as 1729, when he published his pamphlet on paper currency. He remained faithful to the interest of the common people throughout his life, regardless of personal risk—for instance, in the Association for the defense of Pennsylvania (1747); in his passionate appeal to humanity and reason in *A Narrative of the Late . . . [Indian] Massacres* (1764); and at the Constitutional Convention (1787), where, among his "useful" contributions, he successfully opposed property qualifications for the suffrage, declaring that "we should not depress the virtue & public spirit of our common people."[25] Three years before he died he founded the Society for Political Enquiries as an instrument for advancing "the general welfare." "The arduous and complicated science of government," he said, with an eye to the future, had been left too long "to the care of practical politicians or the speculations of individual theorists."[26]

IV *Freedom of Speech and the Press*

The use of a free press to inform and educate the people was an integral part of Franklin's program and method of serving mankind. He stated plainly in his autobiography that he regarded his almanac as "a proper vehicle for conveying instruction among the common people" and his newspaper as "another means of communicating instruction."[27] When he served in London as agent of Pennsylvania and several other colonies, his letters to the press were a potent weapon in his advocacy of the American interest, as they were later, when he represented the United States in Paris. At sixteen, he wrote in *Silence Dogood,* quoting *The London Journal:*

Without freedom of thought, there can be no such thing as wisdom; and no such thing as publick liberty, without freedom of speech; which is the right of every man, as far as by it, he does not hurt or controul the right of another: And this is the only check it ought to suffer, and the only bounds it ought to know . . . in those wretched countries where a man cannot call his tongue his own, he can scarce call anything else his own.[28]

Franklin appreciated the risks involved in freedom of speech and of the press. The remedy, in his opinion, was not repression for the sake of "security," an immemorial excuse, ("He that's secure is not safe," Poor Richard observed)[29] but reasonable self-restraint. He confided to his readers in the *Pennsylvania Gazette:*

I myself have constantly refused to print anything that might countenance vice, or promote immorality; tho' by complying in such cases . . . I might have got much money. I have also always refus'd to print such things as might do real injury to any person, how much soever I have been solicited, and tempted with offers of great pay . . . if all the people of different opinions in this province would engage to give me as much for not printing things they don't like, as I can get by printing them, I should probably live a very easy life; and if all printers were every where so dealt by, there would be very little printed. . . . I consider the variety of humours among men, and despair of pleasing every body; yet I shall not therefore leave off printing. . . . I shall not burn my press and melt my letters.[30]

V *Revolt against Science*

Franklin wrote to Joseph Priestley in 1780: "The rapid progress true science now makes, occasions my regretting sometimes that I was born so soon. It is impossible to imagine the height to which may be carried, in a thousand years, the power of man over matter."[31] He could not have anticipated that it would take only two hundred years, not a thousand. But he did foresee the danger inherent in scientific progress unless there was a concurrent improvement of "moral science" and "human beings would learn what they now improperly call humanity."[32]

In his scientific work, as in everything else that he did, Franklin's constant aim was the good of humanity. While he recognized that the free pursuit of "true science," that is, pure science, was essential for the advancement of knowledge, whether or not a "useful" end was indicated at the outset, he believed that the welfare of people should be the criterion and goal of scientific study and experiment. He confessed to Peter Collinson in the earlier stage of his electrical experiments that he was "chagrin'd a little that we have hitherto been able to discover nothing in this way of use to mankind."[33] It was a great satisfaction to him later that the experiments led to his invention of the lightning rod.

Franklin's pragmatic subordination of science to human welfare without derogation to the spirit of free theoretical inquiry appears in his *Proposal for Promoting Useful Knowledge* through the formation of the American Philosophical Society. He hoped that the Society would encourage studies and experiments that not only "tend to increase the power of man over matter, and multiply the conveniencies or pleasures of life," but also "let light into the nature of things." He achieved this synthesis in his own scientific studies without apparent difficulty.

From a personal rather than a general perspective, this dialectical responsibility of science was stated candidly by Franklin in a letter to "Polly" Stevenson: "There is no rank in natural knowledge of equal dignity and importance with that of being a good parent, a good child, a good husband, or wife, a good neighbour or friend, a good . . . citizen."[34] Is it naive to think that the current disillusionment with science would not have arisen had this responsibility been a cardinal principle of the scientific community?

Franklin himself practiced a morality of science that was consistent with his principles of truth, sincerity, and integrity and that had a marked influence on many other scientists of his time and on the emerging unwritten code of ethics in science. A typical example is found in one of his letters to Collinson detailing his experiments and theories on electricity, in which he acknowledged that in some further experiments made since those described in two previous letters

I have observ'd a phenomenon or two that I cannot at present account for on the principles laid down in those letters, and am therefore become a little diffident of my hypothesis, and asham'd that I have express'd myself in so positive a manner. In going on with these experiments, how many pretty systems do we build, which we soon find ourselves oblig'd to destroy! If there is no other use discover'd of electricity, this, however, is something considerable, that it may *help to make a vain man humble.*[35]

VI Crisis of Education

Franklin did not and could not foresee the vast apparatus of education, public and private, that has developed in this country nor the problems that it has produced, since it is a phenomenon entirely unparalleled in the history of civilization. We know, however, as his friend Condorcet, the French philosopher, attested, that Franklin "did not want any class of citizen to remain without instruction." It is therefore not unreasonable to assume that he would be pleased, as well as astonished, by the awesome development of his ideal of education for all. Though the realization has gone far beyond anything he could imagine, it would not seem quite strange to him, for it bears the imprint in many ways of the ideas and innovations that were embodied in his own self-education and in his educational projects for others.

Probably the most valuable contribution Franklin has made to education is that he broadened the conception of education to mean a process that is a function of life and society, only one part of which goes on in school. Good education cannot be divorced from life. It *is* life and at the same time a continuous preparation for a better life. Franklin's education began years before he entered the Boston Latin School and continued after he was compelled to leave school. He went on learning and growing as long as he lived.

Franklin's original plan for the Academy in Philadelphia, therefore, was designed to create a "useful" model that would bring the education of youth in school closer to the mainstream of Colonial life in America in the mid-eighteenth century. The major step was to make English rather than Latin and Greek the required basic subject for all students, with Latin and Greek (and modern foreign languages) reserved for those who would need them or "have an ardent desire to learn them . . . their English, arithmetick, and other studies absolutely necessary, being at the same time not neglected."[36] His chief authority for this radical shift was the renowned English philosopher, John Locke, whose treatise on the proper education of gentlemen in England was adapted by Franklin; he accepted this and other features of Locke's views to meet the needs of youth and society in colonial Pennsylvania.

The course of study that he outlined included reading, writing, and speaking English, arithmetic and geometry, history, literature, and science,[37] supplemented by physical exercise—"running, leaping, wrestling, and swimming, &c.";[38] the study of "mechanicks"[39] and "excursions . . . to the neighbouring plantations of the best farmers"[40] for observation of their methods. In addition, the students should have access to a well-equipped school or town library.

Franklin intended that the course of study should impart "useful" knowledge and skills, but its fundamental aim was to develop character and the desire to serve others. As he had written in one of his early essays, it is "of much more real advantage" to a man to have acquired self-control, temperateness, fortitude, prudence, and the other qualities of a sound, sturdy character "than to be a master of all the arts and sciences in the world beside."[41] Education meant more to Franklin than the acquisition of knowledge and skills.

Unfortunately, educational tradition and habit proved for the time to be too strong. Franklin's original plan was soon converted, with some features retained, to an academy with two divisions, the Latin and Greek School and the English School, and the English School was consistently neglected and allowed to shrivel away.[42]

However, beginning with the third decade of the nineteenth century, Franklin's original Academy served, with necessary modifications, as a model for secondary schools in the United States until the First World War and the Depression of the 1930s. The war encouraged the expansion of public vocational high schools; and the depression spurred the unprecedented introduction of compulsory education for all to the age of seventeen. There followed varied attempts to adapt free public education to this momentous change. We had finally accepted the validity of Franklin's concept of education as a process of adaptation to changes in life and society.

But, like Franklin, we have been disappointed in our expectations. Though many of those who would have left school at fourteen or fifteen have benefited from the changes in education, many others in school and college now feel that they are getting an education that does not seem useful or satisfying to them or to society. It may be that, in spite of all the changes, the schools are still under the influence of the academic tradition, whereas a large number of their students are not inclined in that direction. They are like the misplaced farmers' sons at Harvard satirized in Franklin's fourth *Silence Dogood* essay.

In the face of this fairly widespread dissatisfaction, much might be gleaned from Franklin's life and his philosophy of education to help us work our way out of our present difficulties. Perhaps, following his practice in time of crisis and confusion, we should initiate a voluntary "association" of the best minds, representing all classes and the major groups of the population, to consider the critical problem created by recent social changes and universal education and to propose a useful plan of education that would take into account the varied needs, talents, and abilities of the young and the aims and needs of our society. While the association might be guided, as Franklin was, by outstanding educational authorities and philosophers, past and present, it would be wise to follow his example and adapt their recommendations to the realities of the present and the probabilities of the future.

The principles of education that Franklin applied in the original plan of the Academy and in his other educational projects still deserve serious study and consideration. Only a few of these principles can be noted here. (1) Education should be "useful," that is, conducive to the development of a more independent individual and a more vigorous society. (2) The opportunity for education should not be closed to anyone because of financial or other handicaps. (3) Knowledge and skills that are "absolutely necessary" should be imparted to all. (4) Instruction should be "both entertaining [i.e., interesting] and useful."[43] (5) Schools should utilize whatever facilities and resources are available in the community to enrich their programs. (6) Education should provide examples and standards of excellence by means of history and literature. (7) It should be "the great aim and end of all learning" to identify and deliberately foster the qualities of character that will tend to produce a richer personal fulfillment and a more just society.

The integrated "Parkway Program" experiment sponsored in 1972 by The Franklin Institute in Philadelphia (which, incidentally, was partly funded by a practical and wise provision of Franklin's last will and testament) illustrates the continuing influence of these principles and of his concept of education as a function of life and society.

The eight hundred students who were enrolled in this public program were selected by random lottery from applicants from all the school districts and from some suburbs of Philadelphia. The program had no school building of its own and no classrooms. Classes were conducted in churches, business conference rooms, vacant offices, and occasionally in a public lobby. Mechanics was taught in a garage, journalism in a newspaper office. The program also utilized the resources of The Academy of Natural Sciences, The Philadelphia Museum of Art, The Franklin Institute Science Museum and Planetarium, and The

Free Library. One of the most remarkable features of the experiment was that it "is committed to operating at a cost equal to or less than the amount required to operate a conventional high school for a comparable number of students."

The students had to meet state requirements for graduation from high school as well as the usual prerequisites for admission to college. Students were essentially responsible for their own education, for they had to choose among the 100–200 courses offered. The teachers, like the students, were volunteers, half from the public school system, and half nonpaid resource people from center city companies and institutions who taught "with almost 'missionary zeal.' "[44]

Franklin's profound understanding of men, women, and children, his great common sense, and his practical imagination would undoubtedly be of great help to the association in its work though it would, of course, have to ponder and extrapolate in many cases, as, for instance, the implications of his notable remarks on the mental abilities of black children. After a visit in 1763 to "the Negro School" in Philadelphia, he wrote:

> I . . . had the children thoroughly examin'd. . . . I was on the whole much pleas'd, and from what I then saw, have conceiv'd a higher opinion of the natural capacities of the black race, than I had ever before entertain'd. Their apprehension seems as quick, their memory as strong, and their docility [i.e., teachability] in every respect equal to that of white children.[45]

And in 1774 he observed in a letter to Condorcet that Negroes were "not deficient in natural understanding, but they have not the advantage of education."[46]

Conversely, one often comes across statements today that seem to echo Franklin. For example, *The New Yorker* in 1972 published a letter that Ralph J. Bunche, first black recipient of the Nobel Peace Prize, had written to a black mother who had asked for his advice on guiding black youth:

> It seems to me that the way to be a good American is do the best you can on every thing you are called upon to do. When you have done your best you can always feel satisfied and no one can ever justly criticize you for not having done better. Try hard and work hard, always. There is a lot of fun and satisfaction in achievement, in doing things right and doing things well. I must admit that at times, only because of my race, I have worked a little harder just to prove that race has nothing to do with ability or achievement.[47]

VII World Peace

Franklin, by temperament and reason, favored the things that help bring people together and maintain peace, and he disliked those who tend to drive them apart and produce strife. Philadelphia was the laboratory in which he tested these opposing forces and learned the power of education and "voluntary association" for a common purpose; and it was in Philadelphia that he used this power to establish or encourage agencies for promoting peace and resisting conflict.

At the age of twenty-one, he founded the prototypical Junto Club "for mutual improvement" and the common good. It worked so well that four years later, with the assistance of the club members, he was able to form The Library Company. In the same year, as a result of his analysis of history, he came to the conclusion that the nations of the world needed an international Junto for the mutual improvement and advancement of men of "virtue" and good will and for the introduction of morality in international relations!

He intended to undertake this ambitious project, which he considered "a practicable scheme," when "circumstances should afford . . . the necessary leisure."[48] Though he retired from business at forty-two, he never found sufficient leisure because of his "multifarious occupations public and private." Yet his American Philosophical Society may be regarded as a kind of intercolonial Junto, and his extensive correspondence at home and abroad grew into a kind of international Junto.

He tried to ensure peace between the colonies and England by proposing the Albany Plan of Union and later by advocating colonial representation in Parliament, and he did everything in his power to avert a break until the British government resorted to force. While he believed that "there never was a good war or a bad peace,"[49] he was not a fanatical pacifist. He had learned from history and experience that "the way to secure peace is to be prepared for war."[50] The universal yearning for peace between nations will probably remain unfulfilled until a practicable plan is devised and accepted by the leaders and people of the world. When that time comes, the federal principle of Franklin, applied with common sense and wisdom, may show the way to world peace.

After the successful termination of the Constitutional Convention of 1787, Franklin, his hope of international peace buoyed by the great charter of a federation of American states united in peace, wrote to a friend in France recommending that Europe form "a federal union and one grand republick of all its different states & kingdoms; by means of a like Convention."[51]

Recently timid steps have been undertaken to realize Franklin's ideal of a United States of Europe. If we continue in his spirit to work for the things that unite people and oppose those that divide them, we may achieve in our common interest a true world federation of nations. Perhaps it is not much farther away from our time than the United States of America was when an unknown young printer in Philadelphia dreamed of a world society "govern'd by suitable good and wise rules."[52]

VIII *Coda*

Anyone who has been privileged to enjoy the company of Benjamin Franklin for any length of time usually takes leave of him with deep regret. Rarely have men as great as he worn their greatness with such modesty, geniality, and grace, or remained as little corrupted by money, fame, and power, or liked people as heartily and received as much affection in return.

Franklin always felt strongly drawn to young people, particularly to those starting out in life with no advantages other than ability and character; and young people were also drawn to Franklin. They found in his example and teachings unfailing encouragement, and a kindred soul in his ever youthful spirit, his lusty sense of humor, his ineradicable altruism, and his concern for their education and future.

The bond between Franklin and the young remained unbroken after his death and has lasted to the present day, notwithstanding the tremendous changes in the intervening years. He still talks sense to those who are diminished by poverty or prejudice anywhere, and he can still give support and guidance to those who are highly critical, as he was, of traditional education, a life of material pleasure devoid of spiritual fulfillment, the abuses of politics, and the wastefulness of war, and who seem to have lost their way and to be wandering in a wasteland. For such people it would help to read his affable and lucid writings, to observe the means by which he reconciled the impetuosity and idealism of his youth with the realities of an imperfect world, and to become familiar with the qualities of mind and heart that enabled him to reach some of his youthful goals.

Perhaps in this generation of disillusioned, drifting youth, waiting only to be awakened by his extraordinary genius and spirit, there is one who will lead them out of the wasteland and back on to the road that Franklin once traveled, toward the time, as he prayed, when a man will be able to set foot in any land on the peaceful earth and say, "This is my country."[53]

Until then, *ave atque vale*, Doctor Franklin.

Notes and References

The texts followed in the quotations from Franklin's writings are *The Autobiography of Benjamin Franklin* (New Haven & London: Yale University Press, 1964) and, in the case of his other writings, *The Papers of Benjamin Franklin* (New Haven & London: Yale University Press, 1959–) for datings from 1706 through 1771, and *The Writings of Benjamin Franklin*, ed. A. H. Smyth (New York: The Macmillan Company, 1905–1907) for 1772 through 1790. These are cited in the references below as *Autobiography*, *Papers*, and *Writings* respectively. See these entries in the Selected Bibliography. The only changes made by the author in quoting from these texts is the discarding of capitalization of common nouns, a printing convention of Franklin's time which is confusing to the modern reader. Franklin's spelling, punctuation, etc., with occasional inconsistencies, have been retained, as the differences are of minor consequence and do not interfere with ease of reading and comprehension.

Chapter One

1. *The Autobiography of Benjamin Franklin*, ed. Leonard W. Labaree et al. (New Haven & London, 1964), p. 55. (Hereafter cited as *Autobiography*).
2. Ibid., p. 47.
3. Ibid., p. 58.
4. Ibid., p. 57.
5. Letter to Barbeu Dubourg, 1773, *The Writings of Benjamin Franklin*, ed. A. H. Smyth (New York & London, 1905–1907), V, 545. (Hereafter cited as *Writings*).
6. *Autobiography*, p. 60.
7. Ibid., p. 62.
8. "Silence Dogood," No. 1, *The Papers of Benjamin Franklin*, ed. Leonard W. Labaree et al. (New Haven & London, 1959–), I, 9–11. (Hereafter cited as *Papers*).
9. *Autobiography*, pp. 67–68.
10. "Silence Dogood," No. 2, *Papers*, I, 12–13.
11. "Silence Dogood," No. 3, *Papers*, I, 13.
12. "Silence Dogood," No. 4, *Papers*, I, 14–18.
13. "Silence Dogood," No. 9, *Papers*, I, 31.

14. *Autobiography*, p. 69.
15. Ibid., p. 71.
16. Ibid., p. 75.
17. Ibid., p. 80.
18. Ibid., p. 81.
19. Ibid., p. 92.
20. Ibid., p. 95.
21. Ibid., p. 98.
22. Ibid., p. 98.
23. Ibid., p. 102.
24. Ibid., p. 105.
25. Ibid., p. 106.
26. "Journal of a Voyage, 1726," *Papers*, I, 73.
27. Ibid., 78–79.
28. Ibid., 85–86.
29. Ibid., 91.
30. *Autobiography*, p. 106.
31. "Plan of Conduct," *Papers*, I, 99.
32. Ibid., 99–100.
33. *Autobiography*, p. 114.
34. "Journal of a Voyage, 1726," *Papers*, I, 98.
35. *Autobiography*, p. 107.
36. Ibid., p. 107.

Chapter Two

1. *Autobiography*, p. 117.
2. "Standing Queries for the Junto," *Papers*, I, 257–58.
3. Ibid., 260.
4. "Articles of Belief and Acts of Religion," *Papers*, I, 103.
5. Franklin agreed with William Wollaston "that there are many lesser Gods, each in his system like a sun." Carl Van Doren, *Benjamin Franklin* (New York, 1938), p. 80. At Palmer's in London, Franklin had been assigned to serve as compositor for the third edition of Wallaston's *The Religion of Nature Delineated*.
6. See *Papers*, I, 101–9.
7. *Autobiography*, p. 148.
8. Ibid., p. 160.
9. Ibid., pp. 115–16.
10. *Papers*, I, 141.
11. *Autobiography*, p. 119.
12. Ibid.
13. *Pennsylvania Gazette*, June 10, 1729, *Papers*, I, 158–59.

14. Ibid., 159.
15. *Pa. Gazette*, June 10, 1731, *Papers*, I, 196.
16. *Autobiography*, p. 165.
17. *Pa. Gazette*, Oct. 23, 1729, *Papers*, I, 165.
18. *Papers*, I, 194–99.
19. Ibid., 195.
20. Ibid., 194.
21. Ibid., 198–99.
22. *Pa. Gazette*, Dec. 16, 1729, *Papers*, I, 163.
23. *Pa. Gazette*, Mar. 13, 1730, *Papers*, I, 169–70.
24. *Pa. Gazette*, Oct. 22, 1730, *Papers*, I, 183.
25. *Pa. Gazette*, Oct. 9, 1729, *Papers*, I, 160–61.
26. *Pa. Gazette*, Aug. 2, 1733, *Papers*, I, 329.
27. Ibid., 330.
28. *Pa. Gazette*, Nov. 20, 1729, *Papers*, I, 162.
29. "Palatines' Appeal," *Pa. Gazette*, Feb. 15, 1732, *Papers*, I, 226–29.
30. *Pa. Gazette*, Jan. 11, 1733, *Papers*, I, 318–19.
31. "On Conversation," *Pa. Gazette*, Sept. 24, 1730, *Papers*, I, 178–79.
32. *Pa. Gazette*, July 30, 1730, *Papers*, I, 187.
33. *Autobiography*, p. 123.
34. For legal complications, see *Autobiography*, p. 129 and 129n.
35. Letter to Peter Collinson, *Papers*, I, 249.
36. *Autobiography*, p. 142.
37. Ibid., p. 143.
38. Carl Van Doren, *Benjamin Franklin*, p. 105.
39. *Papers*, I, 249n.
40. *Autobiography*, p. 142.
41. Ibid., p. 143.
42. John Albee, "Dudley Leavitt's New Hampshire Almanac," *The New England Magazine*, new series, 17 (1893), 545ff.
43. *Autobiography*, p. 164.
44. *Poor Richard* for 1733, *Papers*, I, 311.
45. Ibid.
46. *Autobiography*, p. 164.
47. *Poor Richard* for 1733, *Papers*, I, 312.
48. Ibid., 317.
49. *Poor Richard* for 1736 and again 1744, *Papers*, II, 142 and 398.
50. *Poor Richard* for 1737, *Papers*, II, 166.
51. "The Busy-Body," No. 1, *Papers*, I, 115.
52. "The Busy-Body," No. 3, *Papers*, I, 119.
53. *Poor Richard* for 1738, *Papers*, II, 197.
54. *Poor Richard* for 1733, *Papers*, I, 314.
55. Ibid., 317.
56. Ibid., 316.

Notes and References

57. *Poor Richard* for 1737, *Papers*, II, 170.
58. *Poor Richard* for 1739, *Papers*, II, 222.
59. *Poor Richard* for 1738, *Papers*, II, 193–94.
60. *Poor Richard* for 1734, *Papers*, I, 353.
61. *Poor Richard* for 1738, *Papers*, II, 197.
62. *Poor Richard* for 1735, *Papers*, II, 9.
63. *Poor Richard* for 1738, *Papers*, II, 192.
64. *Poor Richard* for 1741, *Papers*, II, 295.
65. *Poor Richard* for 1737, *Papers*, II, 167.
66. *Poor Richard* for 1740, *Papers*, II, 253.
67. *Poor Richard* for 1735, *Papers*, II, 9.
68. *Poor Richard* for 1744, *Papers*, II, 399.
69. *Poor Richard* for 1742, *Papers*, II, 336.
70. *Poor Richard* for 1743, *Papers*, II, 368.
71. *Poor Richard* for 1733, *Papers*, I, 310.
72. Ibid., 314.
73. *Poor Richard* for 1742, *Papers*, II, 336.
74. *Poor Richard* for 1739, *Papers*, II, 224.
75. Ibid., 227.
76. *Poor Richard* for 1738, *Papers*, II, 194.
77. *Poor Richard* for 1735, *Papers*, II, 10.
78. *Poor Richard* for 1739, *Papers*, II, 222.
79. *Poor Richard* for 1740, *Papers*, II, 251.
80. *Autobiography*, p. 161.
81. Ibid., pp. 161–62.
82. Ibid., p. 163.
83. Ibid., p. 168.
84. Ibid., p. 169.
85. *Papers*, II, 323.
86. *Autobiography*, p. 127.
87. *Pa. Gazette*, Nov. 25, 1742, *Papers*, II, 365.
88. "Virtue" of Moderation; see *Autobiography*, p. 150.
89. *Autobiography*, p. 176.
90. Ibid., p. 170.
91. *Papers*, II, 419–46.
92. Ibid., 441.
93. *Autobiography*, p. 192.
94. Letter to John Perkins, Feb. 4, 1753, *Papers*, IV, 442. "Fluxions" was a popular term in eighteenth-century mathematics and science, used for the flowing of water, blood, light, variable quantities, etc. (O. E. D.)
95. *Pa. Gazette*, June 5, 1740, *Papers*, II, 286–87 and 286, note 3.
96. *Papers*, II, 380–81.
97. Ibid., 382.
98. Ibid., 382.

99. Letter to C. Colden, Apr. 5, 1744, *Papers*, II, 406–7.
100. Quoted in *Papers*, II, 380 (headnote).
101. *Autobiography*, p. 240.
102. *Pa. Gazette*, Apr. 26 and July 26, 1744, *Papers*, II, 450 and 452.
103. Mar. 28, 1747, *Papers*, III, 118–19.
104. *Autobiography*, p. 241.

Chapter Three

1. Letter to George Whatley, May 23, 1785, *Writings*, IX, 333.
2. Quoted in Carl Van Doren, *Benjamin Franklin*, p. 148.
3. *Papers*, III, 123–24.
4. Ibid., 125.
5. Ibid., 120–21 (headnote).
6. Ibid., 121–22 (headnote).
7. Letter to C. Colden, Sept. 29, 1748, *Papers*, III, 318.
8. *Poor Richard* for 1748, *Papers*, III, 248–49.
9. Ibid., 251.
10. "Idea of the English School," *Papers*, IV, 108.
11. "On the Need for an Academy," *Pa. Gazette*, Aug. 4, 1749, *Papers*, III, 385–88.
12. *Autobiography*, pp. 192–93.
13. "Observations Relative to the Intentions of the Original Founders . . ." (1789), *Writings*, X, 30.
14. Letter to Richard Peters, June 9, 1748, quoted in *Papers*, 186 (headnote).
15. Letter to Thomas Penn, Feb. 17, 1750, quoted in *The Works of Benjamin Franklin*, ed. Jared Sparks, 10 vols. (Boston, 1840), I, 570n.
16. Letter to Ebenezer Kinnersley, July 28, 1759, *Papers*, VIII, 416.
17. "Proposals Relating to the Education of Youth in Pennsylvania," *Papers*, III, 397–421.
18. Ibid., 415.
19. "Idea of the English School," *Papers*, IV, 101–8.
20. "Education of Youth in Pennsylvania," *Papers*, III, 404.
21. Ibid., 400.
22. Letter to Samual Johnson, Aug. 23, 1750, *Papers*, IV, 41.
23. "Intentions of the Original Founders," *Writings*, X, 30.
24. Verner W. Crane, *Benjamin Franklin and a Rising People* (Boston, 1954), p. 41.
25. Letter of Peter Collinson to Franklin, Apr. 25, 1750, *Papers*, III, 476.
26. Letter to Collinson, May 25, 1747, *Papers*, III, 131.
27. Ibid., 127.
28. "Opinions and Conjectures," 1750, *Papers*, IV, 19.

Notes and References

29. *Autobiography*, pp. 244–45, note 8.
30. Letter to Collinson, Apr. 29, 1749, *Papers*, III, 364.
31. Quoted from Priestley's *History and Present State of Electricity* (London, 1767), in *Papers*, IV, 127 (headnote).
32. Quoted in *Autobiography*, p. 244, note 7.
33. Letter to C. Colden, Oct. 31, 1751, *Papers*, IV, 202.
34. Same as note 31 above.
35. Letter to John Lining, Mar. 18, 1755, *Papers*, V, 526.
36. *Papers*, V, 79.
37. Dec. 25, 1950, *Papers*, IV, 83.
38. *Papers*, III, 198–99.
39. Ibid., 199–200.
40. Ibid., 200–201.
41. Ibid., 203–4.
42. Ibid., 195.
43. *Pa. Gazette*, Nov. 26, 1747, *Papers*, III, 239.
44. *Autobiography*, p. 184.
45. Ibid., p. 184.
46. Quoted in *Papers*, III, 185, note 6.
47. "Form of Association," *Papers*, III, 206.
48. Ibid., 206–7.
49. Letter of Thomas Penn to Richard Peters, Mar. 30, 1748, quoted in *Papers*, III, 186 (headnote).
50. Ibid., 208.
51. Ibid., 212.
52. Ibid., 212.
53. Letter to James Parker, Mar. 20, 1751, *Papers*, IV, 118–19.
54. *Autobiography*, p. 210.
55. "Short Hints," *Papers*, V, 337–38.
56. Letter to Parker, *Papers*, IV, 117.
57. Written by Franklin Feb. 9, 1789 and published in *The American Museum*, April 1789; see *Papers*, V, 417 and 398–99 (headnote).
58. Letter to William Shirley, Dec. 4, 1754, *Papers*, V, 443.
59. Letter to William Shirley, Dec. 22, 1754, *Papers*, V, 449–50.
60. Samuel E. Morison, *The Oxford History of the American People* (New York, 1965), p. 162.
61. *Autobiography*, p. 226.
62. Letter to Collinson, June 26, 1755, *Papers*, VI, 86.
63. Letter to Collinson, Aug. 27, 1755, *Papers*, VI, 171.
64. Letter to Deborah Franklin, July 17, 1757, *Papers*, VII, 243.
65. *Poor Richard Improved* for 1758, *Papers*, VII, 340.
66. Ibid., 350.
67. For bibliographical history of famous preface, see headnote on *Poor Richard Improved* for 1758, *Papers*, VII, 326–40.

68. Letter of William Strahan to Deborah Franklin, Dec. 13, 1757, *Papers*, VII, 296.
69. Ibid., 297.
70. Letter to Pa. Assembly, June 10, 1758, *Papers*, VIII, 89.
71. Letter to Charles Norris, Sept. 16, 1758, *Papers*, VIII, 156.
72. Letter to Isaac Norris, June 9, 1759, *Papers*, VIII, 402.
73. Letter to Mary Stevenson, May 17, 1760, *Papers*, IX, 117.
74. Jan. 3, 1760, *Papers*, IX, 9.
75. *The London Chronicle*, Dec. 25–27, 1759, *Papers*, VIII, 451.
76. "The Interest of Great Britain Considered," *Papers*, IX, 90–91.
77. Letter from Thomas Penn to Gov. James Hamilton, Apr. 13, 1761, quoted in *Works of Benjamin Franklin*, ed. J. Sparks, VII, 243n.
78. Mar. 25, 1763, *Papers*, X, 232.
79. Letter to David Hall, Aug. 10, 1762, *Papers*, X, 141.
80. Letter to Franklin, May 10, 1762, *Papers*, X, 81–82.
81. May 19, 1762, *Papers*, X, 83–84.
82. As reported in *The London Chronicle*, Dec. 30, 1762 and Jan. 1, 1763, *Papers*, X, 153, note 1.
83. *Papers*, X, 238.
84. *Papers*, XI, 55.
85. Letter from John Waring, Jan. 24, 1757, *Papers*, VII, 100.
86. Letter to John Waring, Dec. 17, 1763, *Papers*, X, 396.
87. *Papers*, XI, 441.

Chapter Four

1. Letter to Lord Kames, Feb. 25, 1767, *Papers*, XIV, 64.
2. *Gentleman's Magazine*, July 1767, quoted in *Papers*, XIII, 126–27 (headnote).
3. "The Examination," *Papers*, XIII, 133–34.
4. Ibid., 139.
5. Ibid., 148–49.
6. Ibid., 159.
7. *Poor Richard Improved* for 1748, *Papers*, III, 255.
8. Letter to C. Evans, May 9, 1766, *Papers*, XIII, 269.
9. Feb. 25, 1767, *Papers*, XIV, 65, 69–70.
10. Letter to William Franklin, Aug. 28, 1767, *Papers*, XIV, 244.
11. See A. O. Aldridge, *Franklin and his French Contemporaries* (New York, 1957), pp. 23–25.
12. Letter to Pierre S. du Pont de Nemours, July 28, 1768, *Papers*, XV, 181–82.
13. Carl Van Doren, *Benjamin Franklin*, p. 370.
14. Letter to Thomas-François Dalibard, Jan. 31, 1768, *Papers*, XV, 35.

Notes and References

15. Letter to C. Evans, Feb. 20, 1768, *Papers*, XV, 52.
16. "Positions to Be Examined," Apr. 4, 1769, *Papers*, XVI, 109.
17. Jan 5–7, 1768, *Papers*, XV, 3–13.
18. Ibid., 5.
19. Ibid., 12–13.
20. Carl Van Doren, *Benjamin Franklin*, p. 378.
21. Letter to William Franklin, Mar. 13, 1768, *Papers*, XV, 74.
22. Letter to William Franklin, July 2, 1768, *Papers*, XV, 162–63.
23. Letter to Dr. Joshua Babcock, Jan. 13, 1772, *Writings*, V, 362–63.
24. *Writings*, VI, 127.
25. Ibid., 128.
26. Ibid., 136–37.
27. "An Edict by the King of Prussia," *Writings*, VI, 118–24.
28. *Writings*, VI, 174.
29. Letter to Thomas Cushing, Feb. 15, 1774, *Writings*, VI, 186.
30. Ibid., 189.
31. "An Account of Negotiations in London . . . " by Franklin, not published until after his death, *Writings*, VI, 370.
32. Ibid., 394.
33. July 7, 1775, *Mr. Franklin*, ed. L. W. Labaree and W. J. Bell, Jr. (New Haven & London, 1956), p. 30.
34. Oct. 3, 1775, *Writings*, VI, 430.
35. Letter to William Franklin, Aug. 16, 1784, *Memoirs . . . of Benjamin Franklin*, ed. William Temple Franklin, 6 vols., 3rd ed. (London, 1818), I, 311.
36. Quoted by Carl Van Doren, *Benjamin Franklin*, p. 537.
37. Quoted by Carl Van Doren, ibid., p. 537.
38. Quoted by Carl Van Doren, ibid., p. 530.
39. *Writings*, VI, 425.
40. Letter to Don Gabriel of Bourbon, Dec. 12, 1775, *Writings*, VI, 436–37.
41. Quoted by Carl Van Doren, *Benjamin Franklin*, p. 549.
42. *Writings*, VI, 306.
43. *Writings*, X, 301.
44. *Writings*, IX, 696.
45. *Writings*, VIII, 304–5.
46. Carl Van Doren, *Benjamin Franklin*, p. 565.
47. Ibid., pp. 571, 632.
48. *The Works of John Adams*, ed. Charles Francis Adams, 10 vols. (Boston, 1856), I, 660.
49. *Les Affaires de l'Angleterre et de l'Amérique*.
50. Carl Van Doren, *Benjamin Franklin*, p. 574.
51. Ibid., pp. 655–56.
52. Ibid., p. 660.
53. *Writings*, VII, 242–43.

54. Letter to David Hartley, Jan. 15, 1782, *Writings*, VIII, 359.
55. June 27, 1780, *Writings*, VIII, 13.
56. *Writings*, VIII, 606.
57. Ibid., 607.
58. *Writings*, X, 97.
59. *Writings*, IX, 162–63.
60. Aldridge, *Franklin and his French Contemporaries*, pp. 80–83.
61. *The Writings of Thomas Jefferson*, ed. Albert E. Bergh, 20 vols. in 10 (Washington, D.C., 1907), VIII, 129.
62. *Writings*, X, 471.
63. Letter to Jean-Baptiste Le Roy, Apr. 18, 1787, *Writings*, IX, 572–73.
64. Letter to William Hunter, Nov. 24, 1786, *Writings*, IX, 548.
65. Quoted by Carl Van Doren, *Benjamin Franklin*, p. 743.
66. *The Records of the Federal Convention of 1787*, ed. Max Farrand, 1911. Rev. ed., 4 vols. (New Haven & London, 1966), II, 65 (Journal of James Madison).
67. See Julian P. Boyd, *Pennsylvania Magazine of History and Biography* 61 (1937), 233–34.
68. Farrand, op. cit., I, 197 (Journal of James Madison).
69. Farrand, op. cit., II, 641–43.
70. Letter to Mr. Grand, Oct. 22, 1787, Farrand, op. cit., III, 131.
71. *Writings*, X, 87.
72. *Writings*, X, 28–30.
73. Dated Mar. 23, 1790. *Writings*, X, 87–88.
74. Ibid., 88–89.
75. Letter dated July 12, 1788 and translated into English, *Works of Benjamin Franklin*, ed. J. Sparks, X, 355.
76. Letter to Le Roy, Nov. 13, 1789, *Writings*, X, 68–69.
77. Dec. 4, 1789, *Writings*, X, 72.
78. Sept. 16, 1789, *Writings*, X, 41.

Chapter Five

1. Quoted by Carl Van Doren, *Benjamin Franklin*, p. 781.
2. Aldridge, *Franklin and his French Contemporaries*, p. 50.
3. *Autobiography*, pp. 30–31. The title of this famous collection: *Works of the late Doctor Benjamin Franklin: Consisting of His Life Written by Himself, together with Essays, Humorous, Moral, & Literary . . .* , 2 vols., published by G. G. J. and J. Robinson.
4. Letter of Jared Sparks to Miss Storrow, Oct. 16, 1817, quoted in Herbert B. Adams, *Life and Writings of Jared Sparks*, 2 vols. (Boston, 1893), I, 6–7.
5. Antonio Pace, *Benjamin Franklin and Italy* (Philadelphia, 1958), p. 199.
6. Ibid., p. 196.

Notes and References

7. Ibid., p. 197.
8. Quoted in Helen and Clarence Jordan, eds., *Benjamin Franklin's Unfinished Business* (Philadelphia, 1957), p. 112.
9. Ibid., p. 29.
10. "Franklin's Last Will and Testament," *Writings*, X, 503.
11. Richard D. Miles, "The American Image of Benjamin Franklin," *American Quarterly* 9 (1957), 134.
12. Quoted by James Parton, *Life and Times of Benjamin Franklin* (New York, 1864), II, 677–78.
13. Thomas Woody, *Educational Views of Benjamin Franklin* (New York, 1931) p. xiv.
14. Mark Twain, "Memoranda—the late Benjamin Franklin," *Galaxy* 10 (1870), 139–40.
15. Aldridge, *Franklin and his French Contemporaries*, p. 59.
16. Charles A. Sainte-Beuve, *Portraits of the Eighteenth Century*, tr. K. P. Wormely (New York & London, 1905), p. 335.
17. The author is greatly indebted in this segment of the chapter to the deeply researched study of Antonio Pace, *Benjamin Franklin and Italy*, Philadelphia, 1958.
18. Ibid., p. 48.
19. Ibid., p. 173.
20. Ibid., p. 178.
21. Ibid., p. 178.
22. Quoted by Pace, ibid., p. 179.
23. Quoted by Pace, ibid., p. 229.
24. Quoted by Pace, ibid., p. 231.
25. Quoting Cesare Correnti, Pace, ibid., p. 257.
26. Pace, ibid., pp. 182–83.
27. Ibid., p. 302.
28. Ibid., p. 302.
29. Ibid., pp. 312–13.
30. Ibid., p. 313.
31. Beatrice M. Victory, "Benjamin Franklin and Germany," (Ph. D. dissertation, University of Pennsylvania, 1915), p. 112. The author has drawn extensively on this well-documented dissertation in this part of the chapter.
32. Herbert W. Schneider, ed., *Benjamin Franklin: The Autobiography and Selections from His Other Writings* (New York, 1952), p. ix.
33. Victory, quoting Herder, op. cit., p. 117.
34. Ibid., pp. 160–66.
35. Ibid., p. 98, quoting Max Kohn.
36. Jordan & Jordan, eds., *Benjamin Franklin's Unfinished Business*, p. 27.
37. Ibid.
38. For example, Francis Jeffrey's review of *The Works of Dr. Franklin*, *The Edinburgh Review* 8 (July 1806), 327–44; the great chemist, Sir Humphry Davy, in his *Collected Works*, ed. John Davy (London, 1840), VIII, 264–65;

the celebrated historian, George O. Trevelyan, *The American Revolution*, condensed and edited by Richard B. Morris (New York, 1964), pp. 342–60; and Sir Esme Howard, ambassador to the U.S., quoted in J. Henry Smythe, Jr., *The Amazing Benjamin Franklin* (New York, 1929), pp. 10–11.

39. D. H. Lawrence, *Studies in Classic American Literature* (New York, 1923), pp. 13–31.

40. Merle Miller, quoting Truman, in *Plain Speaking* (New York, 1973), pp. 400, 431.

Chapter Six

1. *Autobiography*, p. 114.
2. Letter to Joseph Galloway, Feb. 17, 1758, *Papers*, VII, 375.
3. Carl Van Doren, quoting Franklin, in *The Great Rehearsal* (New York, 1948), p. 143.
4. Letter to Joseph Priestley, Feb. 8, 1780, *Writings*, VIII, 10.
5. Carl Van Doren, quoting Franklin, *The Great Rehearsal*, p. 56.
6. Ibid., p. 57.
7. Letter to Benjamin Vaughan, Mar. 14, 1785, *Writings*, IX, 296.
8. Letter to Sir Joseph Banks, July 27, 1783, *Writings*, IX, 72.
9. Letter to Charles Thomson, May 13, 1784, *Writings*, IX, 213.
10. James Parton, *Benjamin Franklin*, I, 525.
11. *Autobiography*, p. 146.
12. May 9, 1753, *Papers*, IV, 480.
13. *Autobiography*, p. 177.
14. Ibid., p. 143.
15. Ibid., p. 200.
16. Aug. 23, 1750, *Papers*, IV, 41.
17. *Proposals relating to the Education of Youth in Pennsylvania* (1749), *Papers*, III, 419.
18. "What Youth Want," New York *Times*, June 13, 1974, p. 42.
19. *Poor Richard* for 1748, *Papers*, III, 257.
20. *Poor Richard* for 1749, *Papers*, III, 342.
21. Diary of Benjamin Franklin, July 27, 1784, *Writings*, X, 357–58.
22. *Poor Richard* for 1747, *Papers*, III, 104.
23. *Autobiography*, p. 197.
24. Ibid., p. 161.
25. Carl Van Doren, quoting Franklin, *The Great Rehearsal*, p. 142.
26. Carl Van Doren, quoting Franklin, from *The Pennsylvania Packet*, Mar. 27, 1787, in *Benjamin Franklin*, p. 743.
27. *Autobiography*, pp. 164–65.
28. No. 8, *Papers*, I, 27.
29. *Poor Richard* for 1748, *Papers*, III, 256.

Notes and References

30. June 10, 1731, *Papers*, I, 196, 198–99.
31. Feb. 8, 1780, *Writings*, VIII, 10.
32. Ibid., p. 10.
33. April 29, 1749, *Papers*, III, 364.
34. June 11, 1760, *Papers*, IX, 121.
35. Aug. 14, 1747, *Papers*, III, 171.
36. *Education of Youth in Pennsylvania*, *Papers*, III, 415.
37. Ibid., *Papers*, III, 405–18.
38. Ibid., p. 402.
39. Ibid., p. 418.
40. Ibid., p. 417.
41. "The Busy-Body," No. 3, *Papers*, I, 119. See the full quotation in Chapter 2 above, p. 63.
42. "Observations Relative to the Intentions of the Original Founders . . ." (1789), *Writings*, X, 9–31.
43. *Autobiography*, pp. 163–64. See also *Pennsylvania Gazette*, June 10, 1729, *Papers*, I, 159.
44. *Franklin Institute News*, Spring, 1972, p. 7.
45. Letter to John Waring, Dec. 17, 1763, *Papers*, X, 396.
46. Mar. 20, 1774, *Papers*, X, 396n.
47. "The Talk of the Town," *The New Yorker*, January 1, 1972, p. 19.
48. *Autobiography*, pp. 162, 163.
49. Letter to Sir Joseph Banks, July 27, 1783, *Writings*, IX, 74.
50. *Plain Truth*, *Papers*, III, 203.
51. *Records of the Federal Convention of 1787*, ed Max Farrand. Rev. ed. (1966), III, 131.
52. *Autobiography*, p. 162.
53. Letter to David Hartley, Dec. 4, 1789, *Writings*, X, 72.

Selected Bibliography

PRIMARY SOURCES

The Autobiography of Benjamin Franklin. Edited by Leonard W. Labaree et al. New Haven & London: Yale University Press, 1964. Standard edition, with admirable introduction, notes, bibliography, and index.

Benjamin Franklin. Edited by Frank Luther Mott and Chester E. Jorgenson. New York, 1936. Revised paperback edition. New York: Hill and Wang, 1962. Representative selections, with excellent scholarly introduction and useful notes and bibliography.

Benjamin Franklin's Letters to the Press. Edited by Verner W. Crane. Chapel Hill: University of North Carolina Press, 1950. Franklin's use of English newspapers for American propaganda before Revolution.

Memoirs of the Life and Writings of Benjamin Franklin. Edited by William Temple Franklin. 3 vols. London, 1818. Vol. I, which includes the *Autobiography* to its conclusion in 1757, is still of special interest as it continues the life of Franklin after 1757, with narrative text and important letters and other papers supplied by the editor, Franklin's oldest grandson (born 1760), who had spent his boyhood in London during Franklin's second mission to England (1764–1775) and had served as his private secretary in France (1776–1785).

Mr. Franklin. Edited by Leonard W. Labaree and Whitfield J. Bell, Jr. New Haven & London: Yale University Press, 1956. Varied selection from his personal letters.

The Papers of Benjamin Franklin. 18 vols. to date. Edited by Leonard W. Labaree et al., vols. 1–14 (1706–1767), and by William B. Willcox et al., vols. 15–18 (1768–1771). New Haven & London: Yale University Press, 1959–. The authoritative edition of the papers so far published, containing letters written to, as well as by, Franklin. A superb work of modern editorial scholarship.

Satires and Bagatelles. Edited by Paul McPharlin. Detroit: Fine Book Circle, 1937. A delightful selection of Franklin's humorous and witty pieces, most of them privately printed in his lifetime for the entertainment and instruction of friends.

The Writings of Benjamin Franklin. Edited by Albert Henry Smyth. 10 vols. New York: Macmillan, 1905–1907. Vol. X contains a biography of Franklin and an index to the letters. The best available edition for the years 1772–

1790, which take in more than half the known papers of Franklin, but it does not include letters addressed to Franklin.

SECONDARY SOURCES

1. Background

BEMIS, SAMUEL FLAGG. *The Diplomacy of the American Revolution.* 1935. Reprint, Bloomington, Indiana: Indiana University Press, 1957. Invaluable in this field.

COHEN, I. BERNARD. *Franklin and Newton.* Philadelphia: American Philosophical Society, 1956. Solid scholarly study of Franklin's part in the development of physical science in the eighteenth century.

PARRINGTON, VERNON LOUIS. *Main Currents in American Thought.* 3 vols. First volume contains chapter on Franklin's place in the liberal tradition of America.

TREVELYAN, GEORGE O. *The American Revolution.* One-volume edition condensed and edited by Richard B. Morris. New York: D. McKay Co., 1964. Contains brilliant historical sketch of Franklin by eminent English historian.

TYLER, MOSES COIT. *The Literary History of the American Revolution 1763–1783.* 2 vols. 1897. Reprint, American Classics series. New York: Frederick Ungar Publishing Co., 1963. Admirable summary of Franklin's major writings in Vol. II, Chapter 38.

VAN DOREN, CARL. *The Great Rehearsal.* New York: The Viking Press, 1948. The Constitutional Convention of 1787 and Franklin's decisive part in the making and adoption of the Constitution.

WEBER, MAX. *The Protestant Ethic and the Spirit of Capitalism.* Translated by Talcott Parsons, pp. 47–78. First published 1930. Reprint, New York: Charles Scribner's Sons, 1958. One-sided ideological view of Franklin as potent influence in development of capitalism.

WYLLIE, IRVIN G. *The Self-Made Man in America.* New Brunswick, New Jersey: Rutgers University Press, 1954. A valuable study.

2. Franklin Biographies

ALDRIDGE, ALFRED OWEN. *Benjamin Franklin Philosopher & Man.* Philadelphia: J. B. Lippincott Company, 1965. An objective, balanced biography, which conveys the impression that the author does not really like Franklin.

BECKER, CARL. "Benjamin Franklin." In *Dictionary of American Biography.* New York, 1931. Reprinted in *The American Plutarch.* Edited by Edward T. James. New York: Scribner, 1964. Best brief account and evaluation.

CRANE, VERNER W. *Benjamin Franklin and a Rising People*. Boston: Little, Brown and Company, 1954. Keen, concise delineation of Franklin, highlighting his political and diplomatic activities.

FAŸ, BERNARD. *Franklin, the Apostle of Modern Times*. Translated by Bravig Embs. Boston: Little, Brown and Company, 1929. Interesting for reflection of love and admiration for Franklin in France in present century.

KETCHAM, RALPH L. *Benjamin Franklin*. New York: Twayne Publishers, Inc., 1966. Well-written, scholarly, presenting Franklin as a great American thinker.

MANNAN, SAYED ABDUL. *Benjamin Franklin*. Dacca, Bangladesh: Majid Publishing House, 1956. A biography in the Bengali language, included merely as an example of the continuing worldwide influence of Franklin.

MORSE, JOHN T., JR. *Benjamin Franklin*. Boston and New York: Houghton, Mifflin and Company, 1889. A sound, lively, late nineteenth-century biography.

PARTON, JAMES. *Life and Times of Benjamin Franklin*. 2 vols. New York: Mason Brothers, 1864. A landmark in Franklin biography, rich in detail, anecdote, and insight.

SAINTE-BEUVE, CHARLES A. "Benjamin Franklin." In *Portraits of the Eighteenth Century*. Translated by K. P. Wormely, pp. 311–75. New York & London: G. P. Putnam's Sons, 1905. Brilliant, perceptive biographical essay; critical, but affectionate.

VAN DOREN, CARL. *Benjamin Franklin*. One-volume edition. New York: The Viking Press, 1938. Still unsurpassed as full-length biography of Franklin; intended "to rescue him from the dry, prim people."

3. Special studies

ALDRIDGE, ALFRED OWEN. *Franklin and his French Contemporaries*. New York: New York University Press, 1957. Throughly researched account of Franklin's reputation and influence in France.

AMACHER, RICHARD E. *Benjamin Franklin*. New York: Twayne Publishers, Inc., 1962. Franklin as a writer; useful bibliography.

BEST, JOHN HARDIN. *Benjamin Franklin on Education*. New York: Bureau of Publications, Teachers College, Columbia University, 1962. Contains his important writings on education and an excellent introduction and topical bibliography.

CLOYD, DAVID E. *Benjamin Franklin and Education*. Boston: D. C. Heath & Co., 1902. First in this field. A limited appraisal of Franklin as a man and an educator.

FARRAND, MAX, ed. *Benjamin Franklin's Memoirs*. Parallel text edition. Berkeley, California: University of California Press, 1949. Important for textual study of *Autobiography*.

Selected Bibliography

FORD, PAUL LEICESTER. *The Many-Sided Franklin*. New York: The Century Co., 1899. Topical arrangement, with copious illustrations and a great many well-chosen excerpts from Franklin's writings.

FORD, PAUL LEICESTER, ed. *The Prefaces, Proverbs, and Poems of Benjamin Franklin*. (Originally printed in *Poor Richard's Almanacks* for 1733–1758.) New York & London: G. P. Putnam's Sons, 1890. Valuable introduction tracing history and influence of Franklin almanacs.

JORDAN, HELEN and JORDAN, CLARENCE, eds. *Benjamin Franklin's Unfinished Business*. Philadelphia: The Franklin Institute, 1957. A summary of the celebration in seventy-two countries of the 250th anniversary of the birth of Franklin; generously illustrated and overflowing with evidence of his worldwide influence.

LAWRENCE, D. H. *Studies in Classic American Literature*. New York: T. Seltzer, 1923. Critical chapter on Franklin is marked by originality and animus.

LUCAS, F. L. *The Art of Living: Four Eighteenth Century Minds*. New York: Macmillan, 1959. A modern appraisal of Franklin, measured and urbane.

MCMASTER, JOHN B. *Benjamin Franklin as a Man of Letters*. Boston & New York: Houghton, Mifflin and Company, 1887. Estimable consideration of Franklin's literary achievement.

MILES, RICHARD D. "The American Image of Benjamin Franklin." *American Quarterly*, Summer, 1957. Excellent survey of Franklin scholarship.

PACE, ANTONIO. *Benjamin Franklin and Italy*. Philadelphia: American Philosophical Society, 1958. Very useful for this area of Franklin's influence.

SANFORD, CHARLES L. "An American Pilgrim's Progress." *American Quarterly*, 6 (1954), 297–310. Significant contribution on Franklin's sense of mission and its source in his Puritan background and his early reading of Bunyan's allegory.

SELLERS, CHARLES COLEMAN. *Benjamin Franklin in Portraiture*. New Haven & London: Yale University Press, 1962. Indispensable in this field—portraits, engravings, cartoons, medallions, china, etc.

STOURZH, GERALD. *Benjamin Franklin and American Foreign Policy*. Chicago: University of Chicago Press, 1954. Exhaustive study of Franklin's influence on American foreign policy.

ULICH, ROBERT. "Benjamin Franklin." In *History of Educational Thought*. New York & Cincinnati: American Book Company, 1945. Interesting assessment by noted German educator.

VICTORY, BEATRIC M. "Benajmin Franklin and Germany." Ph.D. dissertation, University of Pennsylvania, 1915. Thorough, pedestrian study.

WOODY, THOMAS. *Educational Views of Benjamin Franklin*. New York & London: McGraw-Hill Book Company, Inc., 1931. Stimulating comments by author.

Index

For writings of Franklin which are mentioned in the text, see under the entry Works.

Academy of Philadelphia, 86–88, 155, 175, 179–80
Adams, Abigail, 133
Adams, John, 132, 135, 137, 141
Adams, Samuel, 132–33
Addison, Joseph, 27
Albany Congress, 101–102
Albany Plan, 101–103
Almanacs, 61. See also Works, *Poor Richard*
American Magazine, 71
American Philosophical Society, 75–77, 94, 147
Association, the, 96–99. See also Works, "Form of Association"

Bache, Benjamin Franklin (grandson), 125
Bache, Richard (son-in-law), 136
Bache, William (grandson), 136
Bagatelles, 142
Barbéra, Gaspero, 160
Bartram, John, 74, 77
Beccaria, Giovanni, 163
Bigelow, John, 158, 162
Blacks, 111, 113, 150–51
Boston Grammar School (Boston Latin School), 16, 41
Boston Tea Party, 126, 128
Braddock, General Edward, 103–104
Bradford, Andrew, 29, 52, 61, 70–71
Bradford, William, 28
Bray Associates, 113
Bunyan, John, 27; *Pilgrim's Progress*, 16
Burgoyne, General John, 137–38

Burke, Aedamus, 145
Burke, Edmund, 117
Burnet, Governor William (N.Y. and Mass.), 55
Burton, Robert: *Historical Collections*, 16

Canada, 109, 141
Cavour, Conte Camillo di, 164
Chatham, Lord (the Elder William Pitt), 129–30
Clinton, Governor George (N.Y.), 96–97
Cockpit, the, 128
Coercive Acts of Parliament, 130
Colden, Cadwallader, 82
Collins, Anthony, 19, 34
Collins, John, 27, 30–31, 39, 42
Collinson, Peter, 60, 77, 90, 108, 174
Committee of Safety (Defense), Pennsylvania, 133
Concord, Battle of, 132
Condorcet, Marquis de, 158, 179
Constitutional Convention, 147–49, 176
Continental Congress, 130–35
Cook, Captain James, 140
Cornwallis, General Charles, 140
Courant, New-England, 20–21, 23, 26
Courant Club, 42

Daily Courant (London), 20
Dalibard, Thomas-Francois, 91–92, 122
Deane, Silas, 137
Declaration of Independence, 135
Defoe, Daniel, 27; *Essay on Projects*, 16, 26

Index

Deism, 19, 44, 47
Denham, Thomas, 32–35, 39, 42, 44
Dick, Sir Alexander, 109
"Dogood, Silence." *See* "Silence Dogood"
DuPont, Pierre S., 122

Economics, 50–51, 122
Education, aim of, 88, *175;* crisis of, today, *179–82;* inadequacy of formal, 13; methods of, 20; philosophy of, 89, 155; principles of, *20,* 25–26, *46–47,* 69, 88–89, 154–55; value of, at Harvard, 25
Electricity, 77–78, *90–94,* 108
English School (The Academy), *84–89,* 150, 155
Every Man . . . series, 70
Examination, The, 118–20, 139
Experiments, *90–94,* 108, 131

"Father Abraham," 105–106, 140
Federal Gazette, 151
Fire Insurance Company (Philadelphia), 114
Fireplace, improved, 72
Folger, Peter (grandfather), 15–16
Fothergill, Dr. John, 108
Franklin, Abiah Folger (mother), 14–15, 40
Franklin, Benjamin, Works of. *See* WORKS
Franklin, Benjamin (uncle), 14–16, 43
Franklin, Deborah (wife), 104–105, 125, 130. *See also* Read, Deborah
Franklin, Francis Folger (son), death of, 67; 71
Franklin, James (brother), 17–18, 20–21, 26–28, 30, 68
Franklin, Josiah (father), 14–15, 30, 40
Franklin, Sarah (daughter), 77, 125
Franklin, Thomas (uncle), 15
Franklin, William (son), 58, 105, 107, 111, 132, 135, 146
Franklin, William Temple (grandson), 120, 130, 136, 139, 158
"Franklin stove," 72–74
Franklinistes, 122, 152
Free School (The Academy), 86–87

Galloway, Joseph, 136
Garibaldi, 164
Gazette (Boston), 20, 23
Gazette, The Pennsylvania, 52–58, 67, 80, 85, 177
General Magazine, 71
Gentlemen's Magazine, 54, 118
Goethe, Johann Wolfgang von, 165–66
German immigrants (Pennsylvania), 56, 60
Godfrey, Thomas, 61
Grace, Robert, 72
Greeley, Horace, 161
Greene, General Nathanael, 133
Greenwood, Isaac, 74
Grenville, Lord, 116, 118, 128

Hall, David, 82
Hartley, David, 152
Harvard College, 17, *23–25,* 41
Heberden, Dr. William, 72
"Hell-Fire Club," 21
Helvétius, Mme. (Anne-Catherine), 138
Henry, Patrick, 132
Hewson, Mary (Stevenson), 145–46. *See also* Stevenson, Polly
Historical Review of the Constitution and Government of Pennsylvania, 107
Howe, Lord Richard, 135
Hume, David, 109, 111
Hunter, William, 99
Hutchinson, Thomas, 128

Indians, 100–102, *111–12,* 144
Influence, Franklin's: in Argentina, 160; in England, 167; in France, 157–58, 162–63; in Germany, 165–67; in Italy, 160, 163–65; in other countries, 168; in the United States, 169–71
Inoculation, smallpox, 21, 71–72
Irish immigrants, 56

Jay, John, 132, 141
Jefferson, Thomas, 135, 145
Journal of Benjamin Franklin, 1726, 36–39
Junto, *45–47,* 50, 59, 85, 154; idea of, extended to other countries, 68; in Germany, 166; international, 183

Kames, Lord, 109, 120
Keimer, Samuel, 29–30, 44, 49, 52, 61
Keith, Sir William (Governor of Pa.), 30–33, 39, 42
Kite, crossing pond with aid of a, 17
Kite experiment, 92

La Rochefoucauld d'Enville, Duc de, 139, 152
Latin, English subordinated to, at Harvard, 25; Franklin's study of, 23, 69
Latin and Greek School (The Academy), 85, 87, 155
Lawrence, D. H., 167
Lee, Arthur, 138, 142
Leeds, Titan, 62
Library Company of Philadelphia, 59–60, 174
Lincoln, Abraham, 161
Livingston, Robert, 132, 135
Locke, John, 27, 33, 84–87, 179
Logan, James, 60, 97
London Daily Courant, 20
London Journal, 26, 57

Madison, James, 157
Mandeville, Bernard, 34
Mann, Horace, 161
Masonic Lodge of The Nine Sisters, 139, 158
Mather, Cotton, 21, 26, 46; *Bonifacius: An Essay upon the Good,* 16
Mather, Samuel, 23, 26
Mellon, Thomas, 159–60
Mercury (Philadelphia), 52, 71
Meredith, Hugh, 49, 58
Millikan, Robert A., 92
Milton, John, 86
Mirabeau, 145, 157
Montaigne: *Essays,* 60
Moral Perfection, Project for Attaining, 48–49
Moravians, 112
Morris, Robert, 132
"Mrs. T.," 33, 34, 36

New-England Courant, 20–23, 26
News-Letter (Boston), 20
Newton, Sir Isaac, 34, 90

Nine Sisters, Masonic Lodge of the, 139, 158
Norris, Isaac, 107
North, Lord (Frederick), 129

Oliver, Andrew, 128
Osborne, Charles, 31

Paine, Thomas: *Common Sense,* 135
Palmer, Samuel, 33–34
Paper money, 50–51
Parker, James, 109
Parton, James, 162
"Parkway Program," 181–82
Passy, France, 138, 142, 145
Paxton Boys, 112
Pemberton, Henry, 34; *A View of Sir Isaac Newton's Philosophy,* 60
Penn, Thomas, 86, 96–98, 107, 110
Pennsylvania Hospital (Philadelphia), 99, 174
Pennsylvania Gazette, The. See Gazette, The Pennsylvania
Peters, Richard, 86
Philadelphische Zeitung, 60
Physiocrats, 122–23
"Plan of Conduct," 38–39, 44–45
Plutarch: *Lives,* 16
Poor Richard. See under Works
Postal system, reform of Colonial, 99–100
Postmaster general, Franklin as, 99, 104, 124, 128–29
Priestley, Joseph, 91, 93, 132
Pringle, Dr. John, 108, 120–21
Proprietors of Pennsylvania, 104, 107–10

Quakers, 94–95, 137

Ralph, James, 31–35, 39, 42
Raspe, Rudolph Erich, 120
Read, Deborah (wife), 31, 33, 58, 114. *See also* Franklin, Deborah
Religion, Franklin's, 47–48. *See also* Deism
Reynal, Abbé, 82
Robertson, William, 109
Rollin, Charles, 86–87
Romilly, Samuel, 145

Index

Royal Society of London, 21, 75, 90, 140, 158; Franklin elected a fellow of, 94
Royal Society of Sciences (Göttingen); Franklin elected a member of, 120

St. Andrews, University of, 109
Sainte-Beuve, Charles Augustin, 162–63
Sarmiento, Domingo, 160
"Saunders, Richard" (pseudonym), 61–62
Scientific study, 74, 90, 92–93, 125, 143, 146; ethics in, 92–93, 177–78. *See also* Electricity; Experiments
Shaftesbury, Anthony Ashley Cooper, 19, 27, 33
Shirley, Governor William (Mass.), 103, 109, 117
"Silence Dogood" (pseudonym), 21–27, 32, 177
"Six Nations," 100
Slavery, 151
Smallpox inoculation, 21, 71–72
Smith, William, 157
"Snake Cartoon," 101
Society of the Cincinnati, 143–45
Society for Political Enquiries, 147, 176
Sparks, Jared, 159
Spectator, 19–21, 26
Stamp Act, 116–120, 126
Stamp Act Congress, 116
Stevenson, Margaret, 107–108
Stevenson, Polly, 107–108, 110, 178. *See also* Hewson, Mary (Stevenson)
Strahan, William, 106–108, 110

Timothée, Louis, 60
Townshend duties, 123, 125–26
Truman, Harry S, 169
Tryon, Thomas: *The Way to Health, Long Life and Happiness*, 72
Turnbull, George, 86
Twain, Mark, 161

Union Fire Company of Philadelphia, 70

Van Doren, Carl, 122
Vergennes, Comte de, 134–35, 137–38, 141

Virginia Gazette, 99
Volta, Alessandro, 163

Washington, George, 152
Watts, John, 34
Wedderburn, Alexander, 128–29
Whitefield, George, 70–71, 174
Wilberforce, William, 145
Williams, Jonathan (grandnephew), 142
Wilson, James, 149
WORKS
  Account of the New Invented Pennsylvanian Fire-Places, An, 73
  "Advice to a Young Man on the Choice of a Mistress," 80
  "Apology for Printers," 53–54
  "Articles of Belief and Acts of Religion," 47–48
  Articles of Confederation, 134
  Autobiography, 13, 158–61, 165
  "Busy-Body" papers, 52, 63
  Causes of the American Discontents before 1768, 123
  Dissertation on Liberty and Necessity, A, 33–34, 36
  Edict by the King of Prussia, 126–27, 139
  Experiments and Observations on Electricity, 90–91, 125
  "Father Abraham's Speech," 105–106
  "Form of Association," 96–98
  Hints . . . Respecting the Orphan School-House in Philadelphia, 150
  Information to Those Who Would Remove to America, 143–44
  Interest of Great Britain Considered, The, 110
  Maritime Observations, 146
  Narrative of the Late Massacres, 112
  Nature and Necessity of a Paper-Currency, The, 50–51
  Observations concerning the Increase of Mankind, 100, 110
  "Observations on . . . reading history," 68
  Observations Relative to the Intentions of the Original Founders of the Academy in Philadelphia, 150
  "On Literary Style," 56

On the Slave-Trade, 150-51
Plain Truth, 95-96
Plan for Improving the Condition of the Free Blacks, 150
Political, Miscellaneous, and Philosophical Pieces, 140
Poor Richard, 61-67; quotations from, 63-66, 82, 157, 175
Poor Richard Improved, 83-84, 105-106, 164
Proposal for Promoting Useful Knowledge among the British Plantations in America, A, 75, 178
Proposals Relating to the Education of Youth in Pennsylvania, 85, 88

Remarks Concerning the Savages of North America, 144
Rules by Which a Great Empire May Be Reduced to a Small One, 126-27, 139
"Silence Dogood" papers, 21-27, 32, 177
"Speech of Miss Polly Baker, The," 80-82
Way to Wealth, The, 106, 140, 158, 162, 164, 166. *See* "Father Abraham's Speech"
"Witch Trial at Mount Holly, A," 54